e-COMMERCE
OPERATIONS MANAGEMENT

2nd Edition

e-COMMERCE
OPERATIONS MANAGEMENT

2nd Edition

Marc J. Schniederjans
University of Nebraska-Lincoln, USA

Qing Cao
Texas Tech University, USA

Jason H. Triche
Texas Tech University, USA

 **World Scientific**

NEW JERSEY · LONDON · SINGAPORE · BEIJING · SHANGHAI · HONG KONG · TAIPEI · CHENNAI

Published by

World Scientific Publishing Co. Pte. Ltd.

5 Toh Tuck Link, Singapore 596224

USA office: 27 Warren Street, Suite 401-402, Hackensack, NJ 07601

UK office: 57 Shelton Street, Covent Garden, London WC2H 9HE

Library of Congress Cataloging-in-Publication Data
Schniederjans, Marc J.
  E-commerce operations management / Marc J. Schniederjans (University of Nebraska-Lincoln, USA),
Qing Cao (Texas Tech University, USA), & Jason H. Triche (Texas Tech University, USA). -- 2nd edition.
    pages cm
  Includes bibliographical references and index.
    ISBN 978-9814518628 (hard cover : alk. paper) -- ISBN 978-9814518635 (soft cover : alk. paper)
    1. Electronic commerce--Management. 2. Industrial management. I. Cao, Qing. II. Triche, Jason H.
III. Title.
  HF5548.32.S285 2013
  658.8'72--dc23
                                                          2013026846

British Library Cataloguing-in-Publication Data
A catalogue record for this book is available from the British Library.

In-house Editor: Sandhya Venkatesh

Printed in Singapore by World Scientific Printer

To Vicky for your love and support

To Tyson, Glenn, and Brenda for your encourgement, love, and support

PREFACE

These are exciting times in the history of e-commerce and for businesses operating in the growing e-commerce industry. While some companies are making a fortune others are going out of business. How can there be such differences in business performance outcomes? The answer to this question can always be found in understanding the way that e-commerce operations are managed. It is not luck or timing that helps a non-profitable operation become and maintain profitability, it is through the adaptive knowledge and skill of the people who run the business. The managers who run businesses are called, "operations managers" and as this book will show are critical to the success of all e-commerce business operations.

Regardless of whether you are a vice president of operations or working as a supervisor in service shop, this book will help to make you aware of the issues, concepts, philosophies, procedures, methodologies, and practices of running e-commerce operations. The purpose of this book is to provide current research findings, strategies, and practices that can help operations managers run and improve their e-commerce operations. This book has been designed for an upper-level undergraduate course or a graduate business or engineering management course on e-commerce operations management for university students. Decision-makers who have to reengineer e-commerce operations can also use this book. This group of decision makers might include CEO's, vice presidents of operations, general managers, plant managers, supervisors, and industrial engineers. Other operations management and engineering faculty, trainers, and graduate students will also find this book presents a useful variety of new ideas for managing e-commerce operations.

This book assumes that the reader has had some exposure to the terminology and technology commonly found in the field of operations management. The basic operations management or industrial management course that undergraduate students take in business degree programs constitutes sufficient prerequisite knowledge to satisfy the background to fully appreciate the content of this book. While most of the terminology necessary to fully utilize this book are actually defined in the book, readers can consult any basic operations management textbook or in either of the latest versions of the *American Production and Inventory Control Society* (APICS) *Dictionary or Encyclopedia of Production and Manufacturing Management*. Throughout this book, important terms are italicized and are usually followed by a definition. The location of the initial definitions can be found using the index at the end of the book.

The contents of this book are organized into three parts. In Part I, "Introduction and Critical Success Factors in E-commerce Operations Management," two chapters are presented that help to define the basic subject and terminology used in the book, as well as briefly identifying the major topics that make up the rest of the book. In Part II, "Critical Success Factors of E-commerce Operations Management," eight chapters are each devoted to an individual topic that combines the subjects of operations management with leading-edge e-commerce subject material. Part III, "Recent Trends in E-Commerce Technology," consists of two chapters that cover technology developments and in the field e-commerce. These chapters' contents are based on the most recent research in their respective areas. They represent information on both "how-to" manage an e-commerce operation and "what's happening" in e-commerce. Collectively, they help to explain what is meant by the term "e-commerce operations management."

While many people have had a hand in the preparation of this book, its accuracy and completeness are the responsibility of the authors. For all the errors that this book may contain we apologize for them in advance.

CONTENTS

LISTS OF TABLES AND FIGURES

TABLES

Chapter 6

Chapter 7

Chapter 8

Chapter 9

Chapter 10

Chapter 11

Chapter 12

Epilogue

Part I

Introduction and Critical Success Factors in E-Commerce Operations Management

<u>Chapter 1</u> INTRODUCTION

Learning Objectives

After completing this chapter, you should be able to:
  Define and describe "e-commerce."
  Define and describe "operations management."
  Define and describe "e-commerce operations management."
  Explain why e-commerce operations management is important for business success.

Overview of This Chapter

This chapter introduces and defines some of the principle terms that will be used throughout the book. This chapter also tries to help justify why the subject of this book is an important for students of business. The chapter ends with an overview of the book's architecture used to organize the material for student learning purposes.

What is E-Commerce?

Origin of the Term

The need for more timely information leads to the development of world's largest and most widely used networks, called the Internet. The *Internet* is an international collection of hardware and software from hundreds of thousands of private and public computer networks. It represents a global platform that permits digital information to be shared and distributed at very little cost to users. The Internet provides a wide range of information interaction functions, including: communication (i.e., sending e-mails, transmitting data, etc.), accessing information (i.e., searching databases, reading electronic books, etc.), and supplying information (i.e., transferring files, graphics, etc.).

It is no wonder that people of commerce quickly saw opportunities in using the Internet to conduct business. The universality that the Internet offered had to be and was capacitated by businesses into universally accepted standards for storing, retrieving, formatting, and displaying information in a networked environment. This capacitated environment of the Internet is called the *World Wide Web* (WWW) and permits businesses to get online and conduct a variety of business activities. Tim Berners-Lee of the European Labortory for Particle Phyics was credited in 1990 with developing several protocols used in the initial development of the WWW (Deithel, *et al.* 2001, p. 12). One example of the use of the WWW standardization capacity is the use of Web sites in conducting business transactions. It is this capacity of the WWW that allows users of a computer over the Internet to locate and view multimedia documents such as text, graphics, animations, and videos that make up Web sites. As the use of the WWW matured during the 1990's, new terms emerged to more acturately differentiate the different types of business transactions that were taking place over the Internet. One of these new terms was called "electronic commerce" hereafter referred to as "e-commerce."

E-Commerce Definition

E-commerce is the exchange transactions which take place over the Internet primarily using digital technology. These exchange transactions include buying, selling, or trading of goods, services, and information. This encompasses all activities supporting market transactions including marketing, customer support, delivery, and payment. The term, *brick-and-mortar business*, is often used to describe traditional or regular business commerce (i.e., non-e-commerce) exchange transactions.

As we can see in Table 1, there are at least nine different categories of e-commerce (Wood 2001, pp. 1–6; Laudon and Laudon, p. 110; Balasubramanian and Mahajan 2001). The customer can sell items directly to other customers (e.g., like the C2C eBay online auction business that allows people to auction items they own to other people directly), or as a C2B organization where online registrations can be performed for products consumers purchase, or as a C2G organization where individual voters in the United States can contact their governmental representatives directly over the Internet. The B2C organizations are now able, through online registration, to keep better track of their customers for purposes of product recalls and product updates. The B2B organizations can transact product and material purchases, share design specifications for new products, and perform research and development activities all online. The B2G organizations allow businesses to fulfill government obligations on reporting their behavior on such issues of environmentalism, taxes, and legal actions in a timely manner. All of the G2C, G2B and G2G organizations can share information required by law and current legislation that might otherwise take years to convey. These governmental organizations allow for a much needed expedience in the disemination of information concerning the governance of people and assurance that laws will be promptly obeyed.

Table 1. Categories of e-commerce

From	To Customer	Business	Government
Customer	Customer-to-Customer (C2C)	Customer-to-Business (C2B)	Customer-to-Government (C2G)
Business	Business-to-Customer (B2C)	Business-to-Business (B2B)	Business-to-Government (B2G)
Government	Government-to-Customer (G2C)	Government-to-Business (G2B)	Government-to-Government (G2G)

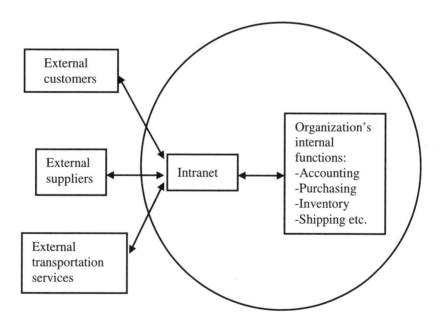

Figure 1. Intranet and extranet

This book takes a very broad view in its definition of e-commerce exchange transactions to include all information sharing that supports business transactions. This would include all transactions internal to the business organizations and those external with customers and government agencies. Also, it incorporates the term "electronic business" or hereafter refered to as "e-business." *E-business* describes the uses of the Internet and digital technology for the management of business processes internal to the organization. The use of *intranets* (i.e., networks within a single organization) as shown in the circled area in Figure 1 are also included in e-commerce. They link internal organization functions together for efficieny, timeliness, and issues of privatacy within the firm. As intranets are expanded to include external organizations (e.g., suppliers) as authorized users of an organization's intranet, they create *extranets* which are also included in the definition of e-commerce in this book.

What is Operations Management?

Operations Management (OM) can be defined as the design, operation, and continued improvement of the system that creates and delivers a firm's products and services (Chase *et al.* 2001, p. 6). It is viewed primarily as a line management function, equal in standing, organizationally, to accounting, marketing, finance, and information systems. As a management function, OM involves all of the basic management tasks of planning, directing, organizing, staffing, motivating, and controlling.

The primary objective of an OM manager is to manage and control the "production process." The *production process* presented in Figure 2 involves taking inputs (e.g., raw materials, human resources, etc.) and transforming them, using technology, processes, and rules, into consumable outputs (e.g., finished products or services) in the most efficient and effective manner. To do this OM mangers must perform a variety of tasks. These tasks include, among other things, managing product and service quality, forecasting demand, managing inventory, scheduling production, purchasing goods and services, managing the supply chain of an organization, aiding in the design and development of products, and managing human and technical resources. OM managers must also control the transformation process and allow for corrective feedback to make sure they are achieving organizational goals. Since OM also involves improving operating systems, additional tasks might include reengineering jobs or processes and working with consultants to alter existing systems for improved efficiency and productivity as changes in technology or markets demand.

Table 2. Types of e-business models

Type of model	Description
Advertiser	Company makes money by selling advertising space on their Web site. The Advertiser then lures target audience by giving them some free service or information. Many companies who maintain a Web site have started using this type of model as an extra source of e-commerce income.
Service	Company creates a Web site that offers customers a service or range of services. Online brokerage houses, travel agencies, etc. are typical examples.
Virtual mall	Company offers a wide range of differing manufactured products on a Web site. One of the most typical examples is AMAZON.COM.
e-tailing	Company can offer a single customized product, like Dell Computers which offers a customized computer system over the Web. They can also offer non-customized products like brand-name appliances.
Information disseminator	Company offers up-to-date source of information of a specific nature. An example would be an online newspaper from a specific city or covering a specific type of news.
Sales facilitator	Company connects buyers with sellers on a Web site that attracts customers with the promise of finding an inexpensive source for the product or service they are looking for while selling access linkage to the seller's site.
e-procurement	Company provides efficient and cost reducing linkages between buyers and sellers of industrial organizations.
Online auction site	Company that provides a market place for buyers and sellers to exchange goods and services to the highest bidder.

While there are many other tasks that OM managers may be asked to perform, those listed in Figure 2 are considered by most OM managers as basic, fundamental, and critical factors necessary for a successful operation. When a task becomes so important that it can determine the successfulness of an organization, it becomes what is called a *critical success factor* (Laudon and Laudon 2001, p. 307). As we will see in Chapter 2, these critical success factors (CSFs) must be included in the development of strategies for successful business operations. Indeed, the rest of this book is devoted to learning how these CSFs can be incorporated in e-commerce operations. While these tasks have been performed by OM managers for many decades, e-commerce is viewed as a revolution, altering how they can and should be performed. This revolution is called "e-commerce operations management."

What is E-Commerce Operations Management?

E-commerce operations management is the application of all operations management tasks applied in an e-commerce setting. It is the combination of the use of the Internet and digital technology to perform the basic OM activities necessary for the successful running of a business. It involves all the typical OM activities (i.e., purchasing management, inventory management,etc) but focuses on managing an e-commerce operation. This includes firms whose business model is completed based on e-commerce transactions and those that are a combination of brick-and-mortar and e-commerce operations. It is not limited to individual or singluar e-business models presented in Table 2, but also includes integration of aspects of e-business models that are combined with regular business operations to help make a modern organization successful. Indeed, it is the advocacy of this book that organizations which can successfully integrate brick-and-mortar with e-commerce operations will be the market winners.

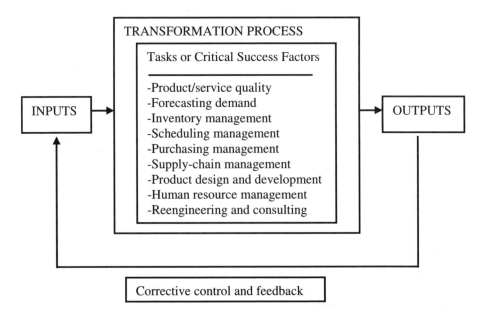

Figure 2. OM production process

For the purposes of this book, the definition of e-commerce does have some limitations. What e-commerce operations management does not include are activities performed by other functional areas in a business organization. While "e-commerce" includes the marketing functions of advertising, promoting, and selling, and accounting and finance functions, including activities such as account management, cash flow, investment, and capital budgeting, these activities are not directly part of the "e-commerce operations management" definition that is more narrowly focused on the OM function. While accounting, finance, and marketing each play critical roles in the successfulness of an e-commerce operation, they are simply not the subject, that will be covered in this book.

Why Study E-Commerce Operations Management?

The introduction of the Internet into activities performed by OM managers required change in virtually everything an OM manager is asked to do. Even if a brick-and-mortar firm chose not to use any of the e-business models, they must interact with firms that do. Hence, e-commerce operations management is not a free choice decision, but a requirement of OM managers who want to be successful in modern business operations.

Fortunately, there are sizable benefits for those OM managers who embrace e-commerce operations and know how to maximize their production process. Some of the OM benefits are stated in Table 3 (Heizer and Render 2001, p. 460; Laudon and Laudon 2002, pp. 122–129; Kamarainen et al. 2001). OM managers are chiefly focused in their jobs on improving operational efficiency. This objective is usually accomplished by cutting costs of resources used in the production transformation process (note Figure 2) and the flexibility of an operation to adapt to changes quickly, thereby avoiding unnecessary increasing costs of not adapting in a timely manner.

While it is more of a marketing function consideration, the potential for new business that e-commerce offers organizations makes it a necessity for OM managers. One forecast has suggested that by the year 2015, e-commerce is expected to worth $1 trillion of business worldwide and $280 billion in the U.S. (Tompkins and Avila 2012). Another forecast suggest e-commerce sales have grown from $995.0 billion in 1999 to $2,385 billion by 2006 in the U.S. alone (Bruce et al. 2009)

Table 3. Benefits of e-commerce

OM benefit	Explanation
Better availability of service	Conveniently allows customers to shop in their homes or anywhere online.
Cost reduction in information processing	Reduces costs of processing and retrieving order and customer information.
Better timeliness of service	Online operations can offer customers 24-hour service for purchasing goods and services.
Better access to customer markets	Online operations go everywhere in the world, opening new and larger markets than brick-and-mortar operations.
Initial cost of operations less expensive	The capital investment in e-commerce operations is considerably less than brick-and-mortar operations.
Operating costs of operations less expensive	The ongoing expenditure of running a virtual or e-commerce operation is less expensive than brick-and-mortar: less people, less physical equipment, less paper work, etc.
Better purchasing prices from suppliers	The nature of the competitive environment in e-commerce allows for more pricing information and results in lowering costs to producers.
Improved product development	The ability to be online with research and development people from around the world can help to reduce the time-to-market for new products and the cost of their development.
Improved scheduling	The online ability to keep track of product or service activities allows schedulers to be more accurate and timely in scheduling and rescheduling production activity, reducing costs.
Better supplier quality	The information driven environment in e-commerce allows purchasers to more easily learn about material and component quality in the items manufacturers acquire.

Of equal importance to both marketing and OM managers is the advantage e-commerce offers organizations to reduce overall costs by eliminating intermediaries in the distribution and retailing of products or services. A process Laudon and Laudon (2002, p. 111) refer to as *disintermediation* is achieved when intermediaries (e.g., distributors, retailers, etc.) are eliminated from the operations and marketing functions of an organization. As can be seen in the simple example in Figure 3, the channel of distribution from the manufacturer to the customers can be reduced by offering customers the product the manufacturer produces directly. By cutting out the intermediaries in the distribution system, the costs the intermediaries normally would add (e.g., their profit, advertising, human resource costs, etc.) are saved. Mougayar (1998, p. 12) found that traditional brick-and-mortar distribution channels may add as much as 135 percent to the cost of the item over its original cost of manufacture. So, a product like frames for eyeglasses that might retail to a customer for $100 using a traditional channel of distribution could be reduced with disintermediation to approximately $42. Clearly, a cost competitive advantage can be achieved using an e-commerce approach to retailing products or services.

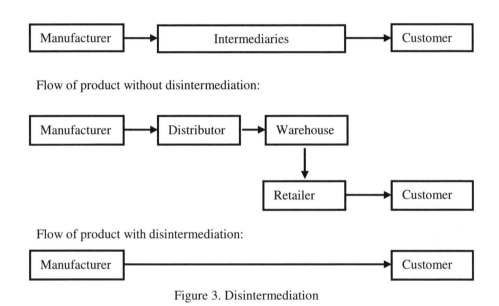

Figure 3. Disintermediation

How This Book is Organized to Help You Learn

Structurally, the remaining chapters in this book all have common educational pedagogy designed to aid the reader in understanding the content material each chapter seeks to present. In addition to the basic subject content, each chapter includes the following seven sections: (1) Learning Objectives: Students should use these declarative sentences as a statement of what they can expect to find in the chapter and as a review tool after they have read the chapter to ensure they have attained the basic knowledge objectives of that chapter. (2) Overview of the Chapter: Students can quickly see in this section a brief statement on the chapter content that follows. This overview is helpful in organizing the content of the chapter, since the content will vary considerably from chapter to chapter. (3) Summary: At the end of each chapter a brief summary of the chapter is presented to remind students of major points and on occasion discussion limitations of topics. (4) Review Terms: Throughout the book the terms are italicized and are restated here to remind students of important terminology. This listing also serves as a quick guide to abreviations. (5) Discussion Questions: A set of discussion questions are presented as a means to stimulate ideas on content and further thinking. (6) Questions: These questions can be used as assignments by faculty or a self-testing check to see if students have learned the basic topics of the chapter. (7) References: All the references used for materials thoughout the chapters are listed here. Students can use these reference citations to locate the publication and further their knowledge of specific content mentioned or referenced in the chapter.

This book's chapters are organized into two parts. Part I, "Introduction and Critical Success Factors in E-Commerce Operations Management," consists of two chapters. In Part I, Chapter 1, "Introduction," the basic definition of e-commerce operations management is presented. Creating a beginning foundation for what e-commerce operations management involves, this chapter's content is further refined in the following chapters. In Part I, Chapter 2, "Reseach on Critical Success Factors in E-Commerce Operations Management," the results of a very recent, extensive research study on e-commerce operations management are presented. This chapter identifies the critical success factors (CSFs) in running an e-commerce operation. Additional journal research is incorporated to contrast the ideas presented and clearly establish select CSFs as the major focus of the rest of the book.

In Part II, "Critical Success Factors of E-Commerce Operations Management," the eight chapters that round out the rest of the book are each devoted to an individual CSF identified in the prior research. These chapters seek to explain their application in e-commerce operations management. The CSFs are easily identified in each of the chapter titles: Chapter 3, "E-Commerce and Supply Chain Management," Chapter 4, "E-Commerce and Product and Process Management," Chapter 5, "E-Commerce and Purchasing Management," Chapter 6, "E-Commerce and Forecasting and Scheduling Management," Chapter 7, "E-Commerce and Inventory Management," Chapter 8, "E-Commerce and Quality Management," Chapter 9, "E-Commerce and Human Resource Management," and Chapter 10, "E-Commerce and Reengineering and Consulting Management." These chapters' contents are based on the most recent research in their respective areas. They represent information on both "how-to" manage an e-commerce operation and "what's happening" in e-commerce. Collectively, they help to explain what is meant by the term "e-commerce operations management."

Summary

This chapter presented basic definitions for a number of important terms that will be used thoughout the rest of the book, including e-commerce, operations management, and e-commerce operations management. A variety of reasons why e-commerce operations management should be studied, including disintermediation, cost reduction, and efficiency in the production process were also presented. The chapter's content ended with an explanation of how the book is organized for student's use and understanding.

Like all introductory chapters, this one overviewed the basic organization of the book's content. In doing so, it provided a preview of the results of research on CSFs that will be discussed in Chapter 2.

Review Terms

Brick-and-mortar business
Critical success factors (CSFs)
Disintermediation
E-business
E-business model
E-commerce
E-commerce operations

Extranets
Internet
Intranets
Operations management (OM)
Production process
World Wide Web (WWW)

◆ Discussion Questions

1. Explain how the nine different categories of e-commerce in Table 1 are different from one another.
2. Explain why "e" preceeds many of the terms in e-commerce.
3. Explain how a "Information disseminator" e-business model can make money for a business.
4. Explain why it is important to study "e-commerce operations management."
5. Describe some of the benefits of e-commerce operations management.

◆ Questions

1. How many categories of e-commerce are their? Give example for each.
2. What is the different between a virtual mall and an e-tailing types of e-business models? Give an example of each.
3. How are intranets and extranets connected to e-commerce operations?
4. What is e-commerce operations management?
5. What are critical success factors? Give examples in operations management.

References

Balasubramanian, S. and Mahajan, V., "The Economic Leverage of the Virtual Community," *International Journal of Electronic Commerce*, Vol. 5, No. 3, Spring 2001, pp. 103–123.

Bruce, D., Fox, W.F., and Luna, L.A., State and Local Government Sales Tax Revenue Losses from Electronic Commerce, Center for Business and Economic Research, The University of Tennessee. Available at http://cber.utk. edu/ecomm/ecom0409.pdf, 2009.

Chase, R. B., Aquilano, N. J. and Jacobs, F. R., *Operations Management for Competitive Advantage.* 9th ed., Boston, MA: McGraw-Hill/Irwin, 2001.

Deitel, H. M., Deitel, P. J. and Nieto, T. R., *e-Business & e-Commerce: How To Program.* Upper Saddle River, NJ: Prentice Hall, 2001.

Heizer, J. and Render, B., *Operations Management*, 6th ed., Upper Saddle River, NJ: Prentice Hall, 2001.

Kamarainen, V., Smaros, J., Faakola, T. and Holmstrom, F., "Cost-effectiveness in the e-Grocery Business," *International Journal of Retail & Distribution Management*, Vol. 29, No. 1, 2001, pp. 41–48.

Laudon, K. C. and Laudon, J. P., *Management Information Systems*, 9th ed., Upper Saddle River, NJ: Prentice Hall, 2002.

Mougayar, W., *Opening Digital Markets*, 2nd ed., New York: McGraw-Hill, 1998.

Pant, S. and Ravichandran, T., "A Framework for Information Systems Planning for e-Business," *Logistics Information Management*, Vol. 14, Nos. 1–2, 2001, pp. 85–98.

Tompkins, J., and Avila, D. 2012. "Keeping up with the E-Giants." *Material Handling & Logistics.* Penton Media Inc.

Wood, M. *Prentice Hall's Guide to e-Commerce and e-Business*, Upper Saddle River, NJ: Prentice Hall, 2001.

Chapter 2 RESEARCH ON CRITICAL SUCCESS FACTORS IN E-COMMERCE OPERATIONS MANAGEMENT

Learning Objectives

After completing this chapter, you should be able to:

Define and describe "strategic planning."

Define and describe "operations strategic planning."

Define and describe "e-commerce operations management strategic planning."

Describe the components of a "strategic planning model."

Explain how a "strategic planning model" can be used to learn about business planning.

Describe "critical success factors" in e-commerce operations management.

Be able to cite recent research studies that explain how "critical success factors" have lead to e-commerce business success.

Overview of This Chapter

This chapter provides an extensive review of the research and published literature that deal with e-commerce operations management. In the process of this presentation this chapter explains how managers should develop an operations management strategy that incorporates e-commerce to achieve business success. The chapter ends with a synthesis of research and its relationship to this book's remaining chapters.

Strategic Planning

All planning in an organization begins at the top with presidents and board members, and works it way down the organization to every member of the firm as presented by the vertical arrows in Figure 1. The planning at the top level of management in most organizations is called *strategic planning*. Strategic plans, such as seeking to increase market share, to become an industry leader in product quality, or growth in the size of operations are usually long-term plans. These strategic-level plans are usually passed down to each of the functional areas within an organization so that each can convert and break down the larger strategic objective into smaller strategies at the functional level. For example, at the functional level an *operations management* (OM) strategy to support a strategic-level growth strategy might be to grow through the acquisition of existing production facilities or the building of new facilities.

A term that is commonly associated with strategic planning is "competitive advantage." A *competitive advantage* is usually a unique process, service, or product that an organization offers its customers is such a way that no other competitor can offer it. For example, Honda Corporation continually sets quality as a major goal in the production of their automobiles. Honda's quality has become so recognized that not only do their customers remain loyal, but also competitors like Ford Motor Corporation has set Honda quality as a quality benchmark goal for excellence in automobile manufacturing. For many organizations a desire to achieve a competitive advantage becomes a goal for which strategic planning efforts are undertaken.

Another functional area important for e-commerce is "information systems." All information technology, including the technology related to e-commerce, its acquisition, maintenance, and improvement clearly falls in the functional domain of *information systems* (IS). Cooperation with other functional areas is critical for e-commerce businesses. The successful e-commerce OM manager knows that all of the functional areas in an organization have e-commerce strategies that they must develop and implement with the help of IS. For example, OM managers might want to support an organizational strategy of growth by the development of new e-commerce operations. The IS functional area might have to then acquire, staff, and train the personnel to run these operations, but it will be the OM manager that will define the job tasks and activities the personnel will perform. Moreover, it will be the OM managers that manage the current operations, seek and recommend improvements in the ongoing operations, and ensure the final product quality that is delivered to the customers. In that regard, IS and OM have a partnership that is critical to the successfulness of an e-commerce operation.

The closeness of IS to OM and the other functional areas in e-commerce businesses can create management problems just by the virtue of the Internet technology that everyone must use. This interconnectivity, represented by the horizontal arrows in Figure 1, can create organizational problems in dealing with lines of authority and decision-making. This in turn can cause firms to incur delays in planning resulting in opportunities missed and a failure to achieve competitive advantages.

One way to overcome these problems is to understand what current research suggests is important in development of OM strategies, what is important in the development of IS strategies, and finally to bring them together to understand what is important in the development of e-commerce OM strategies. These topics are covered in the next few sections of this chapter.

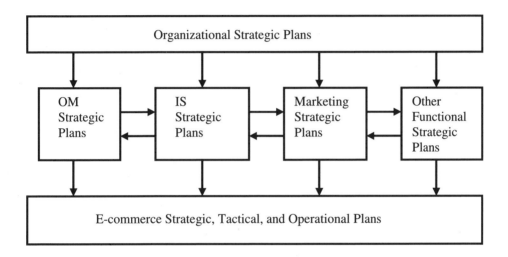

Figure 1. Organizational planning

Research on Operations Management Strategic Planning

As shown in Figure 1, OM strategic plans plays an important role in the successfulness of any organization (St. John *et al.* 2001) and particularly in e-commerce from an operations strategy perspective (Geoffrion and Krishnan 2001). This section reviews relevant OM strategy literature.

The inevitability of research on strategic planning has lead many scholars to devise models by which strategic planning can be explained and further researched. The conceptual framework for an OM strategy model presented in Figure 2 is predominant in most OM strategy research (Ward and Duray 2000; Badri *et al.* 2000; Ward *et al.* 1995; Cleveland *et al.* 1989). Its value in this book is that it provides a theoretical foundation for research studies that have examined the impact of OM strategy on business performance, and in turn helps identify those *critical success factors* (CFSs) that are essential in e-commerce operations management success. The model in Figure 2 prescribes linkages or *constructs* (i.e., the relationships in a model of its variables) among the model's four variables of *business environment* (i.e., the customer markets, labor availability, changes in technology, etc.), *OM strategy* (i.e., in areas such as purchasing, quality, inventory, etc.), *business performance* (i.e., maximizing profit, minimizing costs, improvements in employee attitudes on work, etc.), and *alignment* or *fit* (i.e., which are commonly used measures in strategic planning and refers to harmony or how well aligned one variable in a model is with another). In the case of the model in Figure 2, many research studies have shown that the business environment a firm faces impacts the resulting business performance and also the OM strategies selected to achieve a successful business performance. These impacts directly and indirectly moderate the resulting business performance based on how well they are aligned or fit the environment of the organization. In other words, a good alignment or fit means successful business performance.

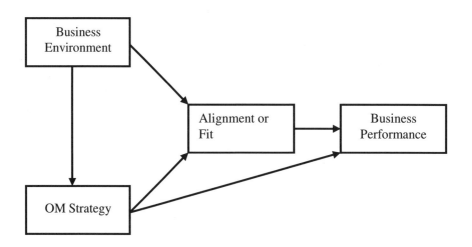

Figure 2. Operations management strategy model

The idea of alignment or fit is very important in the OM research. Tracey *et al.* (1999) examined the effect of the "fit" between advanced manufacturing technology and OM strategy on business performance. In this article *fit* refers to the types and amounts of manufacturing technology and what they should produce in terms of business performance (i.e., profit, sales, improved operations, etc.). The results indicated that firms with a high level of manufacturing technology, and a high level of manufacturing manager's participation in strategy formulation, had high levels of competitive capabilities and improved business performance. In another study Smith and Reece (1999) defined and measured the concept of fit as it applied to OM strategy. They further investigated the interrelationships between business strategy, OM strategy, productivity, and business performance. The findings of their study suggest that the fit between OM strategy and strategic-level strategies is of greater importance than the particular choice of strategy, and that the fit had a significant positive and direct effect on business performance. Using survey responses from 160 US manufacturing firms, Kotha and Swamidass (2000) investigated the fit between OM strategy, *advanced manufacturing technology* (AMT) use, and business performance. The findings of their study suggest that a fit between certain business strategies and AMT dimensions is associated with superior business performance. In summary these research studies suggest that OM managers will be more successful if there are good fits between their OM strategies and their use of technology.

Technology, though, does not work in a vacuum but must interact within the business environment in which it is placed. Ward and Duray (2000) examined the relationship between environment, manufacturing strategy, and business performance. Their study demonstrates that the strategic linkages in manufacturing businesses are clearer among good performers than poor performers. Ward *et al.* (1995) investigated the relationship between environmental factors, OM strategy, and business performance by surveying 1000 firms in Singapore. Their research suggest that environmental factors appear to have a substantial impact on OM strategy, and that good performers adopt different operations strategies in response to environmental stimuli when comparted to poor performers. Badri *et al.* (2000) extended the study of Ward *et al.* (1995) to a different environment, the United Arab Emirates, and expanded the environment dimension to include other variables, such as government regulations and political effects. Their study concurred with the findings of Ward *et al.* (1995), and suggest that proper environmental factors should be a part of any operations strategy framework. In summary, OM managers must include in their strategic plans a consideration of the business environment that they operate in.

Given that the business environment and strategic fit are important in OM strategy development, how do we go about selecting strategies to achieve successful business performance? The answer can be seen in Figure 2's constructs. Gerwin (1993) studied the relationship between business environment and operations strategy and found that the business environment leads to the OM strategy selection. Vickery *et al.* (1993) identified a fit relationship as being critical between environment factors and OM strategy, and its impact on business performance. Ward *et al.* (1995) found with respect to the substance of OM strategy, that the business environment appears to have a tangible impact on strategic choices in operations. OM strategy literature also suggests that operations strategy has a positive impact on performance (Berry and Cooper 1999; Smith and Reece 1999). Kathuria (2000) claimed that the fit between the business environment and the OM strategy was a central tenet of major strategic management paradigms. Research works examining individual dimensions of OM strategy on business performance have shown a positive impact of individual dimensions of operations strategy on business performance. For example, Flynn *et al.* (1994) suggested that quality management positively influenced business performance. Samson and Terziovski (1999) studied the relationship between *total quality management* (TQM) practices and business performance indicated that the relationship between TQM practices and business performance is significant. Numerous researchers found that flexibility positively affected business performance (D'Souza and Williams 2000; Vokurka and O'Leary-Kelly 2000; Koste and Malhotra 1999; Berry and Cooper 1999; Collins *et al.* 1998). This is also very true for e-commerce operations (Feeny, 2001).

What the research in this section reveals in that much of the OM strategy is dependent on the business environment. Equally important is the observation that the successfulness of any OM strategy is both directly and indirectly impacted by how well they are aligned to fit the organization. Because OM strategic planning is important for any type of operation, and particularly an e-commerce operation, this research provides a useful base, both theoretically and applied to understand e-commerce operations. Unfortunately it is only a portion of the total picture of how e-commerce strategic planning is undertaken. What will help complete the picture is understanding how the information system (IS) functional strategic planning is related to OM planning and what is felt to be critically important in that planning process.

Research Relationship of OM on Information Systems Strategic Planning

The relationship between information systems or *IS strategy* (i.e., the existing uses of information technology in organizations) and OM strategy has been the focus of much discussion during the past decade. There have been some empirical studies that sought to determine the extent to which information systems complement OM strategy (Sabherwal and Chan 2001; Chan *et al.* 1997). Chan *et al.* (1997) proposed a conceptual framework similar to that in Figure 3 to establish links between the business strategy orientation, the information system's strategy orientation, and business performance. Like the previous model for OM strategies in Figure 2, the model in Figure 3 presents the constructs between the four variables that explain their relationships to one another. Chan *et al.* (1997) findings suggested that companies with high IS strategic alignment were better performing companies. Although the findings implied that there were several ways to be successful, alignment between OM strategy and information systems strategic orientations was an essential link for successful business performance.

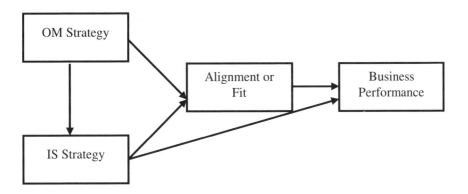

Figure 3. Information systems relationship with OM strategy model

As might be expected there are similarities in the development of IS strategies and OM strategies. Clearly an IS strategy is integral to e-business strategy. The focus of IS strategy is on alignment with all organizational-level strategies (Levy and Powell 2000) and requires a good strategic fit with the organization in which it is developed. Blili and Raymond (1993) showed that information system's strategy in companies became more critical as technology became more central to companies' products and processes, and that the IS strategy needed to be integrated with the organizational-level strategy. Avison *et al.* (1998) showed that without an alignment or good fit between IS strategy and organizational-level strategy, it is likely that information systems would be developed in a piecemeal manner, neither contributing to strategic vision nor enhancing organizational flexibility to respond to market changes. Earl (1996) also argued that IS strategy needed to change in respond to the business environment. According to Levy *et al.* (1998), firms adopting information systems without considering organizational-level strategy are unlikely to gain business benefits. Chan *et al.* (1998) examined IS strategy, OM strategy, and performance. Their research suggested that the fit between IS and OM strategy had a positive impact on business performance. However, the information systems research in this area did not include environmental factors. Reich and Benbasat (2000) investigated factors that influenced the *social dimension of alignment* (i.e., this refers to the state in which business and *information technology* or IT executives understand and are committed to the business and IT mission, objectives, and plans) between business and information technology objectives. They argue that the establishment of strong alignment between IT and organizational objectives is one of the key concerns of information systems managers. Sabherwal and Chan (2001) studied the alignment between business strategy and information system's strategy, which is widely believed to improve business performance. Their study explored and demonstrated the importance of the relationship between environmental factors, information strategic orientation, OM strategy, and business performance in an electronic commerce setting.

In summary, a good strategic fit between IS and OM is necessary in the development of functional-level strategies in order to achieve business performance success. Again, as with OM strategic development, there must be a good fit and consideration of the business environment in the IS objectives with the firm's organizational-level objectives for successful IS strategic planning.

Towards an E-Commerce Operations Management Strategic Planning Model

E-commerce research started in the late 90's and has grown considerably over the last decade (Gupta *et al.* 2009).   Raghunathan and Madey (1999), Badri *et al.* (2001), Bauer and Colgan (2001), Cheng *et al.* (2001), Pant and Ravichandran (2001), Afauh and Tucci (2001), Ngai and Gunasekaran (2007),

Kim *et al.* (2009) and Xiao and Benbasat (2011) proposed several differing conceptual models for e-commerce strategic planning and research. What are in common in these models are constructs of three major variables including: e-commerce business models, the business environment, and business performance as presented in Figure 4.

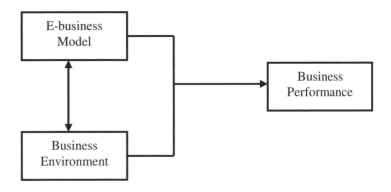

Figure 4. Simplified e-commerce strategy model

One study by Andersen (2001) did examine how the enhancement of an organization's communication capabilities would influence performance through improved strategic decision making, better coordination of strategic actions, and by facilitating learning from strategic initiatives. The results of this study showed a positive construct between Intranet use and innovation. There was also a positive construct to profitability and to innovation in organizations.

In the model in Figure 4 the e-commerce business model variable is the same as was defined in Chapter 1: an *e-business model* is the way an organization conducts its business to make money or achieve financial success. The other variables are the same as previously defined in this chapter. What is conspicuously missing in this model is the "alignment or fit" and, most relevant for this book, the "OM strategy" variables mentioned in the previously models in Figures 2 and 3. To over come these exceptions additional research, based on an extensive empirical study was undertaken by Cao (2001). In this research, the linkages among business environment, OM strategy, IS strategy, and business performance are considered simultaneously using empirical evidence. In contrast to all of the previous research, Cao's research applies OM strategy theory while incorporating the e-commerce elements of the IS strategy model. In this way Cao

(2001) extends the de facto OM strategy models (Badri *et al.* 2000; Ward *et al.* 1995; Skinner, 1969) by incorporating an IS strategic orientation (Chan *et al.* 1997; Chan *et al.* 1998; Reich and Benbasat 2000; Sabherwal and Chan 2001) of an e-commerce setting. In his model in Figure 5 the business environment variable directly influences OM strategy, the alignment between business environment and OM strategy influences business performance, operations strategy has a direct impact on IS strategic orientation, the fit between IS strategic orientation and OM strategy influences business performance, and the IS strategic orientation directly influences business performance.

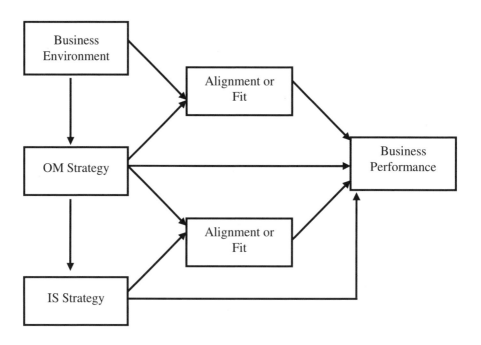

Figure 5. E-commerce operations management strategy model

In the research undertaken to confirm the constructs presented in Figure 5, Cao (2001) demonstrated the importance of the OM strategy and IS strategy variables being aligned in order to achieve successful e-commerce business performance. Along the way, he identified and empirically proved that there exists a number of "critical success factors" (CSFs) that both OM strategy development and IS strategy development must include for e-commerce success.

His research, combined with other research studies identifies the CSFs for e-commerce operations management that are introduced in the next section.

Critical Success Factors in E-Commerce Operations Management

It is impossible for a single book to cover all the critical success factors (CSFs) that may be important to all e-commerce companies. In reviewing recent e-commerce literature a rather consistent set of factors seem to be repeatedly reported as defining what is necessary for business performance success in the area of operations management. Eight of these consistently reported CSFs in e-commerce operations management are presented in Table 1. Some of the related research for the CSFs listed in Table 1 will be discussed here and again later in the remaining chapters of this book. The definitions used in this section to define the CSFs will be purposefully brief for purposes of an introduction only. The CSFs will be substantially expanded each with its own chapter in the remaining chapters of this book.

Supply Chain Management and E-Commerce Research

Supply chain management is all the management tasks necessary to obtain, move, transport, process, and deliver goods from vendors, through manufacturing, to the final customer. The use of Internet technologies to manage supply chain information is a substantial improvement over traditional information systems (Turban *et al.* 2000, 2001; Venkatraman 2000; Applegate *et al.* 1996). Internet information systems allow transactions to be conducted in an integrated and enlarged information space by removing constraints imposed by diverse computing platforms, networks, and applications (Deeter-Schmelz *et al.* 2001; Isakowitz *et al.* 1998; Lederer and Sethi 1998), thereby transforming supply chain management (Cross 2000).

Clark and Stoddard (1996) explored supply chain management coordination issues in e-commerce. They argued that e-commerce linkages were being created between independent organizations in multiple industries, including manufacturing, financial services, transportation, and retailing. Findings of their research suggest that participating firms could gain dramatic benefits from establishing an electronic linkage only when the system is used to increase interdependence and to expand coordination between firms involved in this new inter-organizational relationship. Drawing on the theoretical and empirical research of electronic communications and inter-firm designs, they developed and empirically tested a model explaining the relationships among variables including business performance, interdependence, and coordination of firms involved in inter-organizational relations within the US grocery channel. Both qualitative and quantitative findings indicated that critical success in channel business performance, interdependence, and coordination were closely related to firms with inter-organizational relationships.

Table 1. Critical success factors and related research

CSFs	Related research
Supply Chain Management	Applegate *et al.* (1996), Bhatt and Stump (2001), Cao (2001), Cheng *et al.* (2001), Clark and Stoddard (1996), Cross (2000), Graham and Hardaker (2000), Isakowitz *et al.* (1998), Lederer and Sethi (1998), Turban *et al.* (2001), Venkatraman (2000), Yang and Papazoglou (2000)
Product and Process Design Management	Archer and Yuan (2000), Cao (2001), Emiliani (2000), Guimaraes (2000), Hart *et al.* (2000), Howe *et al.* (2000), Huang and Mak (1999), Marchewka and Towell (2000), Park and Baik (1999), Rao (2000), Rowley (2000), Sarkis and Sundarraj (2000)
Purchasing Management	Cao (2001), Copeland and Hwang (1999), Deeter-Schmeiz *et al.* (2001), Lin and Hsieh (2000), Gattiker *et al.* (2000), Min and Galle (1999), Phau and Poon (2000), Sawabini (2001), Segev *et al.* (1997), Simeon (1999), Turban *et al.* (2001), Wortmann (2000), Wymbs (2000)
Forecasting and Scheduling Management	Boyer (2001), Choi (2000), Culbertson *et al.* (2001), Harrington (1999), Harrington (2000), Heizer and Render (2000), Howells (2000), Reynolds (2000)
Inventory Management	Boyer (2001), Culbertson *et al.* (2001), Heizer and Render (2000), Kamarainen *et al.* (2001), Smaros and Holmstrom (2000), Vlosky (1999)
Quality Management	Cao (2001), Chang and Visser (1998), Dewhurst *et al.* (1999), Finch (1999), Shah and Singh (2001), Shaw *et al.* (1997), Zsidisin *et al.* (2000)
Human Resource Management	Bal and Teo (2000), Reynolds (2000), Sones (2001)
Reengineering and Consulting Management	McIvor *et al.* (2000), Pereira (1999), Wells (2000)

Recognizing the importance of information systems infrastructure in e-commerce, Yang and Papazoglou (2000) examined supply chain management from the standpoint of an architectural framework. They claim that the boundaries of organizations are more fluid than previously observed, and that supply chain management forces companies to streamline the ways they manufacture, distribute, and sell products, which ultimately improve the way organizations conduct business. They argued that an architectural framework that permitted flexibility, interoperability, and openness was a CSF for e-commerce applications. They described the critical elements of interoperability in the context of e-commerce and integrated value chains. They further discussed current development trends and expectations for e-commerce research employing supply chain management.

Cheng *et al.* (2001) proposed a model for an e-commerce infrastructure that could be used to support supply chain activities in construction. In their study, a virtual network structure that acted as a value-added component of an e-commerce infrastructure was used to improve communication and coordination, and also to encourage the mutual sharing of inter-organizational resources and competencies. The e-commerce infrastructure used to support the proposed network structure, as well as the human, organizational, and cultural barriers that might be encountered were presented and discussed. They argued that the proposed e-commerce model would not only benefit those organizations operating in a construction supply chain, but also might fit other types of B2B e-commerce in environments where cooperation between business partners was critical for improving organizational performance and gaining a competitive advantage.

According to Graham and Hardaker (2000), good supply chain management is a CSF for a successful company. Supply chain management can reach beyond the boundaries of a single company to involve sharing information between suppliers, manufacturers, distributors, and retailers. This is where the Internet plays a central role. Shifts towards the development of a virtual supply chain architecture dramatically emphasize the importance of knowledge and intellect in creating value. Adoption of an integrated approach throughout the supply chain requires trade-offs in a unique balance of autonomy and control, a balance that must be developed and maintained for each supply partner relationship. E-commerce communities can target new markets, by offering low entry costs, relatively minimal complexity with more flexibility, and a convenient way of transacting business. It has also been observed that the trend toward outsourcing and strategic alliances in most industries provides an added impetus to support the sharing of supplier, customer, and corporate information that was once proprietary, with competitors and other cross-industry players (Bhatt and Stump 2001).

Product and Process Design Management and E-Commerce Research

Product and process design management refers to the management tasks required in the design and development of products and processes used in both manufacturing and service applications. Internet technology has been increasingly used to support various aspects of the product development process (Guimaraes 2000). Accelerating the process by which new products are introduced to the marketplace has become a strategic imperative in many markets. An emerging precondition for new-product development success is the integration of IT with innovative management practices. Howe *et al.* (2000) explored how the integration of Internet and Intranet applications with the production processes could support and accelerate new product development. This research provided insight into the CSF role Internet technology could play in facilitating information dissemination, process improvements, reductions in time and costs, and improved project management.

Huang and Mak (1999) demonstrated "design for manufacture and assembly" techniques on the Internet. (*Design for manufacture and assembly* or DFMA is an engineering job that seeks to optimize the processes used to produce a final product.) In their research, an experiment was conducted to show how a well-known design for assembly technique could be converted into a Web-based version that was functionally equivalent to its regular standalone workstation version. The Web-based client-server architecture was found to be attractive for collaborative DFMA. The findings of the research suggested that client-side Web scripting could be exploited to develop generic frameworks for developing and applying different *designs for experimental* (DFX) techniques. In addition, Web-based DFX techniques provided more opportunities for integration with other decision support systems such as computer-aided design.

Park and Baik (1999) proposed an intelligent design system environment through agent-based collaborative support via the Internet. This proposed system exchanged process-related features, capabilities, and constraints among design and manufacturing agents. The system, which could enhance manufacturing product development, emphasized the consideration of elements related to process planning and manufacturing concurrent with product design, to materialize the design for manufacturability. In doing so, the Internet-based system supported the concurrent engineering concept of product and process design and could become a CSF to achieve a competitive advantage.

Purchasing Management and E-Commerce Research

Purchasing management includes all the management tasks that are required in setting up, running, and monitoring purchasing activities of an organization. These tasks will include the section of vendors and all purchasing inventory items. The increased popularity of e-commerce in procurement is due to a multitude of operational benefits it can bring to purchasing practices. Many researchers see purchasing management as a primary CSF in e-commerce operations (Tang 2001). Examples of these benefits are cost savings resulting from reduced paper transactions, shorter order cycle time and the subsequent inventory reduction resulting from speedy transmission of purchase order related information, and enhanced opportunities for the supplier/buyer partnership through the establishment of a Web of B2B communication networks.

E-commerce technologies provide effective and efficient ways in which corporate buyers can gather information rapidly about available products and services, evaluate and negotiate with suppliers, implement order fulfillment over communications links, and access post-sales services. From the supplier side, marketing, sales, and service information is also readily gathered from customers. Building and maintaining customer relationships is the key to success in e-commerce, and unless service is maintained, customer loss may result, more than offsetting any cost efficiencies gained by introducing e-commerce technology. Since a prerequisite of e-commerce is information and communications, support for managing customer relationships with technology is critical to those who know how to use it. Archer and Yuan (2000) examined how technology could be used to encourage and facilitate customer-business relationships. The findings of their study demonstrated through a customer relationship life cycle model, how the management of related procurement functions in customer companies could be adjusted to become a CSF in building these relationships.

Through empirical survey research, Min and Galle (1999) investigated factors that influenced purchasing professionals' willingness to adopt or utilize an e-commerce purchasing system, while determining the most suitable e-commerce purchasing strategy for a particular organizational setting. In so doing, their research identified the fact that purchasing was an important CSF regardless of the organizational setting. Their findings suggest that the buying firm with large purchase volumes is a heavy user of e-commerce, and is likely to force its suppliers into the e-commerce network. Their study also pinpointed the fact that such a firm wanting its suppliers to join the e-commerce network would not necessarily provide appropriate support for its non-e-commerce capable suppliers. Finally, they claimed that while the level of a buyer's e-commerce knowledge is factored into its e-commerce usage, the buyer is really concerned about the potential security risk involved in e-commerce usage. Nevertheless, they argued that such a security risk alone did not seem to be viewed as an insurmountable obstacle for e-commerce applications.

Consumer purchasing (i.e., in this case B2C) behavior also plays a crucial role in e-commerce. By comparing purchasing behavior between potential e-commerce buyers and non-e-commerce buyers, Phau and Poon (2000) investigated business to consumer e-commerce in Singapore. They found that the classification of different types of products and services will significantly influence the consumer choice between a retail store and an Internet shopping mall, and that a well managed purchasing function is a CSF in meeting consumer needs. The types of products and services that were suitable for selling through the Internet were also identified. Their findings showed that generally products and services that had a low financial outlay were frequently purchased at a brick-and-mortar store, while products and services that had intangible value and relatively high differentiation were more likely to be purchased via the Internet. Their findings also concurred with Simeon's (1999) results, which indicated that e-commerce shoppers exhibit demographic and psychographic differences.

Before e-commerce became synonymous with Internet-based commerce, e-commerce meant, "electronic data interchange". *Electronic data interchange* or EDI is a technology that enables corporations to exchange data electronically with their suppliers. It has been in use for more than 20 years, and major manufacturers, retailers, and others have spent tens of millions of dollars each year in an ongoing campaign to establish it as the de facto standard for communication. As a new generation of Internet-based technologies emerges, promising to improve the supply chain, many observers leap to the conclusion that EDI is on its way out (Sawabini 2001). Attention has shifted from electronic data exchange-integration with third parties toward applications for e-commerce, leveraging the Internet (Wortmann 2000, Lu 2001). Indeed, Segev *et al.* (1997) argued that the Internet appears to be a cheap, efficient, and ubiquitous channel for transmitting EDI transactions. Their research contrasted two strategies for implementing Internet-EDI systems. The first strategy treated an Internet-EDI system as a traditional information systems development project. The second strategy was used by Bank of America, and built its Internet-EDI system using a prototyping approach. The conditions in which either approach might be appropriate in terms of project goals, time constraints, environmental uncertainty, and organizational structures employed was also discussed by Segev *et al.* (1997). Moreover, they suggested that emerging Internet-EDI applications could transform trading partners' relationships by reducing the import of EDI-capability as a competitive asset, thereby becoming a CSF for many firms.

Forecasting and Scheduling Management and E-Commerce Research

Forecasting management refers to managing the analytic process of determining customer demand and includes determining demand on OM processes. Once customer demand is determined OM managers next have to undertake the development of a production schedule. *Scheduling management* refers to the activities required to formally state what unit production is to be on a timed basis of a day, a week, a month, or a year. Harrington (1999) and Howells (2000) make the connection between the bottom line profitability of an e-commerce organization and it use of forecasting and scheduling as CSFs. Harrington makes the point that integrated systems that include forecasting and scheduling components will be more cost effective than those that don't in e-commerce business environments due to the rapid changes in market demand and the competitive nature of the industry. In a further article by Harrington (2000) the notion of integrating systems, including forecasting and scheduling provides a flexibility in the supply chain of an organization that is necessary to quickly adapt to changes in demand. The integration also allows for positive impacts on other CSFs, such inventory management. Also reported by Boyer (2001), the online integration allows for centralized locations of inventory, which reduce costs and permit production scheduling opportunities to improve efficiency. E-commerce allows companies to centralize their operations in general, which allows for greater task specialization. This permits a less customized demand, particularly for service operations, and a greater standardization of production processes. The efficiencies of this standardization process can result in substantial improvement in productivity and ease of scheduling and task loading. Adding to the integrated theme, Choi *et al.* (2000) described how Internet-based production scheduling is one of several features critical to the successful implementation of computer integrated systems.

Inventory Management and E-Commerce Research

Inventory management is a collection of managerial tasks that are required to acquire, maintain, and deliver inventory to destinations inside and outside production operations. During the last months of 1999 the e-commerce retail (also called *e-retailers*) industry was on the verge of the greatest sales period in its history. Unfortunately the demand far exceeded the available inventory at the e-retailers. The results of this poor inventory planning delayed gift deliveries beyond the holiday period and in thousands of cases caused cancelled orders and frustrated customers who have not returned to doing shopping over the Web. This event made businesses, both brick-and-mortar and e-businesses very much aware that business performance success can rest on a CSF of inventory management.

Since the delivery issues in 1999, e-retailing has shown years of progressive growth and success. Amazon is considered the gold standard for fast order processing and delivery. Other e-retailers try to imitate Amazon processes to increase their own efficiency. Amazon has 18% market share in e-commerce in the U.S., and that is estimated to increase to 33% by 2016. Amazon's worldwide sales are greater than $34 billion, and in 2010, they grew by 39.5%. (Tompkins and Avila 2012).

In a survey conducted by Vlosky (1999) it was observed that the Internet could help customers identify available inventory and help reduce on-hand inventory requirements. They also observed that better inventory control could be achieved by using the Internet, which helped identify in-bound product locations. Culbertson *et al.* (2001) explained how an inventory control system in e-commerce could help make timely adjustments to inventory levels to reduce costs and inventory investments requirements.

One of the many tasks that are a part of inventory management is order picking. Kamarainen *et al.* (2001) reported how inventory costs, in the areas of cost of goods sold, operating costs, and distribution could be improved by using the Web to better coordinate customer demand and inventory planning. Smaros and Holmstrom (2000) similarly found that integrating shop-floor technologies in e-grocery operations allowed for information on inventory to be shared and better used to reduce costs throughout the entire supply chain of an organization.

Other reported aspects of inventory management that are both critical to business success and a benefit of using the Web include the inventory tracking and inventory reduction capabilities (Heizer and Render 2000), improved inventory logistics (Howells 2000), and process planning (Choi *et al.* 2000). All of which clearly demonstrate how critical inventory management is in an e-commerce operation.

Quality Management and E-Commerce Research

Quality management is a set of tasks required to maintain product or service quality in finished products an organization provides its customers. As product quality has become an increasingly important CSF, linking quality management efforts to customer wants and needs has also expanded. For product manufacturers this has resulted in a need to develop more direct links to the customer. Anecdotal reports indicate that firms are beginning to tap into Internet discussions as a source for product quality type of information (Shaw *et al.* 1997). Finch (1999) conducted an exploratory study by monitoring the entire network of user groups for 1 year for messages containing the name of one quality oriented company. The messages were analyzed and revealed the importance of product quality as a CSF.

Using Internet technologies, Chang and Visser (1998) proposed a distributed quality control framework to facilitate quality-related information exchange among members of the supply chain. The proposed framework supported an initiative that integrated state-of-the-art information technologies with quality control tools for swift product design, process design, and quality assurance. The findings of their research suggest that the biggest impact of the proposed approach was that customers could be involved in decision-making about product quality while the manufacturing of ordered products was being planned and produced without physically being there.

Zsidisin *et al.* (2000) examined the relationship between information technology and service quality in a case study situation. The results of this study confirmed the importance of Web-based communication in the delivery of quality oriented services to customers. Interestingly, the study showed that important issues such as a Web site design and the ability to establish competitive advantages in cost and quality are CSFs in being successful.

Cao (2001) empirically demonstrated that quality management was a CSF in determining business performance. Relating the e-commerce operations management strategic model in Figure 5, quality management was determined to be a factor used by successful firms in the alignment of strategies to result in better business performance.

Human Resource Management and E-Commerce Research

To be successful, firms must organize their employees or *human resources* (HR) to take advantage of and build competitive advantages of the e-commerce environment in which they operate. *Human resource management* involves all management tasks of planning, organizing, staffing, and directing HRs. As Sones (2001) points out an e-commerce business must align itself with clear and formal lines of authority to be able to adapt and move as quickly as the needs of e-commerce customers dictate. Without clear and formal lines of authority reporting and control problems can create great disharmony in any organization, but particularly for the fast moving e-businesses. The roles of all HR managers and administrators must be clearly defined so e-commerce operations are responsive. This is particularly true for newly formed organizations, of which most e-commerce departments or organizations suffer from a lack of historic perspective on who really is the "boss". Indeed, Reynolds (2000) reported that a survey had revealed most Web staff was poorly integrated within their organizations and their roles were poorly defined. Reynolds went on to suggest that most firms are adopting a model of organizational change that will help them to identify those aspects of operating in an e-commerce environment and exploiting them by making changes in what their staff should do to take full advantage of skills they bring to their organizations.

One HR strategy that has had some success in organizing staff has been through the implementation of "virtual teamworking" (Bal and Teo 2000). *Virtual teamworking* can be defined as a group of people who interact through interdependent tasks guided by a common purpose but using networking and Web technology for communication purposes. This approach has application to a wide range of HR activities, including engineering, supply chain management, and HR recruitment.

Reengineering and Consulting Management and E-Commerce Research

Since e-commerce operations must by necessity under go continuous revision to meet with their uniquely volatile markets, they require both a process by which change can take place and the necessary expertise to help advise on how best to make those changes. *Reengineering management* also called *business process reengineering* (BPR) is an activity that involves the managing of the restructuring of production processes in an effort to improve efficiency. *Consulting management* involves managing the use of and acquisition of human resources who provide advising and consulting expertise on various OM topics.

Wells (2000) examined factors affecting the implementation of BPR projects using Internet technology. He argued that each IT used during BPR implementation might affect managerial factors differently, and that by determining factors that affected BPR implementation using a specific IT, that these factors could be managed to increase the chance of a successful BPR implementation. The factors examined in the research were: culture, resource management, resistance management, and change management. The findings of the study suggested that the BPR project team should take control of the reengineering effort and that BPR projects using Internet technology could dramatically change how an organization functioned. The findings also showed that regardless of how successful the implementation of the reengineered system using Internet technology was, there was no great need for additional resources. Moreover, the results indicated that adoption and use of Internet technology might prevent employee resistance by allowing them to easily acquire the skills necessary to work with the BPR projects.

During the past two decades both business managers and academic researchers have shown considerable interest in IS networks including the Internet, and their effect on business processes and performance. Bhatt and Stump (2001) built on this interest to examine the nature of IS networks and *business process improvement initiatives* (called BPII), and to delineate the process by which IS networks influenced BPII. A model was developed to elaborate on the interrelationships between these two constructs along with two key contextual antecedents (management support and information intensity). The findings of the study indicated that while network connectivity and flexibility were found to be significantly related to process improvement initiatives, network flexibility had no significant effect on customer focus. Information intensity was also found to be significantly related to BPII and partially mediated by network flexibility with regard to process improvement initiatives.

There are no empirical journal research publications on e-commerce and consulting, but by the dynamic nature of e-commerce it is clear that consulting is commonly used and is essential to successful operations. Chase *et al.* (2001, p. 327) include consulting as an important area of application in e-commerce operations. Greiner and Savich (1998) make it clear that if you are in a business of change one of the best and most costless approaches to change is through consulting expertise. For some e-commerce organizations that can afford consulting expertise but not the investment in permanent staffers, consulting can be a CSF in the acquisition of a essential competitive advantage.

An E-Commerce Operations Management Strategic Planning Model

The CSFs observed in the research discussed in the last section can lead to a more focused e-commerce strategic planning model in the functional area of operations management. Presented in Figure 6, this book proposes that e-commerce organizations must adapt to their external business environments by selecting OM strategies that they can build a successful operation around. The eight strategies proposed in this model are based on the prior research that showed either conceptually or empirically that the eight are critical to the successfulness of e-commerce operations. While it recognized that any one organization might choose to select one or only a few of these OM areas in which to build a competitive advantage, this book advocates that all areas of OM (including areas beyond the scope of this book) should be considered in developing strategic plans in order to lead to business performance success. Each of the chapters that follow are devoted to helping understand these eight basic strategic areas in OM and how they can be adapted, changed, and structured within the context of an e-commerce operation for maximum business performance success.

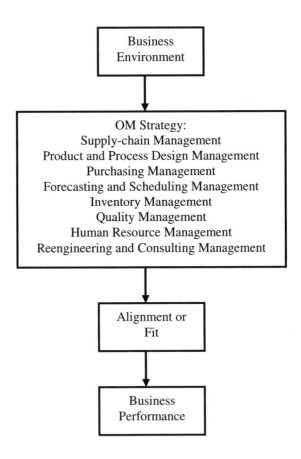

Figure 6. E-commerce operations management strategy model

Summary

Due to the dominance of e-commerce in today's economy, e-commerce research has increased drastically in the past few years. The focus of such research has been in all functional areas of organizations, including operations management. As early as Elofson and Robinson (1998) it was argued that OM strategy research in e-commerce was greatly needed. Keeney (1999) studied the value of e-commerce to the customer and found a set of fundamental OM-related objectives essential or critical for profitable e-commerce operations. Geoffrion and Krishnan (2001), found that OM plays a critical role in e-commerce research. Indeed, some researchers have found that by not paying attention to OM strategies it can be very costly to the growth of e-commerce operations (Han and Noh 2000).

This chapter presented a review of prior research studies dealing first with strategic planning, then focusing on operations strategic planning, and finally on e-commerce operations strategic planning. A series of research models where presented to help convey the ideas discussed in the research. Based on this research a set of eight management-related CSFs (i.e., supply chain, product and process design, purchasing, forecasting and scheduling, inventory, quality, human resources, reengineering and consulting) where identified. These eight CSFs where presented here as the basis of an e-commerce operations management strategic planning model on which the rest of this book will be based.

◆ Review Terms

Advanced manufacturing
technology (ATM)
Alignment (variable in a model)
Business environment (variable in a
model)
Business performance (variable in a
model)
Business process reengineering
(BPR)
Competitive advantage
Constructs (in a model)
Consulting management
Critical success factors (CSFs)
Design for experimental (DFX)
Design for manufacture and
assembly (DFMA)
Electronic data interchange (EDI)
E-retailers
Fit (variable in a model)

Forecasting management
Human resources (HR)
Information systems (IS)
Information system's strategy
Information technology (IT)
Inventory management
Operations management (OM)
Operations management strategy
Product and process design
management
Purchasing management
Quality management
Reengineering management
Social dimension of alignment
Scheduling management
Strategic planning
Supply chain management
Total quality management (TQM)
Virtural teamworking

◆ Discussion Questions

1. Explain how "strategic planning" leads to "e-commerce operations management strategic planning."
2. Explain why a "competitive advantage" is usually the objective in "strategic planning."
3. Explain why "IS strategic planning" should be included in "OM strategic planning" for e-commerce operations.
4. Explain what the purpose is of the strategic planning model variable "alignment."
5. Explain why all the strategic planning models in this chapter end with the "business performance" variable.
6. Explain how the eight "critical success factors" identified in this chapter should be incorporated into all e-commerce strategic planning models.

♦ Questions

1. Why does all OM strategic planning follow the organization-level strategic planning of the organization?
2. What are the four basic variables in the OM strategy model?
3. Why is the variable "fit" so important in strategic planning models?
4. What are the constructs in the IS relationship with OM Strategy model in Figure 3? Explain each.
5. What are the eight CSFs suggested in this chapter? Briefly define each.
6. What is EDI? How is it related to e-commerce?
7. What is BRR? How is it related to e-commerce?
8. Are the CSFs "strategies" or a part of the "business environment"? Explain.

References

Afuah, A. and Tucci, C.L., *Internet Business Models and Strategies: Text and Cases*, Burr: IL, Irwin/McGraw-Hill, 2001.

Andersen, T., "Information Technology, Strategic Decision Making Approaches and Organizational Performance in Different Industrial Settings," *Journal of Strategic Information Systems*, Vol. 10, No. 2, 2001, pp. 101–119.

Applegate, L.M., Holsapple, C.W., Kalakota, R., Radermacher, F.J. and Whinston, A.B. "Electronic Commerce: Building Blocks of New Business Opportunity," *Journal of Organization Computing Electronic Commerce*, Vol. 6, No. 1, 1996, pp. 1–10.

Archer, N. and Yuan, Y "Managing Business-to-business Relationships Throughout the E-commerce Procurement Life Cycle," *Internet Research*, Vol. 10, No. 5, 2000, pp. 385–395.

Avison, D., Eardley, W. and Powell, P. "Suggestions for Capturing Corporate Vision in Strategic Information Systems," *Omega*, Vol. 26, No. 4, 1998, pp. 441–459.

Badri, M., Davis, D. and Davis, D., "Operations Strategy, Environment Uncertainty and Performance: A Path Analytic Model of Industries in Developing Countries," *Omega* Vol. 28, 2000, pp. 155–173.

Bal, J. and Teo, P., "Implementing Virtual Teamwork. Part 1: A Literature Review of Best Practice," *Logistics Information Management*, Vol. 13, No. 6, 2000, pp. 346–352.

Bauer, C. and Colgan, J. "Planning For Electronic Commerce Strategy: An Explanatory Study From the Financial Services Sector," *Logistics Information Management*, Vol. 14, No. 1, 2001, pp. 24–32.

Berry, W.L. and Cooper, M.C. "Manufacturing Flexibility: Methods for Measuring the Impact of Product Variety on Performance in Process Industries," *Journal of Operations Management*, Vol. 17, 1999, pp. 163–178.

Bhatt, G.B. and Stump, R.L. "An Empirically Derived Model of the Role of IS Networks in Business Process Improvement Iinitiatives", *Omega*, Vol. 29, No. 1, 2001, pp. 29–48.

Blili, S. and Raymond, L. "Information Technology: Threats and Opportunities for Small and Medium-sized Enterprises," *International Journal of Information Management*, Vol. 13, 1993, pp. 439–448.

Boyer, K.K., "E-operations: A Guide to Streamlining with the Internet," *Business Horizons*, January-February 2001, pp. 47–54.

Boyer, K.K. and Pagell, M. "Measurement Issues in Empirical Research: Improving Measures of Operations Strategy and Advanced Manufacturing Technology," *Journal of Operations Management*, Vol.18, No. 3, 2000, pp. 361–374.

Cao, Q., "Enhancing Business Performance in an Electronic Commerce Setting: An Empirical Study," An unpublished dissertation, University of Nebraska-Lincoln, June, 2001.

Chan, Y.E., Huff, S.L., Barclay, D.W. and Copeland, D.G. "Business Strategic Orientation, Information Systems Strategic Orientation, and Strategic Alignment," *Information Systems Research*, Vol. 8, No. 2, June 1997, pp. 125–150.

Chan, Y.E., Huff, S.L. and Copeland, D.G. "Assessing Realized Information System's Strategy," *Journal of Strategic Information Systems*, Vol. 6, 1998, pp. 273–298.

Chang, S. I. and Visser J.J. "A Framework of Distributed Quality Control," *Computer & Industrial Engineering*, Vol. 35, Nos. 1–2, 1998, pp. 181–184.

Chase, R.B., Aquilano, N.J. and Jacobs, R.J., *Operations Management for Competitive Advantage*, Burr Ridge: IL, McGraw-Hill/Irwin, 2001.

Cheng, E.W.L., Li, H., Love, P.E.D. and Irani, Z. "An E-business Model to Support Supply Chain Activities in Construction," *Logistics Information Management*, Vol. 14, No. 1, 2001, pp. 68–78.

Choi, H., Kim, H., Park, Y., Kim, K., Joo, M. and Sohn, H., "A Sales Agent for Part Manufacturers: VMSA," *Decision Support Systems*, Vol. 28, 2000, pp. 333–346.

Clark, T.H. and Stoddard, D.B., "Interorganizational Business Process Redesign: Merging Technological and Process Innovation," *Journal of Management Information Systems* Vol. 13, No. 2, Fall 1996, pp. 9–29.

Cleveland, G., Schroeder, R.G. and Anderson, J.C., "Production Competence: A Proposed Theory," *Decision Sciences*, Vol. 20, No. 4, 1989, pp. 655–688.

Collins, R.S., Cordon, C. and Julien, D., "An Empirical Test of the Rigid Flexibility Model," *Journal of Operations Management*, Vol. 16, Nos. 2-3, 1998, pp. 133–146.

Cooper, D.R. and Schindler, P.S., *Business Research Methods*, Saddleback: IL, Irwin/McGraw-Hill, 1998.

Copeland, K. and Hwang, C., "Building Full Service Intranets for Federal Systems Internet Infrastructure," *Journal of End User Computing*, Vol. 11, No. 3, 1999, pp. 23–35.

Cross G.J., "How E-business is Transforming Supply chain Management," *Journal of Business Strategy*, Vol. 21, No. 2, Mar/Apr 2000, pp. 36–40.

Culbertson, S., Burruss, J. and Buddress, L., "Control System Approach to E-commerce Fulfillment: Hewlett-Packard's Experience," *The Journal of Business Forecasting*, Winter 2001, pp. 10–16.

Deeter-Schmelz, I., Bizzari, D., Graham, R. and Howdyshell, K., "Business-to-business Online Purchasing: Suppliers' Impact on Buyers' Adoption and Usage Intent," *The Journal of Supply Chain Management*, Winter 2001, pp. 4–9.

Dewhurst, F., Lorente, A. and Dale, B., "Total Quality Management and Information Technologies: An Exploration of the Issues," *International Journal of Quality an Reliability Management*, Vol. 16, No. 4, 1999, pp. 395–405.

D'Souza, D.E. and Williams, F.P., "Toward a Taxonomy of Manufacturing Flexibility Dimensions", *Journal of Operations Management*, Vol. 18, No. 5, 2000, pp. 577–593.

Earl, M.J., Management Strategy for Information Technology, London: Prentice Hall, 1996.

Elofson, G. and Robinson, W.N., "Creating a Custom Mass-production Channel on the Internet," *Communications of the ACM*, Vol. 41, No. 3, March 1998, pp. 56–62.

Emiliani, M., "Business-to-business Online Auctions: Key Issues for Purchasing Process Improvement," *Supply Chain Management: An International Journal*, Vol. 5, No. 4, 2000, pp. 176–186.

Feeny, D., "E-opportunity," *Sloan Management Review*, Winter 2001, pp. 41–51.

Finch, B.J., "Internet Discussions as a Source for Consumer Product Customer Involvement and Quality Information: An Exploratory Study," *Journal of Operations Management*, Vol. 17, No. 5, 1999, pp. 535–557.

Flynn, B.B, Schroeder, R.G. and Sakakibara, S., "A Framework for Quality Management Research and an Associated Measurement Instrument," *Journal of Operations Management*, Vol. 11, No. 4, 1994, pp. 339–366.

Gattiker, U., Perlusz, S. and Bohmann, K., "Using the Internet for B2B Activities: A Review and Future Directions for Research," *Internet Research: Electronic Networking Applications and Policy*, Vol. 10, No. 2, 2000, pp. 126–140.

Geoffrion, A.M. and Krishnan, R., "Prospects for Operations Research," *Interfaces*, March-April 2001, pp. 1–35.

Gerwin, D., "Manufacturing Flexibility: A Strategic Perspective," *Management Science*, Vol. 39, No. 4, April 1993, pp. 395–251.

Graham, G. and Hardaker, G., "Supply chain Management Across the Internet," *International Journal of Physical Distribution & Logistics Management*, Vol. 30, No. 3–4, 2000, pp. 286–295.

Greiner, L. and Savich, R., *Consulting to Management*, NY, Prentice Hall, 1998.

Guimaraes, T., "The Impact of Competitive Intelligence and IS Support in Changing Small Business Organizations," *Logistics Information Management*, Vol. 13, No. 3, 2000, pp. 117–125.

Gupta, S., Koulamas, C., and Kyparisis, G.J. 2009. "E-Business: A Review of Research Published in Production and Operations Management (1992–2008)," *Production and Operations Management* (18:6), pp. 604-620.

Han, K.S. and Noh, M.H., "Critical Failure Factors that Discourage the Growth of Electronic Commerce," *International Journal of Electronic Commerce*, Vol. 4, No. 2, January 2000, pp. 25–44.

Harrington, L.H., "Collaborating on the Net," *Dot.Com*, February 2000, pp. 8–15.

Harrington, L.H., "Better Forecasting Can Improve Your Bottom Line," *Transportation and Distribution*, July 1999, pp. 21–28.

Hart, C., Doherty, N. and Ellis-Chadwick, F., "Retailer Adoption of the Internet," *European Journal of Marketing*, Vol. 34, No. 8, 2000, pp. 954–974.

Heizer, J. and Render, B., "How E-commerce Saves Money," *IIE Solutions*, August 2000, pp. 22–27.

Howe, V., Mathieu, R.G. and Parker, J., "Supporting New product Development with the Internet," *Industrial Management & Data Systems*, Vol. 100, No. 6, 2000, pp. 277–284.

Howells, R. "ERP Needs Shop-floor Data," *Manufacturing Engineering*, Vol. 10, 2000, pp. 54–62.

Huang, G.Q. and Mak, K.L., "Design for Manufacture and Assembly on the Internet," *Computers in Industry*, Vol. 38, No. 1, 1999, pp. 17–31.

Isakowitz, T., Bieber, M. and Vitali F., "Web Information Systems," *Communications of the ACM*, Vol. 41, No. 7, Jul 1998, pp. 78–80.

Kamarainen, V., Samaros, J., Jaakola, T. and Holmstrom, J., "Cost-effectiveness in the E-grocery Business," *International Journal of Retail and Distribution Management*, Vol. 29, No. 1, 2001, pp. 41–48.

Kathuria, R., "Competitive Priorities and Managerial Performance: A Taxonomy of Small Manufacturers," *Journal of Operations Management*, Vol. 18, No. 6, November 2000, pp. 627–641.

Keeney, R.L., "The Value of Internet Commerce to the Customer," *Management Science*, Vol. 45, No. 4, April 1999, pp. 533–542.

Kim, D.J., Ferrin, D.L., and Rao, H.R. 2009. "Trust and Satisfaction, Two Stepping Stones for Successful E-Commerce Relationships: A Longitudinal Exploration," *Information Systems Research* (20:2), pp. 237-257.

Koste, L.L. and Malhotra, M.K., "A Theoretical Framework for Analyzing the Dimensions of Manufacturing Flexibility," *Journal of Operations Management*, Vol. 18, No. 1, 1999, pp. 75–93.

Kotha, S. and Swamidass, P.M., "Strategy, Advanced Manufacturing Technology and Performance: Empirical Evidence from U.S. Manufacturing Firms," *Journal of Operations Management*, Vol. 18, No. 3, 2000, pp. 257–277.

Lederer, A. L and Sethi, V., "Seven Guidelines for Strategic Information Systems Planning," *Information Strategy*, Vol. 15, No. 1, Fall 1998, pp. 23–28.

Levy, M. and Powell, P., "Information System's Strategy for Small and Medium Sized Enterprises: An Organizational Perspective", *Journal of Strategic Information Systems*, Vol. 9, 2000, 63–84.

Levy, M., Powell, P. and Yetton, P., "SMEs and the Gains From IS: From Cost Reduction to Value Added. In: Larsen, T., Levine, L. and DeGross, J. Eds., *Information Systems: Current Issues and Future Changes*, IFIP 8.2/8.6, Helsinki, Finland, December, 1998.

Lin, B. and Hsieh, C., "Online Procurement: Implemention and Managerial Implications," *Human Systems Management*, Vol. 19, 2000, pp. 105–110.

Lu, E., "A Distributed EDI model," *The Journal of Systems and Software*, Vol. 56, No. 1, 2001, pp. 1–5.

Marchewka, J. and Towell, E., "A Comparison of Structure and Strategy in Electronic Commerce," *Information Technology and People*, Vol. 13, No. 2, 2000, pp. 137–149.

McIvor, R., Humphreys, P. and Huang, G., "Electronic Commerce: Re-engineering the Buyer-supplier Interface," *Business Process Management Journal*, Vol. 6, No. 2, 2000, pp. 122–138.

Min, H. and Galle, W.P., "Electronic Commerce Usage in Business-to-business Purchasing," *International Journal of Operations & Production Management*, Vol. 19, No. 9, 1999, pp. 909–921.

Ngai, E.W.T., and Gunasekaran, A. 2007. "A Review for Mobile Commerce Research and Applications," *Decision Support Systems* (43:1), pp. 3-15.

Pant, S. and Ravichandran, T., "A Framework for Information Systems Planning for E-business," *Logistics Information Management*, Vol. 14, No. 1, 2001, pp. 85–99.

Park, H.G. and Baik, J. M., "Enhancing Manufacturing Product Development Through Learning Agent System Over Internet," *Computers & Industrial Engineering*, Vol. 37, No. 1–2, 1999; pp. 117–211.

Pereira, R., "Factors Influencing Consumer Perceptions of Web-based Decision Support Systems," *Logistics Information Management*, Vol. 12, Nos. 1–2, 1999, pp. 157–181.

Phau, I. and Poon, S.M., "Factors Influencing the Types of Products and Services Purchased Over the Internet," *Internet Research*, Vol. 10, No. 2, 2000, pp.102–113.

Raghunathan, M. and Madey, G.R., "A Firm-level Framework for Planning Electronic Commerce Information Systems Infrastructure," *International Journal of Electronic Commerce*, Vol. 4, No. 1, Fall 1999, pp.121–140.

Rao, S., "Enterprise Resource Planning: Business Needs and Technologies," *Industrial Management and Data Systems*, Vol. 100, No. 2, 2000, pp. 81–88.

Reich, B.H. and Benbasat, I., "Factors That Influence the Social Dimension of Alignment Between Business and Information Technology Objectives," *MIS Quarterly*, Vol. 24, No. 1, Mar 2000, pp.81–113.

Reynolds, J., "E-commerce: A Critical Review," *International Journal of Retail and Distribution Management*, Vol. 28, No. 10, 2000, pp. 417–444.

Rowley, J., "Product Search in E-shopping: A Review and Research Propositions," *Journal of Consumer Marketing*, Vol. 17, No. 1, 2000, pp. 20–35.

Sabherwal, R. and Chan, Y.E., "Alignment Between Business and IS Strategies: A Study of Prospectors, Analyzers, and Defenders," *Information Systems Research*, Vol. 12, No.1, 2001.

Samson, D. and Terziovski, M., "The Relationship Between Total Quality Management

Practices and Operational Performance," *Journal of Operations Management*, Vol. 17, No. 4, 1999, pp. 393–409.

Sarkis, J. and Sundarraj, R., "Factors for Strategic Evaluation of Enterprise Information Technologies," *International Journal of Physical Distribution and Logistics Management*, Vol. 30, No. 3–4, 2000, pp. 196–220.

Sawabini, S., "EDI and the Internet," *Journal of Business Strategy*, Vol. 20, No. 1, 2001, pp. 41–43.

Segev, A., Porra, J. and Roldan, M., "Internet-based EDI Strategy," *Decision Support Systems*, Vol. 21, No. 3, 1997, pp. 157–170.

Shah, J. and Singh, N., "Benchmarking Internal Supply Chain Performance: Development of a Framework," *The Journal of Supply Chain Management*, Winter 2001, pp. 37–47.

Shaw, M.J., Gardner, D.M. and Thomas, H., "Research Opportunities in Electronic Commerce," *Decision Support Systems*, Vol. 21, 1997, pp. 149–156.

Simeon, R., "Evaluating Domestic and International Web-site Strategies," *Internet Research*, Vol. 9, No. 4, 1999, pp. 297–308.

Smaros, J. and Holmstrom, J., "Viewpoint: Reaching the Consumer Through E-grocery VMI," *International Journal of Retail and Distribution Management*, Vol. 28, No. 2, 2000, pp. 55–61.

Smith, T.M. and Reece, J.S., "The Relationship of Strategy, Fit, Productivity, and Business Performance in a Services Setting," *Journal of operations Management*, Vol. 17, No. 2, January 1999, pp. 145–161.

Sones, R., "Resolving the Complexity Dilemma E-commerce Firms Though Objective Organization," *Logistics Information Management*, Vol. 14, Nos.1–2, 2001, pp. 107–118.

St. John, C.H., Cannon, A.R. and Pouder, R.W., "Change Drivers in the New Millennium: Implications for Manufacturing Strategy Research," *Journal of Operations Management*, Vol. 19, No. 2, 2001, pp. 143–160.

Tang, J., "A Conceptual Model for Interactive Buyer–Supplier Relationship in Electronic Commerce," *International Journal of Information Management*, Vol. 21, No. 1, 2001, pp. 49–58.

Tompkins, J., and Avila, D. 2012. "Keeping up with the E-Giants." *Material Handling & Logistics*. Penton Media Inc.

Tracey, M., Vonderembse, M.A. and Lim, J., "Manufacturing Technology and Strategy Formulation: Keys to Enhancing Competitiveness and Improving Performance," *Journal of Operations Management*, Vol. 17, No. 4, 1999, pp. 411–428.

Turban, E., Lee, J. and King, D. and Chung, H.M., *Electronic Commerce: A Managerial Perspective*, Upper Saddle River: NJ, Prentice Hall, 2000.

Turban, E., Rainer, R.K. and Potter, R.E., *Introduction to Information Technology*, NY, John Wiley & Sons, Inc., 2001.

Venkatraman, N., "Five Steps to a Dot-com Strategy: How to Find Your Footing on the Web," *Sloan Management Review*, Spring 2000, pp. 15–28.

Vickery, S.K., Droge, C. and Markland, R.R., "Production Competence and Business Strategy: Do They Affect Business Performance," *Decision Sciences*, Vol. 24, No. 4, 1993, pp. 435–456.

Vlosky, R., "E-business in the Forest Products Industry," *Forest Products Journal*, Vol. 49, No. 10, 1999, pp. 12–22.

Vokurka, R.J. and O'Leary-Kelly, S., "A Review of Empirical Research on Manufacturing Flexibility," *Journal of Operations Management*, Vol. 18, No. 4, 2000, pp. 485–501.

Ward, P.T. and Duray, R., "Manufacturing Strategy in Context: Environment, Competitive Strategy and Manufacturing Strategy," *Journal of Operations Management*, Vol. 18, No. 6, 2000, pp. 123–138.

Ward, P.T., Leong, G. and Boyer K., "Manufacturing Pro-activeness and Performance," *Decision Sciences*, Vol. 25, No. 3, 1995, pp. 435–56.

Wells, M.G., "Business Process Re-engineering Implementations Using Internet Technology," *Business Process Management Journal*, Vol. 6, No. 2, 2000, pp. 164–184.

Wortmann, H., "EDI, Internet and E-commerce," *Computers in Industry*, Vol. 41, No. 2, 2000, pp. 111–112.

Wymbs, C., "How E-commerce is Transforming and Internationalizing Service Industries," *Journal of Services Marketing*, Vol. 14, No. 6, 2000, pp. 463–478.

Xiao, B., and Benbasat, I. 2011. "Product-Related Deception in E-Commerce: A Theoretical Perspective," *MIS Quarterly* (35:1), pp. 169-196.

Yang, J. and Papazoglou, M. P., "Interoperation Support For Electronic Business," *Communications of the ACM*, Vol. 43, No. 6, June 2000, pp. 39–47.

Zsidisin, G.A., Jun, M. and Adams, L.L., "The Relationship Between Information Technology and Service Quality in the Dual-direction Supply Chain," *International Journal of Service Industry Management*, Vol. 11, No. 4, 2000, pp. 312–328.

Part II

Critical Success Factors of

E-Commerce Operations Management

Chapter 3   E-COMMERCE AND SUPPLY CHAIN MANAGEMENT

Learning Objectives

After completing this chapter, you should be able to:

Define and describe "supply chain" and "supply chain management."

Understand the importance of the supply chain management.

Describe the bullwhip effect in the supply chain, its causes, and ways to deal with it.

Explain the supply chain design process and understand what is an ideal supply chain design.

Define and describe the "direct model" and its applications.

Understand supply chain architecture.

Explain how to measure the effectiveness of a supply chain.

Describe the relavance of e-commmerce to the supply chain and describe "e-supply chain."

Define and describe "Electronic Data Interchange" and its relationship with e-commerce and supply chain."

Understand information technology acquisition and justification issues in supply chain management.

Describe the commonly used methods assessing information technology investment.

Describe the relationship between e-commerce and global supply chain management.

Define and describe the "trust" in supply chain.

Explain the major components of the trust in the e-commerce supply chain.

Overview Of This Chapter

This chapter discusses supply chain management in an e-commerce environment. The chapter introduces the concept of supply chain management and related issues, followed by the supply chain design process. The chapter then explains the relevance of e-commerce in supply chain management. It also discusses electronic data interchange and its impact on the traditional supply chain and e-supply chain. Finally, the chapter discusses several important supply chain issues including information technology acquisition in supply chain management, global supply chain management, and trust.

What Is Supply Chain Management?

Competition and globalization are changing the paradigm of traditional logistics strategy. A successful logistics strategy has moved from an internal focus emphasizing integration with other enterprise functions (i.e., operations and marketing) and linking the various enterprise functions to the overall corporate strategy, to an external focus of integrating supply chains and cycle time compression, that is, the complete scope of supply chain management (Gavirneni *et al.*, 1999; Chen *et al.*, 2000).

In a typical supply chain arrangement (see Figure 1), physical goods flow from up-stream to down-stream (i.e., raw materials from suppliers to manufacturers; products from manufacturers to wholesalers, wholesalers to retailers, and retailers to customers), the information flows from down-stream to up-stream along the supply chain. Managing these supply systems is called *supply chain management*.

As Figure 3.1 shows, a supply chain can have multiple tiers of suppliers and vendors as well as multiple levels of distribution channels before the product reaches the end consumer. It is not uncommon to have up to 2,000 second-tier suppliers within the framework of a single supply chain.

The four dimensions of operations strategy: delivery, quality, speed, and flexibility render a whole new level of complexity when coping with a supply chain. Conventional wisdom of lowering inventory levels, outsourcing materials or even changing production technology was considered beneficial for most organizations. However, lowering the inventory level of one firm may raise the inventory level of their supplier firm, which could end up with less optimization of the whole supply chain. The issues surrounding the supply chain management reach a higher complexity level as most organizations belong to several different supply chains simultaneously. Supply chain management directly affects an organization's competitive position. According to Cooke (1993), the Efficient Consumer Response (ECR) estimated a potential $30 billion savings from efficiently streamlining the grocery supply chain.

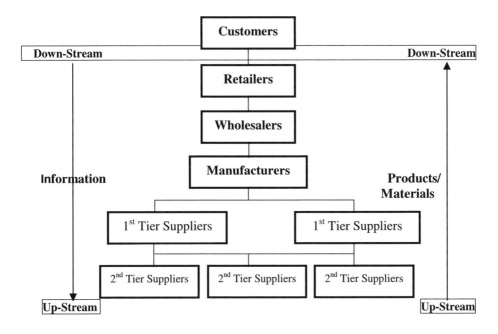

Figure 1. Components of a typical supply chain

Why Is Supply Chain Management So Important?

In order to obtain and sustain a competitive edge, it is crucial for e-commerce companies to effectively deal with the supply chain management. Today's CEO can't simply focus on the performance of the extended supply chain or network in which the company is a partner. The battleground will be supply chain vs. supply chain, with emphasis on continuous improvement across the extended supply chain.

In recent years the topic of supply chain management has received a great deal of attention. Research issues related to supply chain management, such as forecasting, inventory control, and information sharing, are and have been researched for years. Two of the most important issues of the supply chain management are "integration" and "coordination" (Stock *et al.* 2000). *Integration* is e-commerce organizations working closely with both suppliers and customers to reduce or remove organizational boundaries. In most industries today it is not enough to simply optimize internal structures and infrastructures based upon business strategy. The most successful companies are those that have carefully linked their internal processes to external suppliers and customers in unique supply chains. Kim (2000) defined *coordination* as the process of managing dependencies among activities, and suggested different kinds of dependencies associated with such aspects as shared resources, task assignments, producer/consumer relationships, design for manufacturability and so forth. In the supply chain management context, coordination includes the flows within a supply chain. The primary flows in a supply chain are materials, finance, and information. The remaining portion of this chapter will focus on the flow of information and product between supply chain entities.

Controlling Variability Across The Supply chain

According to (Metters 1997), it is generally agreed that a lack of inter-company communication combined with large time lags between receipt and transmittal of information are the root of the supply chain variability. Practitioners and researcher alike are beginning to recognize the supply chain management critically affects businesses' abilities to obtain and sustain competitive advantages. The "bullwhip effect" is one commonly reported type of supply chain information distortion.

The Bullwhip Effect

According to Lee *et al.* (1997b, p. 546), the *bullwhip effect* refers to the phenomenon where orders to the supplier tend to have larger variance than sales to the buyer (i.e., demand distortion), and the distortion propagates upstream in an amplified form (i.e., variance amplification). Figure 2 depicts a visual presentation of the bullwhip effect. The ordering patterns show a common theme: the variability in the ordering process at the upstream sites is always greater than the downstream sites.

The bullwhip effect is not a new phenomenon and numerous researchers from different academic disciplines have researched it. The pioneer work in studying the dynamic behavior of simple linear supply chains was carried out by Jay Forrester of MIT (Forrester 1961). He presented a practical demonstration of how various types of business policy create disturbance, which was often blamed on conditions outside the system. He stated that random, meaningless sales fluctuations could be converted by a system into apparently annual or seasonal production cycles thus sub-optimizing the use of capacity and generating swings in inventory. A change in demand is amplified as it passes between organizations

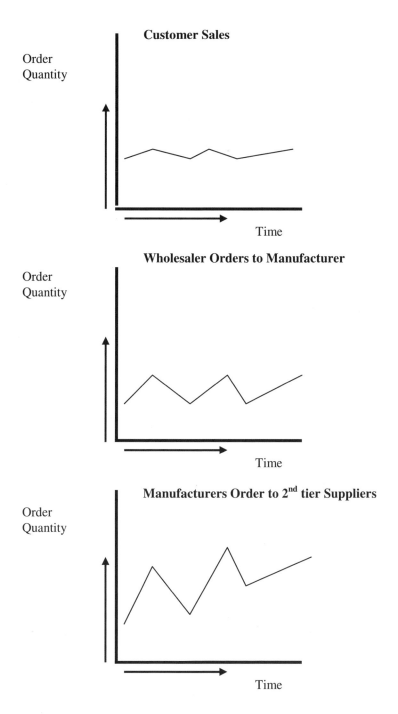

Figure 2. Bullwhip effect in supply chains

in the supply chain. The *beer game*, a management game developed in the 1960's to introduce students and industrialists to the concepts of economic dynamics and management decision-making, has shed further light on the dynamic behavior of supply chains. Participants in the game simulated a supply chain consisting of a beer retailer, wholesaler, distributor, and brewery. As the game proceeds, a small change in consumer demand invariably is translated into wild swings in both orders and inventory upstream: the bullwhip effect.

The bullwhip effect has a major negative impact on the performance of the manufacturing function. For instance, Metters (1997) reported that a major manufacturer of chicken noodle soup increased its production by 11 percent based on the retailers' information in high demand weeks. However, the company cut back its production by more than 10 percent in the low demand weeks, due to the overstock position of the retailers.

Economists have also examined the bullwhip effect. Naish (1994) described the cause of bullwhip effect as the rational actions of profit optimizing managers responding to demand shocks. Kahn (1987) argued that a stylized fact associated with the bullwhip effect was that the variance of production exceeded the variance of sales. His study presented a model of production decisions with demand uncertainty that allowed stock out avoidance. The model indicated that such production decisions caused the bullwhip effect. Metters (1997) also tried to quantify the bullwhip effect from a profitability standpoint. His work aimed at identifying the magnitude of the problem by establishing an empirical lower bound on the profitability impact of the bullwhip effect. He claimed that eliminating the bullwhip effect could increase product profitability by 10 to 30 percent.

Lee *et al.* (1997a, 1997b) investigated four causes of the bullwhip effect: demand signal processing, rationing game, order batching, and price variations.

Demand signal processing: amplification due to increasing safety stock and stock in the pipeline. Forecasts are based on the historical ordering data from the company's immediate customers. However there is a time lag between production and the processing of the orders at the upstream site in the supply chain.

Rationing game: when product demand exceeds supply, organizations often ration sales to retail customers. This results in end customers placing multiple orders with different retailers hoping this will result in a greater chance of obtaining the product. Unfortunately the excess demands for products causes the manufacturing organization to increase capacity to satisfy all the apparent orders.

Order batching: customers tend to order goods at certain times during the week. Organizations running materials requirements planning or distribution requirements planning to generate purchase orders do so at the end of month. These periodic batching of processes result in surges in demand at certain points in time.

Price variations: the impact of promotion results in forward buying. Manufacturers frequently offer promotions and retailers quite frequently "forward purchase" seasonal items. This results in customers buying in quantities that do not reflect their immediate needs. Usually they end up buying in large quantities and stock up for the future. This results in customer buying patterns not reflecting the consumption pattern; the variation of purchased quantities is larger than the variation of the consumption rate creating the bullwhip effect.

As the bullwhip effect receives more and more attention, better strategies to cope with this phenomenon will be developed. As shown in Table 1, various control mechanisms are available to help alleviate the effects of the bullwhip effect, including information sharing, logistics, and operational strategies.

Table 1. Controlling mechanisms for the bullwhip effect

Strategy	Controlling mechanism
Information sharing strategies	– Point of Sale Data Transfer (POS) – Electronic Data Interchange (EDI) – Internet/Extranet Data Exchange (Internet-based EDI) – Enterprise Resource Planning Systems (ERP) – Multi-agent Supply chain Management – Decision support systems (DSS)
Logistics strategies	– Vendor Managed Inventory (VMI) – Direct Purchasing – Logistics Outsourcing
Operational strategies	– Lead Time Reduction (LTR) – Frequent Deliveries – Everyday Low Pricing – General JIT Improvement Efforts

An example of a holistic approach in dealing with the bullwhip effect in the supply chain was proposed by Swaminathan (1998). He suggested a supply chain consisting of different agents (e.g., manufacturer agents, transportation agents, supplier agents, distribution center agents, retailer agents, and end-user agents). Different agents in the multi-agent framework communicate with each other through messages. He claims that this framework is more effective in alleviating the bullwhip effect. Cao and Siau (2000) proposed the multi-agent supply chain framework (parallel decision-making) to replace the traditional sequential supply chain framework (sequential decision-making) to improve the communication among agents in the supply chain, and thus alleviate the bullwhip effect. The empirical results of this research render a 71.3 percent reduction of the bullwhip effect in a four-stage supply chain and hence support the notion that a multi-agent supply chain framework is better than the traditional sequential supply chain framework in bullwhip reduction.

The importance of information sharing throughout the supply chain is critical to achieving superior supply chain performance. Chen *et al.* (2000) quantified the bullwhip effect for simple, two-stage supply chains consisting of a single retailer and a single manufacturer. Their model dealt with demand forecasting and order lead-time; two of the factors commonly assumed to cause the bullwhip effect. They argued that centralizing demand information would result in alleviating the bullwhip effect in a supply chain. Cachon and Fisher (2000) explored the benefits of information sharing in the context of a supply chain with one supplier and a number of identical retailers faced with stationary stochastic consumer demand with a known distribution, and thus expanded the previous information sharing literature in supply chain management. This was accomplished by comparing a traditional information policy that did not use shared information with a full information policy that did exploit shared information. In a numerical study, they found that supply chain costs were 2.2 percent lower on average with the full information policy than with the traditional information policy.

What are the implications for the supply chain based on the bullwhip effect? First, every company is dependent on others in a supply chain. The tenet that effective communication among the companies is one of the key *critical success factors* (CSF) of supply chain coordination to promote to alleviation of the bullwhip effect. Second, organizations must focus on their capabilities supply chain wide. To optimize the entire capabilities of the supply chain, organizations must be willing to cooperate and assist the weaker members of the supply chain.

How Should A Supply chain Be Designed?

The "Ideal" Supply chain

What is the *ideal supply chain*? Every organization is presented with a set of issues that are critical to the design of the perfect supply chain. There is no silver bullet in designing an ideal supply chain. However, supply chain designers must focus on two critical aspects of supply chain design. First, since the company's supply chain consists of virtually all of its operating functions and facilities, and its strategic partners as well, its design is necessarily an integral part of its strategic planning process. To achieve the strategic goal, the company must effectively coordinate all the supply chain functions. In fact, it can be argued that there is no issue more critical to organization success than the design of an effective supply chain from final consumers all the way back to the providers of raw materials (see Fine 1998; Handfield and Nichols 1999). The ideal supply chain then takes into account all the relevant issues related to material suppliers, production facilities, and distribution systems for all entities in the supply chain. Another important aspect of supply chain design is communication and information flow. Advances in computer technology and the Internet have made it possible for suppliers, customers, distribution centers, and shippers to communicate almost instantaneously, thus enhancing the ability to coordinate these different supply chain processes. If all parties involved in the supply chain have access to the same information at the same time, it enables them all to coordinate closely and thus reduce uncertainty, which in turn allows them to reduce inventory levels.

Building a superior supply chain can help a company to obtain a tremendous competitive advantage. Dell is an example of a company that has incorporated the two critical aspects of the supply chain design to achieve a substantial competitive advantage (see Fine, 1998; Margretta, 1998). Found in 1984, Dell has flourished from a mere basement company into a $49 billion Fortune 100 company in 2012 in a short span of time. From the period of 1990 to 1998 its stock price had increased over 26,000 percent outperforming all its major competitors in the market. Dell is ingenious in producing high volume customized PC products and shipping to them on time to its customers. How is Dell able to achieve this remarkable success? Dell's success lies in its superior supply chain design and the use of a true pull system for pre-assembly inventory and distribution.

Dell implements a *Just-In-Time* (JIT) strategy of customer service, strategic supplier partnerships, mass customization, and waste reduction methods in a unique way that has made it a computer giant. In Table 2 some of these basic JIT principles are listed (Schonberger 1982, 1986; Schniederjans 1993; Schniederjans and Olson 1999). These principles will be briefly described in this chapter and throughout the rest of this book as a strategic means of achieving e-commerce business performance success.

Table 2. Basic JIT principles

Principle	Description
Seek to build-to-order	Only produce inventory when a known customer is waiting. This "pulls" the inventory through the system and avoids wasteful time and money in managing inventory.
Seek to eliminate waste	Eliminate wasted labor time waiting for inventory that should have been available, wasted capital in inventory that customers didn't demand, wasted motion in material handling that is unnecessary, etc. Where possible seek zero-inventory.
Seek continuous improvement	Always seek to find new ways to improve products, processes, people, and systems. Continuously enhance the value-added to the product by the operating system.
Seek to eliminate contingencies	Encourage problem identification. Eliminate buffer inventory and surplus human resources to help reveal problems that might go hidden for periods of time (e.g., like defective parts or poor training). Identifying a problem allows it to be solved and improve operations.
Respect people	Respect customer's demands for products and service by focusing on customer needs. Respect employees need to improve and be a real partner in work effort.
Seek long-term commitments from business partners	Establish long-term relationships with all members of the supply chain. Encourage supply chain by investing and helping to build and strengthen its robustness to deal with those times of great change. Establish long-term relationships with customer as a major focus.
Seek production flexibility	Seek to enhance production flexibility in employees and systems to meet with changes in e-commerce operations.
Seek improved quality	Where possible automate for quality consistency reasons. Also provide training and quality knowledge to employees to aid in their efforts to improve product quality.

The business model Dell uses is revolutionizing the PC industry. Traditional PC manufacturers have been highly vertically integrated. Since technology and components were new, manufacturers built large vertically integrated enterprises that produced everything from computer housings to disk drives. The traditional computer industry supply chain is depicted in Figure 3 (see Bendiner 1998; Margretta 1998; Phillips 1998).

Figure 4 depicts the Dell supply chain, which is considered to be a *direct model* (i.e., selling directly to customers) of a supply chain. Rather than being highly vertically integrated, Dell emphasizes on primary value-adding activities. This highly coordinated relationship between suppliers and customers is what is known as the *virtual organization*. *Virtual integration* means piecing together a business with customers and suppliers and treating them as if they are part of your organization. In other words, Dell's considers optimization of the whole supply chain rather than the individual sum of the parts.

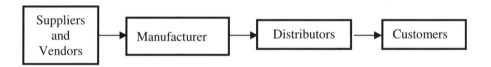

Figure 3. Traditional business computer supply chain

Figure 4. Dell's direct model of a supply chain

The exceptional performance of Dell Computer in recent years illustrates an innovative response to a fundamental competitive factor in the personal computer industry: the value of time. Dell's strategies of direct sales and build-to-order production have proven successful in minimizing inventory and bringing new products to market quickly, enabling it to increase market share and achieve high returns on investment. Dell's case illustrates how one business model may have inherent advantages under particular market conditions, but it also shows the importance of execution in exploiting those advantages. In particular, Dell's use of *information technology* (IT) has been vital to executing both elements of its business model, direct sales and build-to-order, and provides valuable insights into how IT can be applied to achieve speed and flexibility in an industry in which time is critical.

In short, Dell has gained its competitive advantage by using the following elements: the "direct model" for business operations, advanced customer service methods, strong supplier relationships, and advanced demand forecasting (see Fox 1998; Margretta 1998). Each of these components of a successful supply chain operation will be discussed in the following sections.

Direct Model

Rather than build a traditional supply chain system including retailers, distributors and wholesalers, Dell uses the *direct model* to market and sell its products directly to customers (i.e., no wholesalers/retailers). Orders are received via phone, fax, or Dell's Internet Web site. Once an order is completed and payment arrangements are confirmed, a production invoice is electronically forwarded to the production facility and the requisite parts are ordered from the vendors. In other words, Dell receives customer's orders before they actually build a computer. This means Dell does not need to hold any inventory, thereby eliminating most inventory and concomitant risk. As a result, the direct model reduces to an absolute minimum number of steps from the factory to delivery of the finished PC to the customer. In this manner customers are able to get their orders delivered very quickly with a very relatively low cost. Since distribution system costs are essentially removed from the system, Dell is able to keep purchase price to a minimum for its customers.

With direct model, Dell has two significant advantages over their competitors. First, it does need to be overly preoccupied with value erosion caused by throughput discontinuities. Inventories reflect only immediate real need. Since distribution is direct, minute changes in demand are registered immediately and losses attributable to faulty demand forecasts are virtually nonexistent. Second, computer products are built upon receipt of payment so there are no losses from inventory waiting to be sold. In other words, the direct model permits Dell to manage both upstream and downstream inventory.

Company Growth

How has Dell managed to expand its business at an exceptional rate since the very inception of the company? The key for its tremendous success is due to the structure of the company. Dell is leaner and meaner than its vertically integrated competitors. Dell has established JIT-type partnering relationships with its supplier of component parts (i.e., Sony for the monitors) that provide the highest quality component parts for its PC products. Rather than having to build a new facility every time a component part becomes outdated it uses its supplier network to make sure it always has the most current and highest quality parts. In doing so, Dell is also organized to leverage the rapidly declining value of various PC components. Dell has recognized that the decline in value can provide an important competitive advantage to a company able to compress their supply chain and manage logistics time.

Customer Service

Dell is frequently cited as an example of a top *customer-relationship management* (CRM) provider. The CRM activities are integrated with customers' ordering and order fulfillment. Customers can track their orders online, to see if the computers are in production or already on being shipped. They also can access detailed diagrams of the computers and get information about troubleshooting. By using viewer-approved configurations and pricing for its customers and by eliminating paperwork (i.e., waste), Dell has been able to cut administrative-process expenses by 15 percent.

Supplier Relationships

While firms generally outsource their problems or difficult components to regional and specialty suppliers, Dell makes agreements with its suppliers to provide a percentage of its production requirements every year, even when demand exceeds supply. Dell communicates effectively with its suppliers by providing them with its daily production requirements reducing the total amount of inventory in the system and also curtailing the impact of the bullwhip effect. Dell's success is greatly dependent upon its supporting information systems. For instance, Dell is using several information technologies, including: EDI, video teleconferencing, electronic procurement, computerized faxes, an intranet, DSS, a Web-based call center, and more. Computerized manufacturing systems tightly link the entire demand and supply chains from suppliers to buyers. This system is the foundation on which the "build-to-order" strategy rests. This reduces time to the market, creating value that can be shared among buyers, suppliers, and customers. In addition, since there is very little inventory in the supply channel, design and customer service problems can be resolved very quickly.

Being an excellent JIT firm, Dell coordinates effectively with its suppliers to reduce the total inventory in the supply channel. Dell's suppliers typically keep less than two weeks of inventory, whereas its major competitors keep nearly two to three months of inventory. As such, Dell is organized to leverage the rapidly declining value of various PC components. With certain suppliers, Dell can even achieve zero-inventory scenario for its PC components. For example, the arrangements Dell has made with its monitor supplier, Sony, are ingenious. Sony never sends the monitor to Dell; rather, when the Dell computer is completed, UPS or Airborne Express picks up the monitor from Sony's Mexican factory, matches the monitor and the proper computer at its delivery center, and delivers them as a package to the customer. With this system Dell eliminates monitor inventory and saves approximately $30 on shipping costs. Stock is delivered to Dell and placed right in the production line without being warehoused or inspected. The reason why Dell is able to carry out low or sometimes zero inventory policies is because it establishes long and steady JIT relationships with its suppliers.

With the direct model, the variability in the system is greatly reduced and thus production is made easier. Dell receives customer's orders before they actually build a computer as such it does not need to hold any inventory. By shrinking the size of the supply channel, the suppliers are given better information about real demand, which reduces variability, inventory, and costs. Since both Dell and its suppliers are in constant communication, the margin for error is reduced. In turn, suppliers are required to share sensitive information with Dell, such as their own quality problems. It was easy to get suppliers to follow Dell's lead because they also reap the benefits of faster cycle times, reduced inventory, and improved forecasts. Without the demand distortion created by lengthening the supply channel, costs are reduced substantially and savings are shared across the supply chain.

Demand Forecasts

Accurate demand forecasts propel Dell to be a predominant player in the competitive PC industry. The better the demand information used in supply chain the more effective and profitable the company (Phillips 1998; Sanders 1997). Using a very elaborate bottom-up approach to forecasting, sales managers at Dell can work very close with customers and access its current and future computing needs. The close relationship with the customers creates accurate demand information as to the future of the market and allows Dell to create very accurate demand forecasts. Dell considers its customers as an integral part of the supply chain and as a result Dell's supply chain is well managed.

Not every e-commerce-type of company can achieve these types of results, but the principles of supply chain design can be applied to virtually any situation. Ultimately, the application of the Internet to PCs and every other industry means that the direct model pioneered at Dell will be adopted by ever more industries. In this sense, the Dell is a "model system" for managers in almost every other industry. Innovative managers should be able to find much to inspire them from the Dell success of the management of PC production logistics.

Supply Chain Architecture

Drawing from the concept of product architecture, we use the term *supply chain architecture* properly in supply chain design. The traditional trade-off in the design of the supply chain is the make/buy or vertical integration decisions. As exhibited by Dell, a high percentage of the decisions are to contract pieces of their manufacturing to various component suppliers in the industry. However, expanding the decision horizon to include the elements of integral or modular product/process design gains a better understanding of proper supply chain design.

Fine (1998) and Rosenthal (1992) argued that there are four dimensions of proximity measures. Those four dimensions are geographic, organizational, cultural and electronic:

Geographic. Loosely translated means physical distance. *Geographic proximity* plays an important role in the design of "pull" type supply chains, because of the requirements of frequent deliveries in such supply chains. This dimension can be important in the design phase when integrated teams from cooperating firms are used. Physical proximity also makes communication and coordination much easier.

Organizational. This describes the relationship between or among organizations in supply chains. When suppliers and customers have vested interest and ownership rights to a particular organization, this can be referred to as close *organizational proximity*.

Cultural. *Cultural proximity* captures the elements that are common amongst nations or specific regions. Such elements as language, laws and business standards, and ethics.

Electronic. *Electronic proximity* refers to the exchange of information through the "information superhighway." Using tools such as the Internet, EDI, and other e-commerce tools many organizations have been able to speed up introducing their products in the market.

As opposed to an integral supply chain, if the supply chain is modular in nature it will feature low proximity along the four dimensions. It means that modular supply chains can exist over huge geographic expanses, have separate ownership control, have little commonality along culture and use very little exchange of data via e-commerce. Direct model companies are implementing modularized supply chains. Dell is an example of a high modularized supply chain. There is little or no vertical integration in Dell, and parts are virtually interchangeable.

What is the relationship between functionality of product and process, and supply chain architecture? There is a straightforward relationship between them. Generally speaking, firms, which produce modular products, tend to be aligned with the *modularized supply chains* while firms that produce integral products tend to be much closer along the dimensions of proximity. For example, interchangeable parts and a high degree of modularity characterize the PC industry. Of the competitors in the PC industry, those who have designed a modular supply chain have been very successful (e.g., Dell).

Companies whose products are highly integrated and complex tend to have a highly "integral supply chain." One of the examples of an *integral supply chain* can be found in the automotive industry. The nature of the design and complexity of these products force the designers from many firms to be in close proximity to each other on many dimensions: as evident by the high concentration of automotive contractors and producers in the upper Midwest. The automobile industry requires a highly integral supply chain.

The relationship between process and supply chain architecture differs somewhat from the relationship between product and supply chain. Successful organizations can find themselves along any of the dimensions of the process/supply chain matrix. There are still some observable differences. For instance, computers usually are assembled at a very high rate and are done by one or more individuals in a work cell. In contrast, the processing of newspaper information is collected and reported from many locations dispersed across the world.

The challenging part of the supply chain design lies in integrating all of the elements of product, process, and supply chain architecture. While some of the activities throughout the supply chain are still functionally separate, many of the activities overlap and are highly integrated. According to Fine (1998) and others (see Carter and Baker 1991; Cooper 1993), overlapping activities are necessary for firms to ensure success, while not all of the tasks must be performed using integrated development teams. These authors define the overlapping elements as follows:

Product development is divided along the integral or modular architectural and detailed design choices (such as performance and capabilities).

Process development is divided along technology and equipment choices (manual vs. automation) and manufacturing system orientation (such as job shop vs. process flow).

Supply chain development is divided along supply chain architecture and infrastructure decisions. Supply chain architectural decisions include decisions about the integral or modular nature of the product or process. Infrastructural decisions include transportation and information system decisions.

All of these dimensions are common to all supply chains. What separates the successful supply chains from the unsuccessful supply chains is the degree to which they can integrate the overlapping areas. Those overlapping elements have a tremendous impact as to the firms chosen for suppliers and the types of coordination and integration elements that are used in the supply chain. The failure to use the integrated planning teams for the overlapping coordination and planning activities will often result in the introduction of additional variability into the supply chain.

Supply Chain Metrics

As mentioned in the previous sections, there is an emerging requirement for e-commerce firms to focus on the performance of the extended supply chain in which the firm is a partner. Supply chain performance refers to the extended supply chain's activities in meeting end-customer requirements, including product availability, on-time delivery, and all the necessary inventory and capacity in the supply chain. However, organizations have found it difficult to effectively measure their own supply chains because of their cross-functional and boundary-spanning characteristics. Milliken (2001), a supply chain management consultant at BASF, found that most of businesses do not fully know their supply chain performance measures. As such, a different set of measures or metrics that capture all aspects of the supply chain must be developed for helping firms measure their supply chain performance. Caplice and Sheffi (1994) argued that measures used to capture the performance of a transformational process such as a supply chain fall into one of the primary dimensions: utilization, productivity, and effectiveness. Kiefer and Novack (2000) established a taxonomy for supply chain performance metrics comprising of three key dimensions. These three key dimensions are service, assets, and speed.

Service Metrics

Service metrics relate to the ability to anticipate, capture, and fulfill customer demand with personalized products and on-time delivery. In general, it is difficult to quantify the cost of stockouts or late deliveries, so customer service metrics are viable targets to measuring supply chain service dimension.

Customer Service Metrics (Build-to-order)

Quoted Customer Response Time
Percent On-time Completion
Delivery Process On Time
Cost of Late Orders
Number of Late Orders

Dell is an example of the build-to-order manufacturer since it assembles each PC based on customers' order with unique configurations. Dell is very successful in curtailing the quoted customer response time, increasing the on-time completion rate, and enhancing on time delivery process.

Customer Service Metrics (Build-to-order)

Line Item Fill Rate
Complete Order Fill Rate
Delivery Process On Time
Cost of Backordered/Lost Sales
Number of Backorders

Assets Metrics

Assets metrics involve anything with commercial value, primarily inventory and cash. The major asset involved in supply chains is inventory throughout the chain. The two metrics generally used for inventory are:
- Monetary Value
- Time Supply or Inventory Turnovers

Inventory can be measured as a *time supply* (e.g., a 2-week supply of inventory), or as *inventory turnovers*, defined as

Turnover = (Cost of goods sold)/(Inventory Value)

The time supply or turnover measures relate to inventory flows; the *inventory value* in the formula above relates to inventory as an asset on the firm's balance sheet. The time supply and monetary value are useful comparison measures in certain situations. The *Time supply metric* enables managers to make comparisons of inventory levels across categories, such as different lines of business or different divisions, since the data is adjusted to reflect the underlying "run rate" of the business. The *monetary value metric* is most relevant, since it measures funds tied up in inventory (i.e., working capital). One can have a very large time supply of inventory but if the value is relatively low, it is not a major concern.

Speed Metrics

Speed metrics includes metrics that are time-related; they track responsiveness and velocity of execution. The following is a list of possible speed metrics:

Quoted Customer Response
Cycle Reduction Time
Supply chain Cycle Time

We have discussed the *quoted customer response metric* is a build-to-order situation where the company states a quoted time to complete an order and them measures how well it does in meeting the quoted time. The *cycle reduction time metric* is relevant in supply chains in that a supply chain benefits flow from reducing flow time: lowering lead-time and work-in-process inventory levels. Dell, for example, found ways of operating on an 11-day inventory cycle and was able to turn over its inventory thirty-three times per year. The total inventory in the supply chain was reduced significantly, resulting in great improvements in responsiveness to the customer.

The *supply chain cycle time metric* measures the total time it would take to fulfill a new order if all upstream and in-house inventory levels were zero. It is measured by adding up the longest (bottleneck) lead times at each stage in the supply chain. For instance, if we consider a three-tier supply chain with each tier having a two-week lead-time, then the supply chain cycle time should be six weeks. If one of the three tiers can reduce its lead-time to one-week, then the supply chain cycle time will be greatly improved.

An effective performance measurement process is critical to ensure continuous improvement in supply chain management. In this section, integrated performance measures for supply chain, namely a three-dimensional supply chain metrics are proposed as a means to provide managers with more accurate assessment of their supply chains.

The Relevance Of E-Commerce To The Supply Chain

E-commerce is becoming a driving force in today's economic. By and large, e-commerce is still sales and marketing driven. Supply chain management is the most important critical success factor (CSF) of e-commerce operations according to a recent survey by Arthur Anderson of Internet buyers. However the supply chain often neglected or poorly managed in e-commerce practices. As a result, many "dot com" companies lost customers or went out of the business due to their mal-performance of logistical operations. The benchmark e-commerce firms, such as Amazon for instance, paid a heavy price of its logistics woes that ultimately resulted in offsetting the price advantage to the customer and as such lost customers to its major competitors. Industrial experts attributed the downfalls of the "dot com" companies mainly to supply chain failures caused by a lack of rapid reporting structure to identify emerging stock shortfalls, order processing systems to manage the needed repeats, and vendor quality management programs to ensure minimal complaints and returns. E-toy, an Internet-based toy retailer, is one just one example of supply chain mismanagement. In order to be successful in the e-commerce era, companies need to have an integral business model with an emphasis on supply chain management rather than a model solely based on sales and marketing.

The Impact Of E-Commerce On The Supply Chain

E-commerce is an application of interorganizational systems that supports the electronic trading of physical goods and of intangibles such as information. It has major positive impact on supply chain management in several ways. First, e-commerce represents a means of leveraging, for the benefits of buyers and sellers in supply chains, the trend toward increased product customization and personalization. Information technology (IT) allows for the large-scale tracking of customer preferences, including those associated with logistics processes such as ordering and delivery. Second, IT permits the separation of the management and routing of physical goods flows from the processing of information relating to those goods. The information component of logistics can be aggregated or disaggregated for the physical component depending on the context (Lewis and Talalayevsky 2000). Finally, Lee *et al.* (1997a) pinpoint the relevance of information exchange in alleviating the bullwhip effect, one of the major problems in the supply chain management. They argue that IT can help firms to create transparency of orders and operations in providing visibility of demand throughout the supply chain.

E-Commerce and Supply Chain Integration

According to Nissen (2000), an evolution is in progress that is leading to the increasing integration of supply chain management and e-commerce. Hoek (2001) proposes an *e-supply chain* approach which is strategic and integal in nature. He claims that a supply chain needs to be integrated using information from the sales intereface to its logistics operations throughout the entire supply chain. Figure 5 demonstates the two primary dimensions that can be used to assess the e-supply chain. The two dimensions are the supply chain scope of e-business applications (i.e., paritial/fragmented or integral) and the approach of information to be used in the supply chain (i.e., strategic or operational approach). The most desirable e-supply chain falls in the upper right quadrant while the least desirable situation is in the left bottom quadrant. According to Hoek (2001), most of the e-commerce companies fall into the left bottom quadrant. Successful e-commerce firms treat connectivity and transparency in information flow as a neccesety for informaton integration. For example, CISCO credited a 27 percent productivity improvement to its implmenting of an effective e-supply chain concept. There are many parties involved in the supply chain in CISCO and the company alllows as many parties to know about the informaton as early on as possible; everyone sees the same information. That way, everybody in the supply chain is collectively working towards satisfying the end object; delivering the goods to the customer. The aim is to make this work seamlessly, and the company has the appropriate connectivity in place to achieve that.

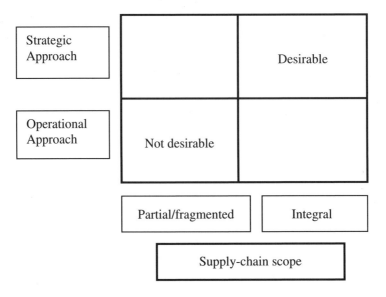

Figure 5. E-supply chain assessment

Traditional E-Commerce vs. E-Supply Chain

There are several major differences between traditional e-commerce and e-supply chain. In fact, e-supply chain renders some improvements in supply chain management in an e-commerce setting. First, since e-supply chain implements a supply chain-wide information infrastructure to disseminate relevant market information directly throughout the supply chain, it helps to alleviate the bullwhip effect of supply chains. Second, with broader and more elaborate co-ordination mechanisms in an e-supply chain environment, the parties involved in a supply chain can coordinate more intensively around market opportunities. Third, e-supply chain uses strategic approach to information, that is, rather than using information for ordering and transactional purposes, e-supply chain uses information for innovation, enhanced consumer relationships and service activities. Finally, e-supply chain can help e-commerce firms to "reengineer" their supply chain to obtain competitive priorities. (We will discuss reengineering in Chapter 10.)

E-supply chain is an evolving concept, which is under practiced by e-commerce firms. However, studies show that with the benefits e-supply chain mentioned above, more and more firms come to realization that e-supply chain must take place in order to compete effectively in an e-commerce era.

The Importance of Electronic Data Interchange in E-Commerce and Supply Chain

Before e-commerce became synonymous with the explosion of Internet: based technology, e-commerce meant "electronic data interchange." *Electronic data interchange* (EDI), a technology that enables corporations to exchange data electronically with their suppliers, has been in use for more than 30 years, and major manufacturers, retailers, and others have spent tens of millions of dollars each year in an ongoing campaign to establish it as the de facto standard for communication. EDI generally refers to the computer-to-computer exchange of high-volume, routine business information between trading partners, using a national or international standard format (Walton and Marucheck 1997). Another definition of EDI, available at *www.whatis.com* (1999), is "a standard format for exchanging business data. The standard is ANSI X12." This definition focuses on EDI as the standard language of electronic business transactions (Attwood 1998). Thus, the EDI standard can be used while transmitting messages or transaction sets computer-to-computer, through a *value-added network* (VAN), or via the Internet (Tyler 1999).

EDI vs. Supply Chain

Developed in the late 1960s and popularized in the last three decades, EDI revolutionized the way many companies managed their business operations. EDI was designed to enable a buyer to extract a purchase order from a purchasing application and send it to a supplier where it would automatically feed into a sales order-entry application. Its intent was to speed information delivery and processing via a "paperless" environment, thereby achieving tremendous cost and time saving efficiencies that would carry over into improved levels of customer service. By and large, for sophisticated suppliers the arrival of an EDI document is the first step in a process that yields enormous benefits. The data is translated by special EDI software from EDI standard data formats and integrated into the supplier's database, where it can be used by the organization's business applications. Generally speaking, once the EDI data is fully integrated, the way a company deals with its supply chain changes.

The benefits that EDI can bring to the supply chain management include the following: (1) EDI affects cycle times as well as the buffer inventory of the purchased items as it can enhance the communications between the supplier and the buyer (e.g., a company might implement a barcode-based inventory monitoring systems to track inventory levels and automatically generate and transmit an EDI purchase order to a supplier.), (2) EDI impacts the relationship between the buyer and the supplier if a company develops its EDI's capacities with a critical supplier to transmit orders directly into the supplier's manufacturing planning and control software, and (3) At a strategic level, EDI has served as a competitive priority or order winner for some companies. For instance, a small electrical supply company in the Raleigh, NC area won contracts over its bigger rivals because it is ready and able to implement EDI for the *purchase order* (PO) transaction.

However, EDI also created a major problem: for EDI to be more than just another tool that runs parallel to the company's existing systems, it must be integrated into corporate business systems. Those companies that have made a significant investment in integrating EDI into their business systems are reaping significant rewards, and they will be unlikely to give up EDI without very good reason. Research shows that EDI, integrated or not, only extends into between 15 percent and 20 percent of a company's trading partner's community. That minimal level of electronic communication makes it extremely difficult, if not impossible, for companies to ever achieve the collaborative, streamlined supply chain that today's global marketplace demands. And unfortunately the explosion of the Internet and e-commerce now posses the added problem as to whether manufacturers want to use EDI today or not.

EDI vs. E-Commerce

According to Walton and Gupta (1999), e-commerce represents a new way of thinking about EDI. In EDI, data is transmitted via a VAN among companies where transaction volume is normally very high. However, in the Internet-based e-commerce environment, data exchange occurs in the Internet with more dispersed customers. Moreover, the transaction volume of e-commerce is more moderate and shipments are more irregular. As such, the data exchange needs to be quick and flexible. With the explosive growth of e-commerce, the temptation may be to adopt an "out with the old, in with the new" attitude that sees EDI being swiftly retired in favor of next generation, Internet-based solutions. Is that so? The jury is not out on this question yet. While some experts believe that Internet-based solutions will dominate how company transmit data, others think that EDI is and will be playing important roles in data exchange for years to come.

Traditional EDI vs. Internet-based EDI

Steggell (1998) notes that Internet access is much cheaper than EDI via VANs. However, Zuckerman and McLymont (1999) believe EDI is alive and well. They observe that industrial giants, such as General Motors, are committed to EDI and that there is a lack of an Internet equivalent to the EDI standards. Sweet (1999) envisions *extensible markup language* (XML) becoming an alternative standard to EDI. However, she also believes "companies that have already implemented EDI will continue to rely on it because it works."

Other authors view EDI and the Internet as complements, rather than substitutes. Smith (1999) suggests EDI for buying in the context of strategic supplier relationships and the Internet for non-strategic repetitive buying. Moreover, the difference between EDI and the Internet is becoming blurred (Burnell 1999). Roberts and Mackay (1998) advocate EDI via VANS to support strategic long-term relationships and EDI standard messages over the Internet for ordering routine, low-value items.

Traditional EDI is thought to work best between two large organizations with a high volume of transactions, while XML and the Internet extend the ability to transmit standard messages to mid-size and smaller organizations (Barrett and Hogenson 1998). Krapf (1999) contrasts traditional EDI via VANs and EDI via the Internet (i.e., Internet-EDI). EDI via VANS links one buyer and one supplier, while Internet-based EDI links one buyer with many suppliers. Many organizations are still using EDI via VANs or with a direct connection (Attwood 1998). The enduring popularity of EDI, coupled with the development of a software bridge between the EDI using ANSI X12 format and XML, inspired Randall Whiting, CEO of CommerceNet, to assert that "EDI is not going to just go away" (Messmer 1998).

One more factor that is often overlooked in answering which data exchange system to choose is the cost. A hard look at the substantial investment of dollars and resources spent on the EDI infrastructure of most large companies, however, makes that a difficult decision to contemplate. So, which technologies to choose: EDI or Internet-based supply chain solutions? The answer is a blending of business needs with business goals; the assessment of both existing tools and new technology capabilities; and the evaluation of where the business wants to be in terms of its existing market and new markets. It is, in short, deciding which opportunities the business wants to-and can-embrace cost effectively, while maximizing its current revenue stream.

An Approach to E-Technology Acquisition and Justification in Supply Chain Management

Businesses around the world have made many investments in IT. It is estimated that $4.4 billion is spent on IT worldwide (Gordon *et al.* 2012). Yet questions about the linkage between business performances including the supply chain performance and IT investments have puzzled researchers and practitioners over the last decade (Hilt and Brynjolfsson 1996). Studies indicate that over 50 percent of IT projects cost more than twice their original estimates, significantly diminishing their payoff. Although many variables contribute to this problem, a lack of foresight in the IT acquisition or investment decision process has been cited as a major factor (Holme 1997).

ITs such as EDI, Internet-EDI, and enterprise resource planning systems are important enablers of effective supply chain management because one of the key ingredients in supply chain management is information processing across all the functional areas of business and its parties in the supply chain. According to Talluri (2000), many companies are taking advantage of advanced ITs for better managing their supply chains. The major IT acquisitions in the areas of supply chain management are in the design and operation phases of the supply chain. These IT systems have major impact on three supply chain management areas: strategic-level planning, tactical-level planning, and operational-level planning (Advanced Manufacturing Research 1998). Strategic-level planning involves supply chain network design that determines the location, size, and optimal numbers of suppliers, production plants, and distributors to be used in the supply chain network. Tactical-level planning is the supply planning phase of the supply chain management and it primarily involves the optimization of flow of goods and services through a given supply chain network. Operational-level planning involves short-term planning that includes production scheduling at all plants on a daily basis.

IT Acquisition Justification Methodologies

Recently, IT acquisition justification issues have caught attentions of both practitioners and researchers of the supply chain management. Many methods can be used to assess IT acquisition justification including empirical survey method, case studies, and quantitative methods. In general, IT investment decisions have traditionally focused on financial or technological issues. Responding to what appears to be a lack of payoff in IT investments, researchers as well as practitioners recently have suggested that traditional valuation analyses are incomplete and have called for additional work to identify hidden or seldom-considered costs and benefits. Ryan and Harrison (2000) attempt to improve understanding of a chief source of these hidden costs and benefits: those changes in the social subsystem brought about by a new IT. Those costs and benefits are not likely to be equivalent among IT investment alternatives, but they are likely to be pivotal in determining the ITs effectiveness. Therefore, to evaluate IT payoffs more completely, these social subsystem costs and benefits must be incorporated into IT investment decisions. Talluri (2000) proposes a goal-programming model, which incorporates both tangible and intangible factors including cost, flexibility, quality, and time for evaluation of IT systems for supply chain management.

E-Commerce and Global Supply Chain Management

As markets for products and services become global, international competition becomes more intense. Global markets are strongly influenced by competitors who drive customer expectations to higher levels. To successfully compete, firms must meet or exceed the pace of rapidly changing technology while also lowering costs, increasing quality, and improving customer service at all stages of the value-chain. These competitive realities face companies and industries worldwide.

A rapidly emerging global market is driving businesses to reorganize manufacturing and distribution operations and to partner with customers and suppliers, forming global supply chains that offer significant competitive value. Effective management of these global supply chains presents challenging strategic, tactical, and operational problems. It involves the integration of all value-creating elements in the supply, manufacturing, and distribution processes, from raw material extraction, through the transformation process, to end user consumption. *Global supply chain management* (GSCM) activities are motivated by the ideals of customer service, lead-time compression and inventory reduction. GSCM is facilitated greatly by communication technologies such as EDI and the Internet. It is inspired by the JIT principles of close supplier relationships, reduced supplier bases, and frequent on-time deliveries by suppliers who are synchronized with a customer's requirement. GSCM also encourages global supply chains to compete against each other, rather than see single firms compete against similar firms. GSCM fosters involvement of members of the supply chain in product development and design, production planning, and quality efforts. Data on market demand and production schedules is shared, and is enhanced by the Internet and by global supply chain information system networks.

Role of IT in GSCM

World-class companies around the world are dependent on their ability to successfully apply IT to GSCM. Motwani *et al.* (2000) proposed a GSCM implementation model, which includes five phases. The five phases are initiation, creation, evaluation, experiment, and implementation. They argue that IT plays important roles in every phase of the GSCM implementation process. In the initiation phase, IT is expected to partner and support. In the second phase of creation, top management work with IT to translate the business vision to technical reality. The role of IT in the evaluation phase is to help the project team in evaluating current capacities and to assess the feasibility and steps for implementing GSCM. In the GSCM experiment phase, IT plays a role of estimating the scope and nature of the IT platform required by the GSCM implementation process. The final stage of implementation involves the deployment of the required IT.

A Success Story of GSCM

In 1999, UPS Logistics Group was chosen by Samsung Electro-Mechanics Co., Ltd. (SEMCO), a division of Samsung, to reengineer and manage its global supply chain. Korea-based Samsung Electro-Mechanics Co. which manufactures, markets and distributes more than 50 product types used in a variety of telecommunications and audio-video devices, computers and computer peripherals. SEMCO sells 80 percent of its products outside Korea.

The project redesigned SEMCO's logistics, transportation, customs brokerage and inventory management for both raw materials and finished goods covering North America, Asia, Europe and Latin America. The goal of the project was to design and implement a global IT infrastructure that would add supply chain visibility to the flow of SEMCO's raw materials, sub-components, and finished goods as they moved from suppliers through manufacturing and on to customers. The project also included the reengineering and management of SEMCO's North American distribution network that connected manufacturing centers in Asia and Latin America with customers in North America. With its global distribution network, great improvements were realized at SEMCO including faster cycle times for finished goods, better customs clearance practices for both raw materials and finished goods, improved inventory and order accuracy, lower returns and lowered inventory carrying costs.

The Issue of Trust in Supply Chain Management

Trust has long been the cornerstone of any successful business relationship. Before the Internet, face-to-face communication typically formed the basis for long-lasting and profitable ventures, instilling confidence in both parties. In fact, recent studies show that face-to-face interaction promotes the greatest trust, followed by the telephone, then text chat, and, last, e-mail. But with the explosion of business-to-business e-commerce, trust can no longer be built on a handshake. We are now expected to collaborate more and more with people we've likely never even meet. Companies that can leverage the power of e-commerce while addressing issues of identity, trust, and performance management will win the race and maximize their business performance.

The Internet has created opportunities for seamless business collaboration between buyers and sellers as well as the collection of service companies that have comprised traditional supply chains. The new Internet model breaks down traditional boundaries between business partners, in essence making all participants in a business transaction part of an expansive extranet. In theory, these business partners will be able to easily and securely communicate and complete end-to-end transactions from within their respective companies-streamlining communications, increasing the precision of forecasts, and driving costs out of day-to-day operations. What the supply chain management in the e-commerce era to date has failed to do is replace or improve the one fundamental attribute required to conduct business: Trust.

What is Trust in E-Commerce?

Ratnasingham (1999) defines trust in e-commerce or *e-trust* as promises, assurances and a demand for high quality products and services. Credibility is a measure of honesty and ethical behavior. Higher levels of credibility create higher levels of trust. The buyer in an e-commerce exchange wants to deal with a seller who is honest. Dishonest behavior, as evidenced in previous transactions, will lead to low trust levels. This dishonest behavior in an e-supply chain may include such serious violations as intentional overcharges, misrepresenting merchandise, and fraudulent use of credit cards or other sensitive consumer information. This dishonest behavior also includes taking advantage of opportunities to do wrong to the other member in the exchange. Dwyer *et al.* (1987) refers to this as "opportunistic behavior" and discourages its use. Participants in an e-supply chain must provide assurance that security issues are important to the marketer as well, and must provide some manner of combating such fear. Security issues may be dealt with by offering a secured server over which all company information and sensitive data are transmitted. This information should be encrypted during transmission for the safety of the consumer. Additionally, privacy policies should be developed for all web sites, explaining to the partners why the data must be gathered, how it will be used, how it will be stored, and who will have access to it. The data gathered should be essential to the supply chain management task at hand.

The Major Components of E-Trust

Sheppard and Sherman (1998) identify factors likely to influence the development and maintenance of trust in the domain of B2C supply chain. The major components of trust in supply chain are listed and defined in Table 3. Sheppard and Sherman (1998) claim that in order to effectively manage the supply chain in an e-commerce setting, companies need to look at all facets of the trust issues.

Summary

This chapter starts with description of supply chain management, one of the most critical success factors in operations management. Suggestions for alleviating the bullwhip effect from operations management research are also discussed. The chapter also establishes the relationship between supply chain management and e-commerce. A discussion of current research on e-commerce and the major issues confronting e-commerce supply chain management were reviewed.

Table 3. Major components of trust in e-commerce

Component of trust	Description
Pre-interactional filters	First of all, it is noteworthy that individuals differ in their general propensity to trust. A second important factor is people's foreknowledge and expectations with respect to a certain industry or company. The latter can be due to *reputation* (i.e., the strength of a company's brand name), previous interactions on- and/or off-line, or reports from trusted third parties (hence, transference of trust).
Interface properties	The development of trust is strongly affected by one's first *impression* of a commercial system. Thus, graphic design and layout are encapsulated in the appeal component. *Overview* refers to the extent to which the site's commercial offerings and resources are made explicit by organizing its content in a manner relevant to the end user. The *usability* component refers to the system's reliability, ease-of-use and familiarity in terms of domain model, classification schemes, and terminology.
Informational content	Information about products and services should be complete, relevant and structured in a way that reduces user costs. A company component here reflects the need to communicate the merchant's history, values and commitment. *Security* refers to the completeness and the understandability of information about financial risk and guarantees. *Privacy* describes the vendor's openness with respect to its privacy policy. The commercial party's competence can be assessed by comparing the first two components, whereas the relationship's inherent risk can be evaluated in the light of the last two components.
Relationship management	The first type of trust to take place is *conversion* trust, where users gain enough trust to engage in a commercial relationship with an online merchant. Whether the trust will be honored in the long term will depend on the follow-up to the initial transaction (e.g., post-purchase communication and customer service). *Communication* trust thus reflects the facilitating effect of frequent and personalized vendor-buyer interactions on trust maintenance.

◆ **Review Terms**

Assets metrics
Beer game
Bullwhip effect
Coordination
Critical success factors (CSFs)
Cultural proximity
Customer relationship management (CRM)
Cycle reduction time metric
Demand signal processing
Direct model
Electronic data interchange (EDI)
Electronic proximity
E-supply chain
E-trust
Face-to-face communication
Four dimensions of operations strategy
Geographic proximity
Global supply chain management (GSCM)
Ideal supply chain
Information technology (IT)
Informational content
Integral supply chain
Integration

Internet-based EDI
Inventory value
Just-in-time (JIT)
Modularized supply chain
Monetary value metric
Multi-agent framework
Multi-agent supply chain
Order batching
Organizational proximity
Pre-interactional filters
Price variations
Quoted customer response metric
Rationing game
Relationship management
Service metrics
Speed metrics
Supply chain
Supply chain metrics
Supply chain architecture
Supply chain cycle time metrics
Supply chain management (SCM)
Time supply metric
Trust
Value-added network (VAN)
Virtual organization
Virtual integration

◆ **Discussion Questions**

1. What is changing the paradigm of the traditional logistics strategy?
2. What is a typical supply chain structure?
3. How can supply chain management be defined in e-commerce operations? Why is supply chain management so important in e-commerce operations management?
4. What are the two important issues of the supply chain management?
5. What is the supply chain variability?

6. What is the "bullwhip effect" and how does it influences the supply chain management?
7. What is the ideal supply chain? How would you design an ideal supply chain?
8. What is the "direct model" of Dell Computers?
9. How can we measure supply chain performance?
10. Why are e-commerce and supply chain relevant?
11. What is e-supply chain?
12. What is electronic data interchange (EDI)? What role does EDI play in supply chain management?
13. What is Internet-based EDI?
14. Why are IT investments so important in supply chain management?
15. What is global supply chain management?

◆ Questions

1. Why is supply chain management such an integral part of e-commerce operations?
2. What are four possible causes of the bullwhip effect? Explain each.
3. What are the major approaches proposed by supply chain researchers to alleviate the bullwhip effect?
4. Why has the "direct model" pioneered by Dell changed the competition landscape in the PC industry?
5. What are four dimensions of "proximity measures"? Explain why they are useful in a supply chain design process.
6. What is the relationship between functionality of product and process, and supply chain architecture?
7. What are three types of supply chain metrics? Explain the importance of supply chain performance measures.
8. How does the e-commerce influence the supply chain? Explain why firms need to achieve e-commerce and supply chain integration?
9. How do you determine the kind of technology investment (Internet-based solutions or traditional EDI) you need to make to compete effectively in the e-commerce environment and what do you do with what you already use (e.g., EDI)?
10. What is trust? How can we define trust in e-commerce?

References

Attwood, R., "E-com Coming," *Supply Management*, July 30, 1998, pp. 37–38.

Avery, S., "Automating RFPs Rids Process of Non-Value-Added Activities," *Purchasing*, July 16, 1998, p. 202.

Barrett, M. and Hogenson, A., "Why and How to Become EDI Enabled," *Transportation & Distribution*, August 1998, pp. 67–70.

Bendiner, J., "Understanding Supply Chain Optimization: From "What If" to What's Best," *APICS: The Performance Advantage*, Vol. 8, 1998, pp. 24–38.

Burnell, J., "Making Information Part of the Package," *Automatic LD. News*, January 1999, pp. 39–42.

Cachon, G. P. and Fisher, M., "Supply Chain Inventory Management and the Value of Shared Information," *Management Science*, Vol. 45, No. 8, 2000, pp. 16–24.

Cao, Q. and Siau, K., "Modeling the Bullwhip Effect in Supply Chains Using Group Problem Solving Approach," *Information Resource Management,* Vol. 13, 2000, pp. 123–140.

Caplice, C. and Sheffi, Y., "A Review and Evaluation of Logistics Metrics," *International Journal of Logistics Management*, Vol.5, No. 2, 1994, pp. 18–32.

Carter, D. and Baker, B., *Concurrent Engineering: The Product Development Environment for the 1990s*. Vol. 1, Reading, MA: Addison-Wesley Publishing, 1991.

Chen F., Drezner Z., Ryan J. K. and Simchi-Levi D., "Quantifying The Bullwhip Effect in A Simple Supply Chain: The Impact of Forecasting, Lead times, and Information", *Management Science*, Vol. 46, No. 3, March 2000, pp. 436–443.

Cooke, J. A., "The $30 Billion Promise," *Traffic Management,* Vol. 32, February 1993, pp. 57–59.

Cooper, R. G., *Winning at New Products: Accelerating the Process from Idea to Launch*, 2nd ed. Reading, MA: Addison-Wesley Publishing, 1993.

Dwyer, F. R., Schurr, P. H. and Oh, S., "Developing Buyer–Seller Relationships," Journal of Marketing, Vol. 51, April 1987, pp. 11–27.

Fine, C., Clockspeed: Winning Industry Control in the Age of Temporary Advantage. Reading, MA: Perseus Books, 1998.

Forrester, J. W., Industrial *Dynamics: Systems Dynamics Series*, Productivity Press, MIT Press, Portland, OR, 1961.

Fox, M. L., "Charting the Course to Successful Supply Chain Management," *APICS: The Performance Advantage*, Vol. 8, 1998, pp. 44–48.

Gavirneni, S., Kapuscinski, R. and Tayur, S., "Value of Information in Capacitated Supply Chains," *Management Science*, Vol. 45, No. 1, 2000, pp. 16–24.

Gordon, R., Hale, K., Hardcastle, J., Graham, C., Kjeldsen, P., Shiffler, G. III, and Lovelock, J.D. 2012. "Forecast Alert: It Spending, Worldwide, 1Q12 Update." Gartner Research

Handfield, R. and Nichols, E., *Introduction to Supply Chain Management*. Upper Saddle River, NJ: Prentice-Hall, 1999.

Hilt, L. M. and Brynjolfsson, E., "Productivity Business Profitability, and Consumer Surplus: Three Different Measures of Information Technology Value," *MIS Quarterly*, Vol. 20, No. 2 1996, pp. 121–141.

Hoek, R. V., "E-supply Chains – Virtually Non-Existing," *Supply Chain Management*, Vol. 6, No. 1, 20001, pp. 21–28.

Holme, M. R., "Procurement Reform and MIS Project Success," *International Journal of Purchasing and Materials Management*, Vol. 33, No.1, 1997, pp. 2–7.

Judge, C., Burrows, P. and Rheinhardt, A., "Tech to The Rescue?" *Business Week*, 1998, pp. 30, 31.

Kahn, J. A., "Inventories and The Volatility of Production," *American Economics Review* Vol. 77, No. 4, 1987, pp. 667–679.

Kiefer, A. W. and Novack, R. A., "An Empirical Analysis of Warehouse Measurement Systems in the Context of Supply Chain Implementation," *Transportation Journal*, Vol. 38, No. 3, Spring 1999, pp. 18–29.

Kim, B., "Coordinating an Innovation in Supply Chain Management," *European Journal of Operational Research,* Vol. 123, No. 3, 2000, pp. 89–100.

Krapf, E., "Can Businesses Find Common Ground for E-Commerce?" *Business Communications Review*, April 1999, pp. 43–46.

Lee, H. L., Padmanabhan, V. and Whang, S., "The Bullwhip Effect in Supply Chains," *Sloan Management Review*, Vol. 38, No. 3, 1997a, pp. 93–102.

Lee, H. L., Padmanabhan, V. and Whang, S., "Information Distortion in A Supply Chain: The Bullwhip Effect," *Management Science*, Vol. 43, No. 4, 1997b, pp. 546–558.

Lewis, I. and Talalayevsky, A., "Third Party Logistics: Leveraging Information Technology," *Journal of Business Logistics*, Vo. 20, No. 2, 2000, pp. 173–185.

Margretta, J., "The Power of Virtual Integration: An Interview with Dell Computer's Michael Dell," *Harvard Business Review*, March–April 1998, pp. 73–84.

Messmer, E., "Software Aims to Bridge EDI/XML Traffic," *Network World*, July 13, 1998, p. 6.

Metters, R., "Quantifying the Bullwhip Effect in Supply Chains," *Journal of Operations Management,* Vol. 15, No. 1, 1997, pp. 89–100.

Milliken, A. L., "Key Ingredients of Successful Performance Metrics in The Supply Chain," *The Journal of Business Forecasting*, Summer 2001, pp. 23–28.

Motwani, F., Madan, M. and Gunasekaran, A., "Information Technology in Managing Global Supply Chains," *Logistic Information Management*, Vol. 13, No. 5, 2000, pp. 320–327.

Naish, H. F., "Production Soothing in The Linear Quadratic Inventory Model," *Quarterly Journal of Economics*, Vol. 104, No. 425, 1994, pp. 864–875.

Nissen, M., "Agent-based Supply Chain Disintermediation versus Re-intermediation: Economic and Technological Perspectives," *International Journal of Electronic Commerce*, Vo. 3, No. 4, 2000, pp. 237–256.

Petersen, K. J., "An Empirical Investigation of Global Sourcing Strategy Effectiveness," *Journal of Supply Chain Management*, Vol. 36, No. 2, Spring 2000, pp. 29–39.

Phillips, S., "A Total Business Systems Approach to the Supply Chain," *APICS: The Performance Advantage*, Vol. 8, 1998, pp. 54–58.

Ratnasingham, P., "Implicit Trust in The Risk Assessment Process of EDI," *Computers & Security*, Vol. 18, No. 4, 1999, pp. 317–321.

Ratnasingham, P., "Implicit Trust in The Risk Assessment Process of EDI," Computer & Security, Vol. 18, No. 4, 1999, pp. 318–321.

Roberts, B. and Mackay M., "IT Supporting Supplier Relationships: The Role of Electronic Commerce," *European Journal of Purchasing and Supply Management,* Vol. 4, Nos. 2, 3, 1998, pp. 175–184.

Rosenthal, S., Effective Product Design and Development: How to Cut Lead Time to Increase Customer Satisfaction. Homewood, IL: Business One Irwin, 1992.

Ryan, S. D. and Harrison, D. A., "Considering Social Subsystem Costs and Benefits in Information Technology Investment Decisions: A View from The Field on Anticipated Payoffs," *Journal of Management Information Systems*, Vol. 31, No. 4, Spring 2000, pp. 9–25.

Sanders, N. R., "The Status of Forecasting in Manufacturing," *Production and Inventory Management Journal*, Vol. 38, 1997, pp. 32–39.

Schniederjans, M. J., *Topics in Just-In-Time Management*, Needham Heights, MA: Allyn and Bacon, 1993.

Schniederjans, M. J. and Olson, J. R., *Advanced Topics in Just-In-Time Management*, Westport, CT: Quorum Books, 1999.

Schonberger, R. J., Japanese Manufacturing Techniques: Nine Hiddent Lessons in Simplicity, New York: The Free Press, 1982.

Schonberger, R. J., World Class Manufacturing: The Lessons of Simplicity Applied, New York: The Free Press, 1986.

Sheppard, B. H. and Sherman, D.M., "The Grammars of Trust: A Model and General Implications," *Academy of Management Review,* Vol. 23, No. 3, 1998, pp. 422–437.

Smith, M. T., "Are Procurement Cards Compatible with Internet-based E-Commerce?" *Technology Guide*, October 1999, pp. 4–8.

Steggell, D., "EDI versus The Internet," *Technology Guide*, November 1998, pp. 24–28.

Stock, G. N., Greis, N. P. and Kasarda, J. D., "Enterprise Logistics and Supply Chain: The Role of Fit," *Journal of Operations Management*, Vol. 18, No. 5, 2000, pp. 531–547.

Swaminathan, J. M., "Modeling Supply Chain Dynamics: A Multi-agent Approach," *Decision Sciences*, Vol. 29, No. 3, 1998, pp. 607–632.

Sweet, L. L., "Giving Them The Business," *Infoworld*, July 26, 1999, pp. E2–E4.

Talluri, S., "An IT/IS Acquisition and Justification Model for Supply Chain Management," *International Journal of Physical Distribution & Logistics Management*, Vol. 30, Nos. 3–4, 2000, pp. 221–237.

Tyler, G., "Identity Crisis," *Supply Management*, March 4, 1999, pp. 42–43.

Walton, S. V. and Marucheck, A.S., "The Relationship between EDI and Supplier Reliability," *International journal of Purchasing and Materials Management*, Vol. 33, No. 3, Summer 1997, pp. 30–35.

Walton, S. V. and Gupta, J., "Electronic Data Interchange for Process Change in an Integrated Supply Chain," *International Journal of Operations & Production Management*, Vol. 33, No.3, Summer 1997, pp. 30–35.

Zuckerman, A. and McLymont, R., "EDI: Not Dead Yet," *Purchasing*, September 16, 1999, pp. 26–29.

Chapter 4   E-COMMERCE AND PRODUCT AND PROCESS DESIGN MANAGEMENT

Learning Objectives

After completing this chapter, you should be able to:

Define and describe concepts "product design" and "process design."

Understand the difference between the sequential and concurrent engineering in product design.

Explain the major benefits of the concurrent engineering.

Describe various product design improvement approaches.

Be able to categorize processes from different perspective.

Understand how to use break-even analysis in process selection.

Explain why product and process management is important for e-commerce operations.

Explain e-commerce strategies for product and process design.

Explain how e-commerce supports product development.

Explain how to use Web technology in "design for manufacture and assembly" and the benefits of doing so.

Describe the relationship between "enterprise resource planning" and e-commerce operations.

Overview of This Chapter

This chapter discusses the topic of product design and process management in an e-commerce setting. The chapter first presents an overview of product design and process management. Next the chapter describes the relevance of e-commerce in product design and process management and how e-commerce can help in enhancing product design and process management by reducing costs. Finally, the chapter explains how "enterprise resource planning" plays an important role in product/process management.

What are Product Design and Process Management?

Product design specifies which materials are to be used, determines dimensions and tolerances, defines the appearance of the product, and sets standards for performance. Product design is a very critical activity for a company. From a strategic standpoint, it defines a company's customers, as well as its competitors. A firm can gain a competitive advantage through designs that bring new ideas to the market quickly. One approach that many companies have introduced to their product design is a customer-focused or market-driven methodology that places data collection, processing and analysis in the hands of a cross-functional team of product developers within a company. In other words, the product design process links customer needs and expectations to the activities required in manufacturing the product.

The design process generally involves *multi-functional department groupings* comprised of such as functional areas as marketing, design, manufacturing, sales, and logistics. There are two types of product design processes, namely "sequential engineering" and "concurrent engineering." *Sequential engineering* (SE) refers to a simple serial approach in which product design proceeds one phase (department) to another. When the steps of the design process are performed sequentially, physical and mental "walls" tend to build up between functional areas and departments. *Concurrent engineering (CE)* emphasizes cross-functional integration and simultaneous development of a product and its associated processes. CE helps improve the quality of early design decisions and thereby reduces the length and cost of the design process. For instance, design engineers do not have a good understanding of the capabilities or limitations of their company's manufacturing facilities. Increased interaction with manufacturing can bring attentions to them of the realities of making a product. Simply consulting manufacturing personnel early in the design process can help identify critical factors or constraints that considered in the design can improve the quality of product design. Product design has a major impact on sales strategies, efficiency of production, speed of maintenance, and manufacturing cost. As such, improving the design process is very critical for a company to sustain its competitive edge. Table 1 shows several methods that help improve the design process.

A *process* is any part of an organization that takes inputs and transforms them into outputs that, it is hoped, are of greater value to the organization than the original inputs (Chase *et al.* 2001, p. 92). Processes can be categorized in different ways. One way to categorize processes is based on what they do.

Table 1. Design improvement methods

Design improvement methods	Description
Design for Manufacture (DFM)	Design for manufacture describes designing a product so it can be manufactured easily and economically. DFM identifies product design characters that are easy to manufacture, focuses on the design of component parts that are easy to fabricate and assemble, and integrates product design with process planning. It ensures that manufacturing concerns are systematically incorporated into the design process. There are several key elements of DFM including simplification, standardization, modularization, and *design for assembly* (DFA). *Simplification* refers to the reduction of the number of parts, assemblies, or options in a product. *Standardization* makes possible the interchangeability of parts among products. *Modularization* combines standardized components or modules to create unique finished products. Design for assembly (DFA) is a set of procedures for reducing the number of parts in an assembly, evaluating methods for assembly, and determining an assembly sequence.
Design for Environment (DFE)	Design for environment involves designing products from recycled material, using materials or components that can be recycled, designing a product so that it is easier to repair than discard, and minimizing unnecessary packaging, and minimizing material and energy usage during manufacture, consumption, and disposal.
Quality Function Deployment (QFD)	Quality function deployment translates the voice of the customer into a set of technical design requirements. QFD promotes better understanding of customer demands and design interactions. It also breaks down barriers between functions and departments by fostering teamwork. As a result, QFD increases customer satisfaction while reducing the cost of design and manufacturing.
Design for Robustness (DFR)	Superior quality is derived from a robust design. Robust design in turn yields a product designed to withstand variations. Design for robustness tackles the issue of design consistency.
Technology in Design	Due to the advancement of the technology, product design has experienced drastic changes in the past decade. Major computer-based design tools include *computer-aided design* (CAD), *computer-aided engineering* (CAE), and *computer-aided manufacturing* (CAM). CAD assists in the creation, modification, and analysis of a design. CAE tests and analyzes designs in CAD. CAM refers to control of the manufacturing process by computers.

There are four types of such processes: job shop, batch shop, assembly line, and continuous flow. A job shop is the one-of-kind production of a product to customer order. Batch shop processes items in small groups or batches and is characterized by fluctuating demands, short product runs of a wide variety of products. Assembly line produces large volumes of a standard product for a mass market. Continuous flow is used for very high volume commodity products that are extremely standardized. A second way to categorize a process is to base it on how they are designed. For instance, a process can be a single-stage or a multiple-stage process. Another way to characterize a process is whether the process make-to-stock (i.e., production that goes into inventory) or make-to-order (i.e., production that is shipped per prior customer order).

Process management involves process selection, planning, analysis and reengineering and it is the essence of operations management. Process management is also subject to the well-known rule that "time is money." One of the commonly used quantitative methods in process selection is *break-even-analysis*. The variables in the model of break-even analysis can be volume, cost, revenue, and profit. The break-even analysis mathematical formula is shown below:

Total cost = fixed cost + total variable cost

Total variable cost = variable cost per unit * volume

Total revenue = volume * price

Profit = total revenue – total cost, or
$\qquad$ = volume * price – (fixed cost + variable cost per unit * volume)

In selecting a process, it is useful to know at what volume of sales and production we can make a profit. By letting total cost equal total revenue, we can derive the volume of production/sales at which profit is zero. This volume is the so-called the "break-even point." At any volume above the break-even point, we will earn a profit.

$$\text{Volume break-even point} = \frac{\text{fix cost}}{\text{price} - \text{variable cost per unit}}$$

To illustrate the use of this formula lets take a simple technology process decision. Suppose we must choose between two process technologies, A or B. These technologies, each providing the same single service product to individual customers. Technology A has a fixed cost of purchase of $1 million and allows a service product to be delivered that we can charge (i.e., price) our customers $50 to perform while only requiring a labor cost (i.e., variable cost per unit) of $10 per unit of service. Technology B has a fixed cost of purchase of $500,000 and allows a service product to be delivered that we can charge our customers $35 to perform while only requiring a labor cost of $10 per unit of service. Which technology process should we choose if obtaining our investment in the technology quickly is the criteria for selection?   For Technology A the volume break-even point is:

volume break-even point (A) = $\dfrac{1,000,000}{50 - 10}$

= 25,000 units of service or customers served

For Technology B the volume break-even point is:

volume break-even point (B) = $\dfrac{500,000}{35 - 10}$

= 20,000 units of service or customers served

We can interpret the break-even point for Technology A as requiring 5, 000 (i.e., 25,000 – 20,000) more customers to be served before revenue and cost break-even than Technology B. Clearly, Technology B is preferable to Technology A since the revenues can be recouped more quickly, thereby leading to a shorter period of time in which the technology has an opportunity to start generating profits.

Process planning is used in determining how a product will be produced. Process planing usually involves major issues such as "make-or-buy decisions" and "equipment selection." *Make-or-buy decision* refers to a decision such as which components will be purchased and which components will be manufactured internally (Arslan 2001). Table 2 shows key factors in the make-or-buy decision. *Equipment selection* includes using, replacing, or upgrading existing equipment or purchasing new equipment. Some of the factors need to be considered here are purchase cost, operating costs, annual savings, revenue enhancement, and replacement analysis.

Table 2. Key factors in make-or-buy decisions

Key factors	Description
Cost	Companies need to use cost-benefit analysis to determine whether it is cheaper to make the item or buy it?
Capacity	Companies that are operating at less than full capacity usually make components rather than buy them, especially if maintaining a level work force is important.
Quality	It is easier to control the quality of items produced in house.
Speed	Sometimes components are purchased because a supplier can provide goods sooner than the manufacturer.
Reliability	Suppliers need to be reliable in both the quality and timing of what they supply.

Process analysis is the systematic approach to examine all aspects of a process to improve its operation. Some of the tools used in process analysis include process flowcharts, process diagrams, process maps, and graphic user interface (GUI)-based simulation (Jacobs 2000). (Note: We will discuss some of these in Chapter 10.)

Business process reengineering (BPR) is a relatively new concept. Thong *et al.* (2000) defined BPR as the fundamental rethinking and redesign of operating processes and organizational structure, focused on the organization's core competencies, to achieve dramatic improvements in organizational performance. BPR has been defined in different ways with different emphases by different researchers and practitioners. Despite the differences in definitions, and terminology, the emphasis in all these definitions is on redesigning business processes using a radical *information technology* (IT) enabled approach to organizational change. This suggests essential components within BPR, which make it distinct from other management tools and paradigms.

BPR versus TQM

In the last several decades, two main organizational development models dominated the organizational world, namely, total quality management (TQM) and business process reengineering (BPR). Organizations have used either or both to achieve the required change and ensure success. Jarrar and Aspinwall (1999) studied the relationship between BPR and TQM by pointing out the differences between and major strengths and weaknesses of TQM and BPR approaches (see Table 3).

It is apparent that there are major problems within the foundations of each individual approach. However, there is also a clear opportunity to unite them to fill each other's gaps. Jarrar and Aspinwall (1999) proposed a model that integrates of the best practices of TQM and BPR. The aim of the model is to help organizations achieve performance excellence by ensuring a healthy balance between stability and continuous change. Although "processes" and IT (the main focal areas in TQM and BPR, respectively) are crucial components for success, they are the easiest to perfect in an organization, and can easily be replicated by competitors, thus providing little competitive advantage. (Note: The importance of these subjects as agents of change in e-commerce organizations are such that we will be discussing them more fully in later chapters. TQM is discussed in Chapter 7 and BPR is discussed again in Chapter 10.) People and knowledge are perceived to be the main sources for competitive advantage in the future.

Why is Product and Process Design Management so Important?

According Moore *et al.* (1999, p. 28), "when industries are competing at equal price and functionality, design is the only differential that matters." As previously mentioned, the customer-focused or market-driven methodology of product and process design is in high demand. However, a major drawback in market-driven product/process design procedures are that they often do not consider operating capability, constraints, and other managerial decisions. This is problematic because it is quite likely that a profit-maximizing product profile would be relatively difficult to produce under an existing operating setup. Moore *et al.* (1999) proposed the Effective Product/Process Design (EPPD) model that incorporates customer preferences, production cost, and operating difficulty/capability into an analysis scheme.

Because engineering resources are limited and fast time-to-market is essential in e-commerce today, it is not surprising that the issue of product support is often neglected during new product development. However, failing to give appropriate attention to product support at the design stage a missed opport-

Table 3. BPR vs. TQM

Description	BPR	TQM
Initiated by	Panic External pressure from customers, competitors and stakeholders	Conventional know-how Common sense
Starting point	Clean slate: throw everything out and start afresh (total design)	Existing processes: analyze, standardize and improve
Frequency of change	One-time (occasional)	Continuous (continuous and incremental)
Focus	Macro processes Core processes	Components of the system Individual processes
Customer focus	Emphasis on external customers. Internal customers are a distraction	Equal emphasis on internal and external customers
Level of change	Radical change. Whole new process Revolutionary	Incremental improvement for existing processes Evolutionary
Employee involvement	The BPR and implementation teams	Total involvement from everyone is essential (all individuals, work groups and some teams)
Participation	Top-down (intensive)	Bottom-up (built within culture)
Empowerment	Important in certain area	Very important
Disadvantages	Could discard good with bad High cost in most cases	Difficult to get excited about and commit time to, since it involves many small improvements
Advantages	Erases old paradigms	Appropriate when resources are at their lowest Provide consistent improvement over time

Table 3. (Continued)

Description	BPR	TQM
Typical scope	Broad-cross-functional – a single BPR project sweeps across many functions or the whole organization	Narrow, within functions. Process improvement efforts are often within single teams or a few functions
Risk	High	Moderate
Primary enabler	Information technology	Statistical process control
Payback period	Quick dramatic payback	Slow continuous small improvements

unity. Good product support-including installation, customer training, maintenance, and repair is essential to achieving customer satisfaction in many markets. In addition, support can be a major source of revenue and can bring sustainable competitive advantage.

Product support, also known as *customer support* or *after-sales support*, is the name given to the various forms of assistance that companies offer customers to help them gain maximum value from manufactured products. Typical forms of support include installation, training on a product, maintenance and repair services (i.e., generally termed service), documentation, availability of spare parts, upgrades (i.e., enhanced functionality), customer consulting, and warranty schemes. Product support plays a key role in the marketing of both high-tech and engineering products. For example, both car owners and personal computer owners expect prompt and efficient service, while users of mainframe computer systems and communication networks derive maximum value from their equipment only when good support is available to help them understand its full capabilities and keep it running without interruption.

Product design influences both the amount of support necessary and the way it can be delivered. Decisions taken at the design stage affect product reliability and, consequently, how often products require maintenance. Similarly, modular design can reduce repair costs, and fault-finding is made easier by good diagnostics. Leading companies recognize both the importance of product support and the significance of evaluating support requirements at the design stage by using *Design for Supportability* (DFS) techniques. This enables them to gain competitive advantage from customer support and earn significant revenues (Goffin 2000).

"Agility" is a way for firms to obtain competitive advantage in the time-based competition today. *Agility* refers to the ability of an enterprise to respond quickly and successfully to change. According to Goldman *et al.* (1995), agility can be further divided into four dimensions: 1) enriching the customer, 2) cooperating to enhance competitiveness, 3) organizing to master change and uncertainty, and 4) leveraging the impact of people and information. Product and process design plays an important role in achieving the agility. McGaughey (1999) pinpointed the fact that Internet technology (i.e., Intranet and Extranet) help companies to achieve agility through the product/process design process. Table 4 summarizes the contributions of Internet technology on achieving the agility.

E-Commerce Strategies for Product and Process Design

Lee and Whang (2001) examined the efficiency of e-commerce operations and propose five strategies for product/service and process design in an e-commerce setting. The five e-commerce strategies include "logistics postponement", "dematerialization", "resource exchange", "leveraged shipments", and the clicks-and-mortar model. These strategies are based on two core e-commerce operations concepts, namely improving the use of information and leveraging existing resources. While the first core concept emphasizes using information well and addresses the complexity of the e-commerce operations, the second core concept is to leverage existing resources to perform order fulfillment.

Logistics Postponement

Logistics postponement means to delay product shipments until more accurate information becomes available. In doing so, logistics can be run efficiently because accurate information helps improve timeliness and reduces delivery cost. Logistics postponement is in line with the just-in-time (JIT) philosophy as the companies ship their products when needed. It also avoids unnecessary reshipments due to lack of accurate information and thus curtails the cost of inventory management and reshipments. The logistics postponement strategy is used when products are of high value and if customers' demands are highly unstable.

Table 4. How internet technology helps to achieve agility

Agility dimensions	Contribution of Internet technology
Customer enrichment	Company Web site can be used to solicit feedback about the depth and breadth of its product offering and the quality of its products and to solicit customer ideas for product modifications or new products. Internet makes it possible for customers to experience certain types of products after which a company might solicit feedback about consumers' experiences. (For example, see software demos at www.download.com.) The Internet also helps manufacturing company's prompt customer involvement in product design processes. For example, Ford Motor Company used online conferences and e-mail to support online interaction with designers working on its Taurus model (Preiss *et al.* 1996).
Competitiveness enhancement via cooperation	Internet based technology is a viable tool of enhancing cooperation. The need for cooperation goes beyond a company itself but includes the company customers, suppliers, stockholders, government, and even competitors. Intranet and *groupwares* (e.g., Lotus Notes, electronic meeting or scheduling software) that can facilitate cooperation among individuals or groups in either inter-organizational or intra-organizational situations. For instance, an Intranet-based groupware software could enhance the sharing of information regarding customer needs and it could also support collaborative work on product and process design.
Change and uncertainty mastering	Internet technology provides rich communication facilities using common protocols across software, platforms, and networks. Internet technology also allows *knowledge workers* to form, change and dismantle virtual intra- or inter-organizational teams in response to changes and uncertainties.
Impact of people and information	Internet technology provides a channel for data flows to and from any internal or external source. Intranet can selectively provide individuals and groups, within or outside an organization to access the data gathered. The intranet and the Internet can also provide support for education and training.

Dematerialization

With the advancement of IT, information flow is less expansive than material flow because it does not incur logistic costs such as handling, loading and unloading, warehousing, shipping, returns, spoilage, and damage. Thus, it is often tempting to substitute material flow with information flow in the digital age we are living in. Dematerialization is an extreme case where the physical product is totally replaced by information. Dematerialized products include software, airline tickets, publications, documents, music, videos, photos, stamps, banking, and financial services to name a few.

Resource Exchange

Resource exchange refers to pooling resources among different divisions in an organization to satisfy the demands of customers, regardless of their location. For instance, the product a customer needs may be stocked at many locations. If the stock at all the locations can be pooled to form a virtual resource, then whenever customer demand shows up, companies can utilize the nearest location. Enterprise resource planning (ERP) can facilitate information flow activities to allocate demand and resource availability.

Leveraged Shipments

In order to reduce the cost logistics for small shipments and/or in dispersed locations, the leveraging shipments approach is often employed. Leveraged shipments make use of the physical channels already in place for the delivery of other products. Because those channels already exist, the cost of shipping is relatively small.

The Click-and-Mortar Model

The click-and-mortar model (CAMM) is used to get customers to handle the last mile of the delivery journey. The CAMM model is popular among not only bricks-and-mortar companies (e.g., Circuit City, Best Buy, and Barns and Nobles) but also virtual retailers (e.g., Egghead.com, Amazon.com). For instance, Best Buy (an electronic-product retailer) allows customers to order their products online and then pick them up at the nearest outlet locations. For virtual retailers, tight links between suppliers and the external outlets must be formed to achieve CAM. For example, VooDoo Bicycle Co. of Sunnyvale,

California uses its Web site to let customers create customized bicycles and then links customers directly to a local dealer for placing the final order and receiving the product.

So, what is the best strategy in e-commerce operations? The answer is that it depends on the company's business environment and on the nature of its products. The logistics postponement strategy is used when products are of high value and if customers' demands are highly unstable. Dematerialization works best when physical products can be transformed into a digital format. The resource exchange strategy becomes a viable business process choice when the company already has access to stock and resources widely distributed across a geographical region and when the company has information systems to management information flow. Leveraged shipment maybe applicable in the situation where products have a stable demand. Finally, the CAMM model can be implemented when logistical outlets are near customers.

Using empirical survey research, Guimaraes (2000) examined the impact of the Internet and e-commerce activities on the organizational change in product and process. The findings of his study suggest that Internet-based e-commerce is a critical requirement for implement organizational change. By reducing clerical procedures and eliminating paper handling, e-commerce can accelerate ordering, delivery, and payment for goods and services while reducing operating and inventory costs. In reality, e-commerce is about next generation manufacturers and their consumers adopting a new process or methodology in doing business. These processes are in essence supported by electronic interactions that replace traditional means of conducting business (Soliman and Youssef 2001). Gide and Soliman (1998) studied the success factors for the implementation of e-commerce and were able to identify the following ten *critical success factors* (CSFs) for the implementation of e-commerce in manufacturing:

1. Management commitment and support for e-commerce.
2. Organizational and management objectives for e-commerce.
3. Communication between users and e-commerce department.
4. E-commerce system security and reliability.
5. E-commerce department's service function.
6. Integrating e-commerce into existing business functions.
7. Change management for e-commerce system implementation.
8. Appropriate e-commerce system applications.
9. User participation and satisfaction for e-commerce implementation.
10. Technological competence for e-commerce implementation.

McIvor *et al.* (2000) suggested that e-commerce is not just a single technology but a combination of technologies, applications, business processes, business strategies and practices necessary to do business electronically. This leads to the need to discuss how e-commerce facilitates product development.

How E-Commerce Supports Product Development

Shortening the product development process is one of major ways in dealing with the time-based competition. Howe *et al.* (2000) explored how e-commerce can support product development by examining the impact of the integration of Internet and intranet applications with the stage-gate product development system on supporting and accelerating new product development. A stage-gate system is a process model for developing new products from idea to launch. Stage-gate system is widely used in managing the new product process and has shown to be effective in achieving time reduction of launching new products to market, earlier detection of failures, higher success rates, permitting more projects to come in on time and at their cost targets, better cross-functional communication, and greater customer satisfaction.

Major components of stage-gate systems includes those presented in Table 5. The possible impacts of e-commerce on the various stage-gate system steps in Figure 1 are described in Table 6.

In a study by Soliman and Youssef (2001), the role of *knowledge management* (i.e., a set of processes in an organization to create, gather, maintain, and disseminate a firm's knowledge) in improving the product development in an e-commerce setting was investigated. Today's global economies create an international competitive environment in which commercial success of individual firms is strongly conditioned by their belonging to a network of collectively interacting firms. As such, the knowledge-building requirements are not confined to the organization itself, but transcends to a network of organizations. Foss (1999) stated that inter-firm relations are not given but developed and that knowledge sharing, trust relations, and standardization must be built up and allowed to gradually emerge. His research concludes that firms may benefit from network capabilities, such as collective learning, when these capabilities are: valuable (i.e., collective technological learning in Silicon Valley), rare (i.e., very seldom different networks will possess the same network capabilities), hard to imitate, non-substitutable (i.e., highlighting the need for continued process innovation), characterised by imperfect competition in acquisition/development, such as time compression economies from collective learning and their effects relative to would-be imitators. As knowledge management becomes a vital prerequisite for competitive management, the efficiency of sharing across the enterprise or network of enterprises must be evaluated and managers must devote attention to network options such as the Internet, intranets and extranets.

As described above, e-commerce can contribute a greatly to new product development processes. E-commerce offers opportunities fo cost reduction and a shortened product development life cycle.

Design for Manufacture and Assembly in E-Commerce Operations

As discussed in the previous sections, design for manufacture and assembly (DFMA) is one of the critical elements of product design process. Computer-aided DFMA tools have been used in the past three decades and have some benefits. For instance, computer-aided DFMA tools are systematic and have overcome traditional tedious and time-consuming DFMA processes. However, they also have some disadvantages. For example computer-aided DFMA tools are difficult to maintain and administer. Moreover, they also suffer from disintegration just like other decision support systems (e.g., CAD and CAM). According to Huang and Mak (1999), Internet-based e-commerce is often involved in support various activities of the product development process. For instance, the University of Iowa developed a general client-server model of collaborative design using the Web technology. Huang and Mak (1999) examined the impact of e-commerce on design for manufacture and assembly (DFMA), particularly on using the Web technology to support DFMA on the Internet. Their research demonstrated that e-commerce oriented DFMA (e-DFMA) not only offered equivalent functionality as those of traditional computer aided DFMA on standalone workstations, but also had some unique advantages. First, e-DFMA can significantly reduce the cycle time of DFMA and thus product design process in general. Second, since e-DFMA uses the client-server architecture where the client side no longer needs to be concerned about installation or maintenance issues. As long as the user connects the network with a Web browser, they can have instant access to any e-DFMA technique available on the network. Third, one of the greatest benefits of using e-DFMA is the universal platform that the Web technology provides. Both client and server use the same protocol (i.e., TCP/IP) to communicate to each other, regardless of their hardware configurations (e.g., PCs and mainframes) and operating systems (e.g., Windows, Unix, and Linux). Finally, by nature, the client-server architecture of e-DFMA facilitates the integration between other Web-based decision support systems such as e-CAD and e-CMA in the product development process.

Table 5. Stage-gate system components

Component	Description
Parallel processing	Stage-gate systems use *parallel processing* rather than sequential processing. As a result, at each stage of the system, many activities take place simultaneously.
Stages	There are five stages in a stage-gate system. They are preliminary investigation, business case preparation, development, testing, and launch. Figure 1 shows a typical stage-gate system.
Gates	As shown in Figure 1, there is a so-called "gate", that is, a quality control checkpoint between each stage. The gate has a set of quality criteria that the product must pass before moving to the next stage. Fives gates included in stage-gate systems are initial screen, second screen, decision on business case, post-development, and decision to launch.
Product development project teams	Project teams are cross-functional teams involving members from customers, marketing, design, manufacturing, logistics, and sales.

Roy and Kodkani (1999) proposed an approach to the development of an open collaborative design environment in the CAD setting of a networked enterprise. They ascertained that demands for high quality, a variety of low to medium quality products or mass customization has led to the concept of *virtual organizations* and that the de-centralized design teams of such an organization required a framework to manage the CAD product information. By integrating the emerging standard for 3D geometry on the World-Wide-Web (WWW) with conventional CAD packages, a framework was described in their study for the development of a product model with various levels of abstractions. The syntactic content of the product model was accessible through any Internet interface, such as Google Chrome, and by other associates with a centralized database for embedding technological information at the face and feature levels. The semantic and syntactic content of the product model could then be accessed and manipulated through the single Internet interface. The system was also deployed on a test-bed utilizing both a UNIX box and a machine operating under the Windows NT system, to demonstrate its open architecture and interoperability.

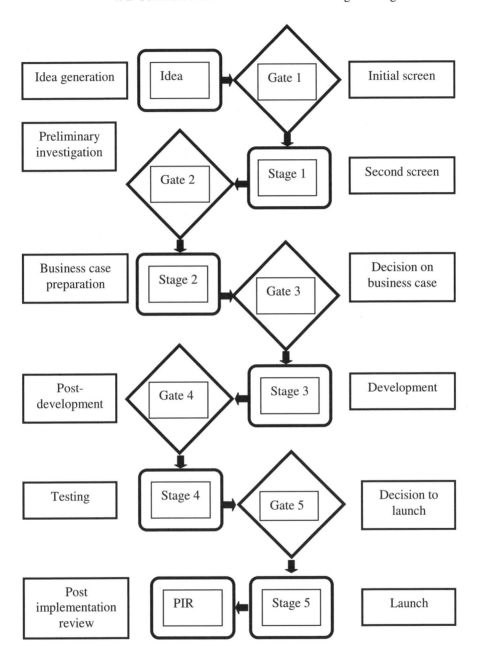

Figure 1. Stage-gate system

Table 6. Impact of e-commerce on stage-gate system

Gate or stage	Impact of e-commerce
Idea generation	Idea generation is the first step of stage-gate systems. Ideas are generated from both internal and external sources in this step. The Internet offers a great tool to gather ideas from external sources such as customers, channel members, and competitors. The major Internet-based venues of idea generation include newsgroups, forums, and bulletin board. The ideas gathered in this step then submitted to Gate1 for screening. Ideas from internal sources can be gathered through Intranet and groupware applications.
Gate 1: Initial Screen	In this step, a feasibility study of project is conducted. The intranet can enhance communications of among employees who monitor the quality criteria, while Internet newsgroups can serve as a window to inform customers and gather feedback from them.
Stage 1: Preliminary Investigation	The goal of this step is to determine the project's technical and marketplace merits. Groupware can be a viable tool for facilitating technological feasibility assessment. Market research at the stage can be through the Internet.
Gate 2: Second Screen	This step is similar to gate 1. However it reevaluates the project as new information added in stage 1. This stage involves a more detailed investigation and requires detailed market research information. Once again, the Internet is a useful and cost saving tool to conduct a detail-oriented market research and can provide more timely information than previously used methods.
Stage 2: Business Case Preparation	In this stage, the objective of the market research is to determine consumers' needs, wants, and preferences. The Internet is a great place to conduct customer survey. It is also less costly than traditional survey methods such as mail or phone surveys.
Gate 3: Decision on Business Case	This gate renders the decision whether to accept the business case and move the project into development. The intranet can be used to disseminate and exchange information of financial criteria such as sales, cost, and profit projections that are needed to make the decision on the business case.
Stage 3: Development	Product prototype is developed at this stage. Both Internet and intranet can arm product development teams with multi-media information infrastructure that facilitates communications among members either locally or in dispersed locations. The Web can help reduce the set-up cost and time for product development project.

Table 6. (Continued)

Gate or stage	Impact of e-commerce
Gate 4: Post-development Review	The post-development review aims at evaluating the progress the product development process supported by the intranet.
Stage 4: Testing	Testing is used to validate the product developed. The Internet is a major outlet for testing of information products such as software. Many software companies including Microsoft and Netscape provide their beta versions browsers for users to try out via download from the Internet. According to MacCormack (2001), successful development is evolutionary in nature. Companies first release a low-functionality version of a product to selected customers at a very early stage of development. Thereafter work proceeds in an iterative fashion, with the design allowed to evolve in response to the customer's feedback. This approach contrasts with traditional models of software development and their more sequential processes.
Gate 5: Decision to Launch	Gate 5 is the final checkpoint before launching the product. The decision making process can again be enhanced through the use of the intranet.
Stage 5: Launch	Promotion through advertisement is critical in launching new products. The Internet is an attractive venue for advertisement due to this lost cost and wide audience exposure.
Post Implement Review (PIR)	This step involves reviewing the performance of new products. The Internet can again be used here to gather feedback from customer's on the new products developed.

Roy and Kodkani (2000) also presented an approach to develop and implement an architecture to support geographically dispersed designers, to effectively develop and select the product concept through a collaborative effort. Their approach is based on the WWW, which allows designers to represent their concepts and also aids them to search existing ideas on similar products is developed.

Greek (2000) reported that the idea of a seamless design process has been around for years, but appeared to be an unattainable dream. The problem wasn't a lack of interoperability between modeling software; many sectors, notably automotive, have online design processes, usually via extranets and intranets, and they tend to ensure that their suppliers and contractors work on the same platforms and modeling software packages to allow easy interchange. The research claimed that the big problem had been the transmission of traditional CAD models. This is because models even for simple products can reach many hundreds of megabytes and these can prove impossible for Internet connections to cope with. So attempts have been slow, unreliable, and systems have become overloaded and crashed. But a new technology called 3D streaming, is bringing CAD truly into the Internet age.

Integrating ERP and E-Commerce Operations

Enterprise resource planning (ERP) systems are a new type of software that enables companies to integrate business functions-including finance, human resources, operations, sales and distribution, and marketing, across their organizations. Companies throughout the world are increasingly converting to these systems. An ERP system promises more and better information, which can lead to lower costs. It integrates and automates most business processes and shares information enterprise-wide in real time. Because the system tracks production by job, work center, person, and activity, there's evidence that it improves cost system quality. It's especially useful to companies pursuing a low-price/high-volume strategy-rather than a market niche strategy-such as manufacturers of mass merchandise items.

Benefits of ERP

Interestingly, firms initiating ERP projects rated their cost management systems significantly higher than did non-ERP firms. With far more cost-driver information available, ERP systems enable a greater variety of allocation-bases to be used. Pillowtex, for example, previously used plant-wide overhead rates spread evenly by department. Now with its ERP system providing access to information by activity, the company's accountants can do a better job of allocating specific overhead to different cost objects, such as customers, according to Krumwiede and Jordan (2000). Another benefit of ERP systems is that activity-based costing (ABC) is finding a new home within ERP systems at many companies. Partnership agreements between major ERP vendors and ABC software developers now exist, such as the one between SAP and ABC Technologies. These alliances may help ABC proponents overcome some of the traditional problems such as lack of top management buy-in and infrequent updates.

E-Commerce and ERP

Now the elusive goal of integrating business and production operations is getting a new twist via the Internet. ERP vendors such as SAP, PeopleSoft, Oracle, Baan, and JD Edwards are rolling out new programs that use Internet technologies such as eXtensible markup Language (XML) and Java for gluing together an enterprises' various computer systems. These so-called "post-ERP" programs are available under a variety of acronyms: ERP portals, EAI (Enterprise Application Integration), EPS (Enterprise Production Systems) and XRP (eXtended Resource Planning), among others. The goal is to use the Web to help companies with make-to-order operations, enabling them to link purchase orders, whether actual or forecasted from a customer instantly to the plant floor. Simultaneously, a host of other processes would update a plant's logistics, inventory control, maintenance, production quality, accounting, and sales functions. Then, domino-like, the system would update related operations in an enterprise, and those of its customers and suppliers.

ERP and Lean Philosophy

For the past decade, organizations have spent billions of dollars and countless employee hours installing huge integrated ERP software packages. Now many manufacturing companies are realizing that the infrastructure they spent years creating is deficient on their plant floor. The ERP systems of the 1990s have become a liability for many manufacturers because they perpetuate some of the legendary material requirements planning (MRP) (i.e., a software used to schedule production and plan materials usage) problems such as complex bills of materials, inefficient workflows, and unnecessary data collection. Lean manufacturing, a concept with roots in the production processes of Toyota, aims at improving efficiency, eliminating product backlogs, and synchronizing production to customer demand rather than a long-term forecast (Schniederjans and Olson 1999).

Organizational Preparedness for ERP

There are many factors that a company needs to consider in their implementation of ERP. Some proposed by Rao (2000), Chase *et al.* (2001, pp. 420–428), and Turban *et al.* (2002, pp. 254–259) are presented in Table 7:

Table 7. CSFs in the implementation of ERP

Area of application	Description
Infrastructure planning	Information infrastructure such as networks is a basic requirement implementing ERP and the major concerns for such networks include adequate bandwidth, reliable LAN, and network compatibility.
Local area network (LAN)	The LAN needs to have a centralized server location even on a widely dispersed place.
Server hardware	Low-end servers are required even in the preliminary ERP selection stage to train and show the ERP demos. Adequate server/network also needs to be available in the modeling phase.
Computer hardware	All computers need to be upgraded to run ERP system.
Training and education	ERP systems require a lot of personnel training and constant updated education. There is, therefore, a need for educational and training facilities and resources.
Human resources (HRs)	ERP is HR dependent. These systems need co-operations from all the functional areas and their successful integration together.
Commitment of HRs	ERP implementation is a very difficult process. The best people in the organization have to be assigned or released to form a cross-functional ERP implementation teams.
Top management commitment	ERP is a time-consuming and financial-drain process. Without the top management's commitment, the ERP project will most likely to fail.
Commitment to default system	Although most of the ERP systems can be customized, it is always highly recommended that the company need to test and implement a default version first before a full-scale ERP system goes live.

Table 7. (Continued)

Area of application	Description
New site consideration	Implementation an ERP system on a new site is always much easier than an existing site. When dealing with an on-going site, focuses should be on learning and implementing only the new procedures. In doing so, implementation could be speeded up considerably.
Commitment to a manual system	A good manual system can serve as the backup of the ERP system for auditing purposes.
Strategic Decision on Centralized vs. Decentralized Implementation	Most companies have dispersed locations and thus whether to place servers in centralized locations or locally become an important question. The answer to the question is it depends. Often a hybrid strategy (both centralized and decentralized infrastructures) is implemented.

These guidelines are essential basics to begin the process of implementing an ERP system. Because they are mostly IT related, they also serve to help in the integration of ERP with e-commerce operational activities.

Summary

This chapter introduces the concept of product and process management and describes various approaches used in produce/process enhancement. The importance and uniqueness of product and process design in an e-commerce setting are also explained in this chapter. Drawing upon product and process design research literature, this chapter presents e-commerce strategies for product and process design, e-commerce support for product development, e-commerce based design for manufacture and assembly (DFMA), and the integration of ERP and product/process design concepts.

♦ Review Terms

Activity-based accounting (ABC)
Agility
Assembly line process
Batch shop process
Break-even analysis
Business process reengineering
Competitive advantage
Computer-aided design (CAD)
Computer-aided engineering (CAE)
Computer-aided manufacturing
(CAM)
Concurrent engineering (CE)
Continuous flow
Cross-functional teams
Customer support
Dematerialization
Design for assembly (DFA)
Design for environment (DFE)
Design for manufacture (DFM)
Design for robustness (DFR)
Design for supportability (DFS)
Effective product/process design
(DPPD)
Enterprise resource planning (ERP)
Gate
Groupware
Initial screen
Just-in-time (JIT)
Knowledge workers
Knowledge management
Lean management
Lean philosophy
Leveraged shipments
Local area network (LAN)

Logistics postponement
Make-or-buy decision
Make-to-order
Make-to-stock
Material requirements planning
(MRP)
Modularization
Multi-functional departments
Parallel processing
Post implement review (PIR)
Post-development review
Preliminary investigation
Process
Process analysis
Process management
Process planning
Process selection
Product design
Product support
Quality function deployment (QFD)
Resource exchange
Second screen
Sequential engineering (SE)
Stage
Stage-gate product development
system
Stage-gate system
Standardization
The click-and-mortar (CAM)
Time-based competition
Total quality management (TQM)
Virtual organization
World-Wide-Web (WWW)

♦ Discussion Questions

1. How can organization gain a competitive edge with product and process design?
2. What types of decisions are involved in process planning?

3. What are the different ways to categorize process types?
4. How does the role of the design engineer change under concurrent engineering?
5. What are the major elements of process management?
6. What is the difference between business process reengineering (BPR) and total quality management (TQM)?
7. Why product and process design management is so important in an e-commerce setting?
8. Why product and process design management is so important in an e-commerce setting?
9. How can e-commerce contribute in achieving agility?
10. How does e-commerce support product development?
11. What are some of the benefits of ERP?

♦ Questions

1. How is simplification, standardization, and modularization related to process design?
2. What are the commonly used methods in facilitating product design process? Name three of them.
3. What are the benefits of concurrent engineering as compared to the sequential engineering?
4. What are the key factors in rendering make-or-buy decisions? Explain.
5. What are the major problems of both BPR and TQM? What is the solution to these problems?
6. What is agility? What are the four dimensions of agility?
7. What are the five e-commerce strategies for product and process design? Briefly explain each of them.
8. What is the best e-commerce strategy for product and process design? Where to use a particular e-commerce strategy?
9. What is a stage-gate system? Describe the major steps involved in the stage-gate system.
10. How can e-commerce support the collaboration in product and process design?

◆ Problems

1. If a computer has a fixed cost to a small B2B operation of $18,500, requires labor costs of $250 per order processed, and operation charges its customers a flat fee of $1000 per customer, how many customers will they have to process before their total revenues will break-even with their total costs?

2. If a piece of automated technology used in transmitting orders has a fixed cost to a B2G operation of $1,375,000, requires labor costs of $170 per order processed, and operation charges its customers an average service fee of $1700 per customer, how many customers will they have to process before their revenues will break-even with their costs?

3. If expected total volume in sales of a B2C operation is only 32,000, they have a fixed cost of $660,000, and a variable cost of $30 per customer, what price would the B2C have to charge to at least break-even?

4. Suppose we must choose one of three possible knowledge management systems, A, K, or Z. These systems provide the same service to customers. System A has a fixed cost purchase price of $1,070,500, and generates a service product that we can charge our customers $1,500 to perform while only requiring a labor cost of $805 per unit of service. System K has a fixed cost purchase price of $647,300, and generates a service product that we can charge our customers $700 to perform while only requiring a labor cost of $500 per unit of service. System Z has a fixed cost purchase price of $1,503,950, and generates a service product that we can charge our customers $1,200 to perform while only requiring a labor cost of $1,100 per unit of service. Which system should we choose? Generate a break-even analysis in volume for each system to support your decision.

5. A startup e-commerce operation must decide between using people to process orders manually from e-mails or let a software application do the processing. The cost of processing an order using a team of people is $73 while the costs of the technology to support the manual people option are only $18,125. The cost of the software application is $26,221 and the only cost for technology is a single computer for $1,800. To maintain the software per order will cost $2. If the price the company can charge its customers is $160 per customer, which of the two processes should be selected? Compare break-even values for both processes.

References

Arslan, H., "Analytic Models for When and How to Expedite in Make-to-order Systems," *IIE Transactions*, Vol. 33, No. 11, 2001, pp. 1019–1030.

Chase, R. B., Aquilano, N. J. and Jacobs, F. R., *Operations Management for Competitive Advantage*. 9th ed., Boston, MA: McGraw-Hill/Irwin, 2001.

Foss, N. J., "Networks, Capabilities, and Competitive Advantage", *Scandinavian Journal of Management,* Vol. 15, 1999, pp. 1–15.

Gide, E., Soliman, F., "Framework for the Internet-based E-commerce in Manufacturing and Business Operations", *Proceedings of 4th International Conference on Networking Entities: NETIES '98: Networking for the Millennium*, Leeds, 1998, pp. 66–72.

Goffin, K., "Design For Supportability: Essential Component of New Product Development," *Research Technology Management*, Vol. 43, No. 2, 2000, pp. 40–48.

Goldman, S., Nagel, R. and Preiss, K., *Agile Competitors and Virtual Organizations*. Nostrand Reinhold, New York, NY, 1995.

Greek, D., "Design Grasps the Net," *Professional Engineering*, Vol. 13, Nos. 2000, pp. 36–38.

Guimaraes, T., "The Impact of Competitive Intelligence and IS Support in Changing Small Business Organizations," *Logistics Information Management*, Vol. 13, No. 3, 2000 pp. 117–122.

Howe, V., Mathieu, R. G. and Parker, J., "Supporting New Product Development with the Internet," *Industrial Management & Data Systems*, Vol.100, No. 6, 2000, pp. 277–284.

Huang, G. Q. and Mak, K. L., "Design for Manufacture and Assembly on the Internet," *Computers in Industry*, Vol. 38, No. 1, 1999, pp. 17–31.

Jarrar, Y. F. and Aspinwall, E. M., "Integrating Total Quality Management and Business Process Reengineering: Is It Enough?" *Total Quality Management*, Vol. 10, Nos. 4/5, 1999, pp. S584–S594.

Krumwiede, K. R. and Jordan, W. G., "Reaping the Promise of Enterprise Resource Systems,"*Strategic Finance*, Vol. 82, No. 4, pp. 48–53.

Lee, H. L. and Whang, S., "Winning the Last Mile of E-commerce," *MIT Sloan Management Review*, Vol. 42, No. 4, 2001, pp. 54–63.

MacCormack, A., "Product-development Practices that Work: How Internet Companies Build Software," *MIT Sloan Management Review*, Vol. 42, No. 2, 2001, pp. 75–85.

McGaughey, R. E., "Internet Technology: Contributing to Agility in the Twenty-first Century," Vol. 1, No. 1, 1999, pp. 7–13.

McIvor, R., Humphreys, P. and Huang, G., "Electronic Commerce: Re-engineering the Buyer-Supplier Interface," *Business Process Management Journal*, Vol. 6, No. 2, 2000, pp. 122–131.

Moore, W. L., Louviere, J. J. and Verma, R., "Using Conjoint Analysis to Help Design Product Platforms," *Journal of Product Innovation Management*, Vol. 16, No. 1, pp. 27–39.

Preiss, K., Goldman, S. L. and Nagel, R. N., *Cooperate to Compete: Building Agile Business Relationships*. Nostrand Reinhold, New York, NY, 1995.

Rao, S. S., "Enterprise Resource Planning: Business Needs and Technologies," Industrial *Management & Data Systems*, Vol. 100, No. 2, 2000, pp. 81–88.

Roy, U. and Kodkani, S. S., "Collaborative product conceptualization tool using Web technology," *Computers in Industry*, 2000, Vol. 41, No. 2, pp. 195–209.

Roy, U. and Kodkani, S. S., "Product Modeling within the Framework of the World Wide Web," *IIE Transactions*, Vol. 31, No. 7, 1999, pp. 667–678.

Schniederjans, M. J. and Olson, J. R., *Advanced Topics in Just-In-Time Management*, Westport, CT: Quorum Books, 1999.

Soliman, F. and Youssef, M., "The Impact of Some Recent Developments in E-business on the Management of Next Generation Manufacturing," *International Journal of Operations & Production Management*, Vol. 21, Nos. 5/6, 2001, pp. 538–564.

Thong, J. Y., Yap, C. Y. and Seah, K. L., "Authors: Kin-Lee Business Process Reengineering in the Public Sector: The Case of the Housing Development Board in Singapore," *Journal of Management Information Systems*, Vol. 17, No. 1, 2000, pp. 245–270.

Turban, E., McLean, E. and Wetherbe, J., *Information Technology for Management*, 3rd ed., New York: John Wiley & Sons, 2002.

Chapter 5 E-COMMERCE AND PURCHASING MANAGEMENT

Learning Objectives

After completing this chapter, you should be able to:
Define and describe "purchasing management."
Understand JIT (just-in-time) purchasing principles.
Describe the supplier selection process in JIT purchasing.
Explain why firms implementing JIT purchasing process perform better than non-JIT firms.
Describe the eight dimensions of excellence in purchasing management.
Describe the new trends in purchasing management.
Explain the importance of e-commerce purchasing.
Describe the benefits of e-commerce purchasing as compared with traditional purchasing practices.
Explain what factors influence professional's decisions of purchasing to utilize the e-commerce purchasing.
Describe the purchasing life cycle and explain why it is important in e-commerce purchasing management.
Describe the e-commerce purchasing behavior model.
Describe how to develop strategies for increasing e-commerce purchasing.
Explain how the business-to-business auction model enhances e-commerce purchasing.

Overview of This Chapter

This chapter presents the topic of purchasing management in the context of e-commerce. The chapter presents JIT purchasing principles and talks about purchasing management benchmarking. The chapter then explains why purchasing management is so important in an e-commerce setting. Finally, the chapter concludes with several research models that describe how e-commerce purchasing can be improved.

What is Purchasing Management?

The traditional role of purchasing management is to ensure that there is a supply of parts and materials to support a business's operations and save money in the process. Purchasing management must make certain that the parts and materials required by the product specifications are of the desired quality and are delivered on time. Purchasing statistics show that historically about half of U.S. manufacturing cost comes from purchased materials and that many manufacturing companies purchasing more than half of their parts rather than make in-house. As such, purchasing cost is also a major issue of purchasing management.

Supplier selection is extremely important in purchasing management to enhance quality, reduce delivery time, and to curtail purchasing cost. Suppliers selected must share the purchasing company's commitment to quality and delivery scheduling and main their own quality assurance program such as *total quality management* (TQM) for providing high quality materials and parts. A strategic partnership needs to be built between the supplier and the buyer. The supplier needs to be in line with the purchasing company in terms of the safeguarding the quality by monitoring its own materials and parts quality before delivery. This process will not only control the quality of the materials delivered but also reduce the delivery cycle time in that, in so doing, it is unnecessary for the buying company to spend time to inspect incoming materials and parts. However, JIT purchasing is often implemented as a major strategy to tackle the issue of customer service in purchasing, namely, the on-time delivery (see next section for details about JIT purchasing principles). Common practices for cost savings in purchasing include reducing the number of suppliers to obtain volume discounts (i.e., smaller number of buyers allows larger quantities to be ordered from the remaining suppliers) and maintaining stronger control by using competitive bidding to ensure the suppliers provide their materials and parts at a competitive price.

JIT Purchasing

A just-in-time (JIT) purchasing system is critical to the success of any production operation. It is harder to implement than other aspects of the JIT because it involves an external element of the supplier. A buyer seeks a single, reliable supplier that is willing to deliver quality items, in the amount and at the time needed. A long-term contract is generally negotiated between the two parties where the order quantity, delivery frequency, quality level, and price are specified.

In a traditional purchasing environment, the buyer and supplier often have an adversarial relationship. Each party tries to enhance their own position, which can considerably increase the costs for the other party. For JIT to be effective, there should be a cooperative relationship between the two parties. They should work together to enhance both positions. JIT purchasing is not new. Schonberger (1982) was one of the first researchers who pointed out the importance of purchasing and of suppliers' involvement in JIT product systems. Mehra and Inman (1992) defined JIT purchasing as a purchasing strategy that yields higher levels of productivity and quality by minimizing vendor lot sizes and their leadtime through the use of single sourcing and quality certification of suppliers. Drawn from several JIT purchasing studies (Schniederjans and Olson 1999, pp. 71–77; Germain and Droge 1998; Landry *et al.* 1997; Richeson *et al.* 1995; Leavy 1994; Schniederjans 1993, pp. 33–37; Mehra and Inman 1992; Wantuck 1989; pp. 300–302; Schonberger 1982), Table 1 lists some of the major *JIT purchasing principles*.

Table 1. JIT purchasing principles

Area of decision-making	JIT purchasing principles
Supplier Relation principles	• Seek to reduce purchasing costs: Implement continuous replenishment • Seek timely communications and responsiveness • Seek ordering flexibility: Permits changes in order quantities to better synchronize inventory with actual demand • Seek long-term relationships with suppliers • Seek single-source suppliers • Seek certification in quality of items purchased • Seek to continuously identify and correct all supplier related problems

Seek to Reduce Purchasing Costs

JIT purchasing treats suppliers and buyers as partners that share risks and benefits (Leavy 1994). Sharing benefits means that if the supplier manages to achieve some productivity improvement, which lowers net product costs, part of this improvement will accrue to the buyer in the form of price reductions and part will accrue to the supplier in the form of benefits.

Cost saving can also be obtained with "continuous replenishment" in JIT purchasing. *Continuous replenishment* is by the continuous updating of data shared between suppliers and customers such that replenishment, as managed by supplier, may occur daily or even more frequently. The customer pays a premium for regular daily deliveries instead of weekly deliveries; however, continuous replenishment reduces the need for warehouse space and inventories, thus saving inventory storage costs to the buyer.

Seek Timely Communications and Responsiveness

An extensive exchange of information and frequent communications is an essential part of JIT purchasing. Chapman and Carter (1990) pinpointed the importance of internal as well as external communications in the JIT environment. Handfield (1993) observes that the volume of shared information between buyer and supplier increases before JIT purchasing is implemented. Frequent communications contribute to generating trust and to assure the success of co-operative relationship between the buyer and the supplier.

Seek Ordering Flexibility

A buyer and supplier relationship can be seen as one more step in the value-added chain (i.e., like the supply chain, the value-chain shows linkages of organizational activities that can add value to the customer and profits to the firm), and small batch delivery are essential to eliminate incoming stocks, gain production flexibility, and extend the JIT philosophy up through the entire supply chain. Frequent and small delivery batches and reduced inventory can be considered essential elements of JIT purchasing.

Seek Long-Term Relationships with Suppliers

The buyer and supplier as partners approach is one of the cornerstones of the whole JIT philosophy, which has had enormous impact on international competition in many industries from automobiles to computers. In this perspective, the emphasis for the buyer is placed on the development of close cooperative relationships with a relatively small number of carefully selected suppliers, with long-term partnership in mind. This strategy encourages a high degree of interdependence between buyer and supplier and offers significant economies of cooperation, which can help to improve the profitability of both parties.

Seek Single-Source Suppliers

With near or single-sourcing, a company purchases materials from very few suppliers, sometimes only one. With single-sourcing, a company has more directly influence and control over the quality and delivery performance of a supplier. In JIT purchasing, the supplier and buyer form a partnership. Supplier agrees to meet the quality standards of the buyer in terms of parts, materials, service, and delivery, while the buyer offers a long-term purchasing agreement with the supplier that includes a stable order and delivery schedule. Also, less purchasing agents saves labor in keeping tract of the agents (Wantuck 1989; pp. 300–301).

Seek Certification in Quality of Items Purchased

Quality certification has become one the strategies to ensure supplier's quality and consistent competence. Quality certification provides some guarantees about the capacities of the supplier before initiating a relationship. The ISO 900 certification is the most popular quality standard. However, it only assures that the supplier has implemented certain quality management systems and does not assure product quality itself. As a result, many companies have designed their own quality certifications for suppliers.

Seek to Continuously Identify and Correct All Supplier Related Problems

More and more companies are moving toward closer relationships with key suppliers to support TQM and JIT systems. Because these systems dictate closer working relationships with suppliers, supplier evaluation systems will also undergo changes. Evaluation systems under TQM/JIT must be broader in scope and oriented toward proactive problem solving and continuous improvement on the supplier and buyer relationships.

JIT Supplier Selection

JIT purchasing focuses on developing long-term, cooperative partnerships between companies and their suppliers. As such, supplier selection process is extremely critical in reaping the benefits of JIT purchasing. Table 2 summarizes, from operations management (OM) literature, eight criteria that make an ideal supplier selection (see Holmstrom 1998; Lummus *et al.* 1998; Schorr 1998, pp. 29–43):

Table 2. JIT supplier selection criteria

JIT supplier selection criteria	Description
Delivery	Suppliers need to be able to make frequent deliveries and be flexible enough to cover unexpected at least minor demand surges that were expected and negotiated as a part of the long-term contract.
Quality and reliability	Suppliers need to deliver high quality products at the right time. Suppliers with high quality standards such as ISO 9000 and quality certifications are desirable.
Price	JIT purchasing is characterized by cost-based rather than price-based negotiation. Both buyer and supplier work out the cost involved in the production of a component and determine a fair margin for the suppliers. Supplier selection and evaluation in JIT purchasing should be based on quality and delivery performance as well as price, rather than solely a price decision.
Leadtime	Purchasing small batches in JIT purchasing implies frequent exchange of orders and receipts between buyer and supplier. Furthermore, the exact quantities are known only a short time before they are processed, so that speed is essential. These needs have often been covered with the implementation of technology like *electronic data interchange* (EDI). Information sharing also plays a critical role in reducing the leadtime.
Location	Geographical concentration of suppliers around the buyer is another characteristic JIT purchasing practice. Proximity has direct effects in the reduction of costs and leadtime because it reduces the need for transportation.
Technological capabilities	Suppliers need to have the technological infrastructure to deal with the dynamic market conditions.

Table 2. (Continued)

JIT supplier selection criteria	Description
Financial stability	JIT purchasing creates a long-term buyer and supplier relationship, so the financial well being of the supplier becomes an important issue in supply selection.
Supply chain management	As described in chapter 2, *bullwhip effect* is one of the primary barriers in supply chain management. Information sharing is the most viable approach in alleviating the bullwhip effect in supply chain. Suppliers need to be willing to share information with all parties involved in the supply chain.

JIT Purchasing and Performance

It has been well documented that the implementation of JIT purchasing systems can result in reduced inventory costs, shorter leadtimes, and improved productivity for purchasing organizations (Germain and Droge 1998; Vonderembse *et al.* 1995; Ansari and Modarress 1990).

Germain and Droge (1998) examined the differences in the organizational design and performance between JIT buying and non-JIT buying firms. The findings of their research indicated that JIT purchasing is appropriate across a wide spectrum of competitive environments because JIT purchasing firms are not different from non-JIT purchasing firms on absolute size, size related to suppliers, industry level concentration, industry growth, or variance in demand. It was found that the organizational design of JIT buying firms is significantly different from non-JIT buying firms. In JIT buying firms the level of performance control is very high. JIT buying firms are more likely to monitor profitability, costs, and productivity level, from both internal data, and that relative to the competitors. They also tend to be more in tune with supplier performance keeping a close eye on supplier price, delivery, and manufacturing capacity. In addition, JIT buying firms are more likely to be proactive in developing a purchasing mission and establishing a performance monitoring systems. Finally, the performance is higher for JIT buying firms versus non-JIT buying firms. The evidence from the study indicated that JIT buying firms reported superior performance in terms of both market share and financial performance measures. The findings also suggested that a JIT purchasing firm could still receive benefits even if their suppliers were non-JIT based.

However, it is less clear to what extent suppliers will benefit from engaging in JIT purchasing with buyers. For instance, researchers have found that JIT purchasing results in inventory costs being transferred from buyers to supplier (Romero 1991; Zipkin 1991). This transfer of cost may be due to poor implementation of JIT purchasing by suppliers or to poor information flow between buyers and suppliers. Dong *et al.* (2001) explored the issue whether JIT purchasing benefits suppliers as well as buyers. An important finding of the study was that the extent of JIT purchasing has a direct effect on reducing costs in the buyer organization but not in the supplier organization. However, significant relationships were found between supplier JIT manufacturing and supplier logistics costs. This result indicates that JIT purchasing could indirectly lead to lower logistics costs for suppliers, that is, if suppliers implemented JIT manufacturing in conjunction with a JIT purchasing program. The study also suggests that purchasing integrating between buyers and suppliers was positively associated with JIT purchasing for both buyers and suppliers. This finding is further supported in a study by Narasimhan and Das (2001). Using an empirical research, Narasimhan and Das (2001) examined the impact of purchasing integration on manufacturing performance. *Purchasing integration* refers to the integration and alignment of strategic purchasing practices and goals with that of the firm, while manufacturing performance has four dimensions including cost, quality, delivery, customization, and new product introduction time. The findings of the study suggested that purchasing integration has a beneficial effect on manufacturing performance and integration of purchasing practices with the strategic priorities of a firm is associated with manufacturing gains.

Purchasing Management Framework

Based on an empirical survey research of 463 of the world's largest companies, A. T. Kearney, Inc., a global management consulting firm, proposed an eight-dimensional model for excellence in purchasing management (Cavinato and Kauffman 1999). The eight dimensions in their model include purchasing and supply strategy, organization, sourcing, supplier management and development, day-to-day purchasing, performance management, information management, and human resource management. Their survey research indicated that excellence in purchasing management involves all eight dimensions. In doing so, the leader companies set up benchmarks for others to follow. Table 3 summaries the benchmark activities along the eight dimensions of excellence in purchasing management by purchasing leaders.

Table 3. Dimensions of excellence in purchasing management: *Benchmarking*

Dimensions of excellence in purchasing management	Benchmarking activities
Purchasing and supply strategy	Seek opportunities to shape corporate strategy by exploiting supply market opportunities.
	Establish policy and allocate resources based on opportunities and risks across their entire portfolio of purchases.
	Proactively define how purchasing activities will be organized, conducted, and managed to capitalize on opportunities.
Purchasing and supply organization	Employ a center-led approach to direct, set policy, and coordinate purchasing activities throughout the organization.
	Adapt the organizational structure for purchasing to fit the overall organization structure.
	Use teaming approaches to embed purchasing expertise into the company's key processes.
	Elevate purchasing organizationally to management board-level decision-making.
Sourcing	Develop sourcing strategies differentiated by expenditure category and based on market dynamics.
	Deeply involve end-users in the sourcing process for knowledge and buy-in.
	Apply a rigorous sourcing approach that examines internal needs against supply market options to find the lowest total cost solution.
	Challenge specifications and usage patterns to ensure that each expenditure is providing the best value for the company.
	Identify, select, and negotiate with strategically advantaged suppliers, not just the ones with the lowest price today.

(Continued)

Table 3. (Continued)

Dimensions of excellence in purchasing management	Benchmarking activities
Supply management	Manage supplier, relations to ensure continuous improvement and two-way learning.
	Integrate with suppliers to wring out excess cost and increase value from the relationship.
	Develop suppliers where needed capabilities do not exist in a current supply market.
Day-to-day purchasing	Automate day-to-day activities or delegate them to users or suppliers.
	Cut waste from routine transactions.
	Redeploys purchasing people onto high-value-added activities.
Performance management	Demonstrate senior management commitment and leadership to improve procurement process performance.
	Implement and operate formal improvement programs with suppliers.
	Carry out ongoing formal improvement processes internally.
Information management	Share information extensively, internally, and with suppliers.
	Employ powerful analytical tools that enable management of performance.
	Exploit the emerging generation of information technology.
Human resource management	Recruit and attract talented people for the purchasing organization from a variety of sources, both internal and external.
	Invest heavily in developing purchasing capabilities and skills both inside the "formal" purchasing organization and throughout the network.

Future of Purchasing Management

According to Fung (1999), there are more major trends that appear most likely to shape the future of purchasing management. These trends include among other things global sourcing, industry consolidation, technology advancements, and supply chain synchronization.

Globalization is revolutionizing the scope of purchasing management (Petersen *et al.* 2001). *Global sourcing* or international purchasing management used to be a defensive tactic to maintain competitive edge by reducing cost in response to foreign entrants who were penetrating domestic markets. Today, companies realize international purchasing management as a key driver of business performance and thus competitive advantage. Companies with global sourcing capabilities seek to reduce costs, improve quality and flexibility, and enter markets faster. Sunil and Sameer (1998) observed that political, social, economic and technological factors have all contributed to the purchasing management.

Industrial consolidation will lead to greater purchasing management efficiencies as newly formed companies leverage their size and influence to push suppliers for more services and lower costs (Teo 2001). Suppliers will respond through consolidations and strategic alliances of their own. Through consolidation and/or alliance, suppliers in the future will offer a greater breadth of products, cost-cutting technologies, value-added services, and global networking.

Technology advancements, especially information technologies (IT), are redefining all aspects of business' operations from sales and marketing to process control, production, and delivery. The major IT applications in purchasing management include electronic procurement (called "e-procurement"), *enterprise resource planning* (ERP), and *electronic data interchange* (EDI). *E-procurement* refers supply chain, business-to-business purchasing). ERP applications can fully integrate a supply chain's request, order, receipt, and inventory processes to facilitate direct B2B transactions. Transactions can be also made via EDI systems or through Internet that automate high frequency, high value communications between suppliers and buyers (Banerjee and Sriram 1995).

Why is Purchasing Management So Important in E-Commerce?

E-commerce purchasing or e-procurement (i.e., purchasing in e-commerce) has grown astronomically in recent years. One reason may be that it offers such a strong return on investment. Companies using online purchasing report cost savings of up to 80 percent, and a recent study by Deloitte Consulting shows more than 200 survey respondents will average a 300 percent return on investment over the first two to three years.

But the value of e-procurement is extending beyond cost savings. Len Prokopets, senior manager at Deloitte Consulting suggested that traditional purchasing departments will cease to exist and instead will focus on coordinating information exchanges and improving relationships with suppliers by managing them more efficiently (Roche 2001, pp. 57).

Benefits of e-commerce purchasing are also well documented in the academic arenas. For instance, Min and Galle (1999) suggested that benefits of e-commerce purchasing included cost savings resulting from reduced paper transactions, shorter order cycle time and the subsequent inventory reduction resulting from speedy transmission of purchase order related information, and enhanced opportunities for the supplier/buyer partnership through communication networks. A study done by (Radstaak and Ketelaar 1998) suggested that e-commerce purchasing could enhance supply chain efficiency by providing real-time information about product availability, inventory level, shipment status, and product requirements. Karoway (1997) also suggests that e-commerce purchasing has a great potential to facilitate collaborative planning among supply chain partners by sharing information on demand forecasts and production schedules that dictates supply chain activities. More recently, Kehoe and Boughton (2001) argued that the Internet technologies made it possible for demand data as well as supply capacity data to be visible to all companies within a manufacturing supply chain. It is perceived that manufacturing supply chains will change from an order-driven-lot-sizing approach to one more akin to a capacity-availability-booking approach supported by appropriate search engines. Furthermore, using Internet-based information transfer, supply networks will replace the traditional linear movement of information within supply chains, thereby facilitating a more interactive approach to supply chain partnering.

Min and Galle (1999) examined factors that influenced decisions of purchasing professionals to utilize the e-commerce purchasing by addressing issues such as security and legality. The findings of the study where that:

1. In general, the purchasing firms have not valued the suppliers' e-commerce purchasing infrastructure as a critical attribute for supplier selection. However, larger firms with greater annual purchasing volume are more inclined to mandate the use of e-commerce infrastructure as an important part of an on-going business relationship with their suppliers than their smaller counterparts.

2. Although e-commerce purchasing success depends on the degree of acceptance and the extent of participation among suppliers due to the interdependent nature of e-commerce purchasing, only the buying firms with a relatively large number of purchasing employees indicated that they are willing to help suppliers to establish e-commerce purchasing networks.

3. Despite the fact that security and legality issues remain the most serious obstacles for utilizing e-commerce purchasing, purchasing professionals still think that the benefits of e-commerce purchasing out-weight the security risk and potential legal problem.

Turban (2000, pp. 210) and Balakrishnan *et al.* (1999) have claimed that purchasing professionals must focus on more strategic purchasing management in the e-commerce era to achieve the goals of e-commerce purchasing, including: reducing purchasing cycle time and cost, enhancing budgetary control, eliminating administrative errors, increasing buyer's productivity, lowering prices through product standardization and consolidation of buys, improving information management (e.g., supplier's information and pricing information), and improving the payment process.

E-Commerce Purchasing

As described in the last section, e-commerce purchasing is becoming one of the hottest topics in e-commerce because of its cost reduction capabilities, and other tangible and intangible benefits in operations. However, e-commerce purchasing is not new. According to Banerjee and Sriram (1995), in the 1980s and early 1990s, many companies used EDI to handle purchasing-related activities. As mentioned in previous chapters, the nature and extent of EDI implementation varies across organizations. In its simplest form, EDI implementation involves conversion of standard business documents into a readable format so that computers of the trading partners can communicate directly with one another. The purpose of such implementation is to increase the speed and accuracy of document transfer between organizations. A study of 15 corporations (Emmelhainz 1988) showed that EDI does improve the productivity of purchasing but does not significantly change the purchasing process (i.e., the manner in which purchasing decisions are made and how the procedures are performed). Another study involving purchasing executives explored the extent of computerization (not necessarily EDI) in purchasing and concluded that use of computers is going to increase in purchasing but a major impediment to the implementation of such systems is their cost (LaLonde and Emmelhainz 1985). Since the potential impact of EDI adoption on the purchasing function is high, it is important to examine its nature.

Banerjee and Sriram (1995) investigated the impact of a set of EDI adoption factors on purchasing policies and procedures. The results of the study indicate that the fewer the number of years after EDI adoption, the more important were computer skills for buyers and the greater the need for buyer retraining. Conversely, these factors become less important the longer the time after EDI adoption. The higher the percentage of purchasing transactions using EDI, the greater the perception of purchasing inflexibility. Since EDI requires data transmission in a standard format, increased use of such standardized format may cause an inflexible environment. (i.e., how can you make something standard without formalizing the standardizing the process, thereby creating inflexibility in its continued use). Interestingly, encouraging vendors to use EDI creates significant changes in purchasing procedures (e.g., less monitoring of vendors, automatic reordering, simplified order approval processes) and also reduces operating inefficiencies, possibly because companies, which encourage their vendors to use EDI best, understand how to capitalize on its benefits.

E-commerce purchasing is a step ahead of purchasing using EDI in that there is no need for traditional client/server technology and thus avoiding the private networks as required by EDI. Using the Internet to replace private networks can have substantial cost savings resulting from simplified supply chain communications. ERP vendors such as SAP, Oracle, PeopleSoft, and among others, have developed modules of e-commerce purchasing in their ERP software packages. As such, ERP pertains to the overall management system of a corporation's undertaking of market distribution, product design, customer satisfaction, production, logistics, suppliers, inventory, and procurement (Huang *et al.* 2001).

Lin and Hsieh (2000) claimed that companies are using e-commerce purchasing to reduce costs while improving access to suppliers and they are reaping substantial benefits of e-commerce purchasing as following:

1. The most significant savings are from the reduction in processing of paper requisitions, purchase orders and invoices.
2. It could shorten the delivery time by cutting time waiting for documents in the mail.
3. It reduces administrative hours, freeing them up to do other work.

4. It helps to consolidate purchasing practices that will lead to deeper discounts and better service form suppliers.
5. It eliminates time zone obstacles, as the e-commerce purchasing can be used any time of the day.
6. It accelerates the flow of important information between the buyer and supplier.
7. It reduces inventory levels, hence costs associated with inventory.
8. It improves buyer/supplier relationships, as mutual cooperation is required.
9. It maximizes labor by empowering the employees who want the product to make the transactions that are right for their work.

In conclusion, more and more companies are implementing e-commerce purchasing and reaping benefits in both cost saving and service enhancement.

E-Commerce Purchasing Life Cycle

Building and sustaining customer relationships is the key to the success in e-commerce purchasing. The "purchasing life cycle" serves as a corner stone to establish strong and long-term customer relationships. Purchasing life cycle involves seven stages of purchasing activities that include information gathering, supplier contact, background review, negotiation, fulfillment, consumption/maintenance/disposal, and renewal. Table 4 shows purchasing life cycle adapted from Archer and Yuan (2000). Buyers can follow the seven phases of purchasing life cycle to conduct purchasing activities for their organizations, while suppliers can use these phases to create opportunities for marketing, sales, and supply chain management.

A Model for E-Purchasing

Based on a variety of disciplines such as management, information systems, sociology, psychology, and marketing, Gattiker *et al.* (2000) proposed a conceptual framework to investigate and understand the mechanisms of e-commerce purchasing behavior. Figure 1 shows the proposed model, which is comprised of variables such as predictors, mediator, moderators, and criterion.

The model indicates that predictors or independent variables (i.e., information processing and purchasing context) influence the criterion or dependent variable (i.e., *Web beliefs and behavior*) through mediator variables (i.e., *privacy and security*). Moderators (i.e., socio-demographic characteristics, cultural factors, attitudes towards information technology, and economic factors) help explain when predictors (i.e., information processing and purchasing context) influence or fail to influence the criterion (i.e., Web beliefs and behavior). Table 5 summarizes and explains relationship among variables.

Table 4. Purchasing life cycle

Phase	Description
Information gathering	If the potential customer does not already have an established relationship with sales/marketing functions of suppliers of needed *products and services* (P/S), it is necessary to search for suppliers who can satisfy the requirements
Supplier contact	When one or more suitable suppliers have been identified, *request for quotes* (RFQ), *request for proposals* (RFP), *request for information* (RFI) or *request for bids* (RFB) maybe advertised, or direct contact may be made with suppliers.
Background review	References for product/service quality are consulted, and any requirements for follow-up services including installation, maintenance, and warranty are investigated. Sample of the P/S being considered may be examined, or trials undertaken.
Negotiation	Negotiations are undertaken, and price, availability, and customization possibilities are established. Delivery schedules are negotiated, and a contract to acquire the P/S is completed.
Fulfillment	Supplier preparation, shipment, delivery, and payment for the P/S are completed, based on contract terms. Installation and training may also be included.
Consumption, maintenance and disposal	During this phase the company evaluates the performance of the P/S based on contract terms. Installation and training may also be included
Renewal	When the P/S has been consumed and/or disposed of, the contract expires, or the product or service is to be re-ordered, company experience with the P/S is reviewed.

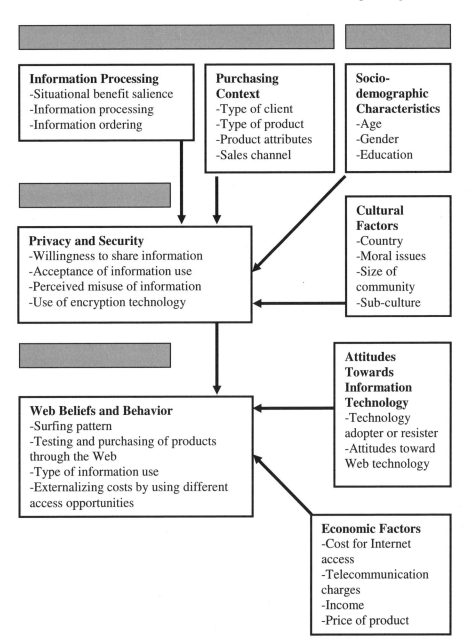

Figure 1. A model for e-commerce purchasing behavior

Table 5. Variables of the model for e-commerce purchasing behavior

Variables	Description
Predictors Information processing	Web beliefs and behavior are influenced by situational benefit salience, such that more salient benefits will be used as more important information than others. They are also influenced by how people order information and situational benefit salience: factors that are more salient based on subsequent use of the product will provide more important information than others.
Purchasing context	Purchasing context will have an impact on Web beliefs and behavior, more specifically, corporate clients will differ form consumers in that: • An important Web application is to obtain information in contrast to private users who will look for entertainment and freeware. • Important criteria used when shopping on the Web is documented quality, while consumers will be more influenced by warranty. • Great importance will put on delivery conditions. • Favorable terms, so that in the case of delivery, which fails to meet specifications, product or parts can be replaced without difficulty and quickly, will be important. Type of products will have an impact on Web beliefs and behavior. Specifically, industrial products will differ from consumer products, in that, for industrial products: • Pre-sale support on the Internet will often be a required service. • After-sales service at the industrial customer's site will be important criterion for evaluating products. • Leadtime and terms of replacement will be used to evaluate possible suppliers. Web beliefs and behavior are influenced by product attributes with different intensities. Specifically, Web shoppers will differ from their conventional store shoppers in that: • Price and brand will be more important product attributes used to assess a product. • Recommendations from others will matter more. • Warranty will be taken into more careful consideration. Web beliefs and behavior are influenced by type of buyers. More specifically, corporate purchasing agents will differ from private shoppers towards using the Web in that they: • Will be more reluctant to use the Web for purchasing. • Will prefer person-to-person sales channels. • Are more concerned about security issues when using the Web. • Spend few hours for purchasing using Web compared to others.

Table 5. (Continued)

Variables	Description
Moderators Socio-demographic characteristic	Gender, age, and education have impact on Web beliefs and behavior.
Cultural factors	Cultural variables and community size have impact on Web beliefs and behavior.
Economic factors	Economic factors will play a significant role for Web users access to the Internet. Specifically, Web users accessing the Internet from home will differ from Web users accessing the Internet from work in: • The cost of Internet access will influence how much time is being spent on the Internet from home. • Policies permitting Internet use for private purposes from work will encourage surfing and searching on the Internet for information for private matters. • A person's income is likely to influence expenditures incurred for private Internet use from home and an Internet café.
Attitudes towards information technology	Web beliefs and behavior are influenced by information technology attitudes. More specifically, a direct relation exists between attitudes and experience in testing and/or purchasing a product or service on-line.
Mediator	Web beliefs and behavior are influenced by privacy and security matters. The impact of information processing, attitudes towards information technology, and purchasing context on Web behaviors can be explained by the perception of privacy and security threats.
Criterion	Internet access costs influence Web beliefs and behavior. More specifically, users whose Web access is being metered will differ from others in trying to externalize costs by using work facilities as much as possible for non-work-related Web use. Internet access costs influence Web beliefs and behavior. Specifically, Web users access costs are variable, resulting in: • Spend less time on the Web. • Have less positive Internet/Web attitudes towards using the Web for shopping. • Visit their favorite sites less frequently and during off-peak hours. • Be less likely to have tested and purchased a product via the Web, or have done so less often.

This study tackled several issues in the e-commerce purchasing. First, it explores relationships between cross-national differences, demographics, perceived treats and Web use. Second, it examines the assessment of online information for different categories of product. Third, the study investigates the influence of people's technology resistance on attitudes toward and behaviors regarding the e-commerce purchasing and how these factors affect people's attempt to externalize costs. Finally, the study compares e-commerce purchasing in the context of corporate purchasing with individual shopping.

E-Commerce Purchasing Strategies

The potential for dramatic cost savings and productivity improvements suggests that both buying and selling firms would benefit from increased use of the Internet for corporate-related purchasing activities. Thus, suppliers with online purchasing capabilities, as well as those considering an implementation of such a system, need to devise ways to increase the usage of online purchasing among their industrial customers (Hill 1999; Weber 1999). Developing effective strategies for increasing e-commerce purchasing requires an understanding of the factors that contribute to buyers' adoption of the Internet for e-commerce purchasing. Deeter-Schmelz *et al.* (2001) developed and empirically tested a research framework of the impact of supplier support on buyer's adoption of the Internet. Figure 2 shows the model of the relationship between supplier support and buyers' adoption of Internet. Supplier support and communication convenience are independent variables, while buyer adoption behavior and Internet purchase intent are two dependent variables. Supplier support underscores the degree to which purchasing professionals perceive that their suppliers are providing encouragement, guidance, and incentives for purchasing via the Internet. Communication convenience refers to the extent to which purchasing professionals believe that the Internet is a more convenient information source when compared to salespeople and other supplier representatives. Communication convenience can be viewed as an independent variable for both dependent variables and as a dependent variable for supplier support. Buyer adoption behavior depicts the degree to which the purchasing professional decides to adopt this new method of purchasing earlier than other buyers, while Internet purchase intent represents the extent to which organizational buyers are likely to use the Internet for purchasing activities.

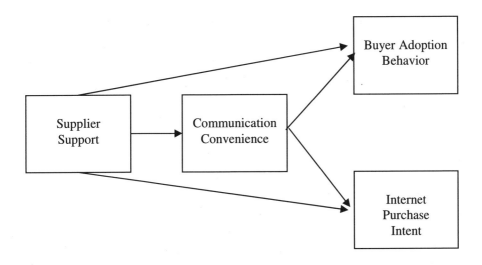

Figure 2. A model of supplier's impact on buyers' adoption and purchase intent

This model indicates that there is a direct positive impact of supplier support on both of the dependent variables, buyer adoption behavior and Internet purchase, as well as variable communication convenience. Also, the variable communication convenience influences positively on both dependent variables, buyer adoption behavior and Internet purchase.

The results of this study suggest that suppliers play a critical role in organizational buyers' adoption of and intent to use the Internet of e-commerce purchasing. The findings of the study also indicate that buyers who perceive the Internet to be a more convenient source of information and communication are more likely to adopt and intend to purchase on the Internet. Finally, the results of the study underpinned the importance of incentives provided by the suppliers in encouraging e-commerce buyers purchasing among the industrial buyers.

Improving E-Commerce Purchasing Process

As e-commerce purchasing is becoming an important part of the business operations, its processes need to be enhanced to obtain and maintain competitive advantages. One of the major issues in e-commerce purchasing is price negotiation. Price negotiation is a time-consuming process, especially for high volume purchasing situations. One way to improve this process is to use the B2B online auctions model (Emiliani 2000). Business-to-business online auctions are downward pricing, or reverse auctions performed in real time over the Internet or through a private network (i.e., intranet or extranet). It would work by an intermediary accepting bids on behalf of a corporate purchaser for goods or services provided by current or new suppliers using proprietary software. Buyer and supplier benefits of using B2B online auctions model are listed in table 6 (Emiliani 2000).

Summary

This chapter introduces the concept of purchasing management and describes JIT purchasing principles and other trends in purchasing management. Importance and uniqueness of purchasing management in an e-commerce setting are explained in this chapter. Drawing upon business procurement research literature, this chapter also presents strategies for an e-commerce purchasing model, e-commerce purchasing management, and e-commerce purchasing process improvement.

Table 6. Benefits of using B2B online auctions for both buyer and supplier

Benefits to Buyers	Benefits to Suppliers
1. Only potential suppliers will bid on consolidated volumes of products that have similar characteristics, which should help improve cost, delivery, and quality performance - especially if the supplier practices JIT or lean production.	1. Leveling the field removes some of the advantage enjoyed by incumbent suppliers. Suppliers that bid have a fair opportunity to win the work.
2. The involvement of an intermediary in the auction process brings valuable experience and facilitates adherence to project milestones.	2. Qualified suppliers may be invited to participate in future online auctions sponsored by their current customer and as such suppliers can grow sales or diversify their customer base, which can reduce expenses related to sales/marketing.

Table 6. (Continued)

Benefits to Buyers	Benefits to Suppliers
3. Only potential suppliers will bid on consolidated volumes of products that have similar characteristics, which should help improve cost, delivery, and quality performance — especially if the supplier practices JIT or lean production.	3. Leveling the field removes some of the advantage enjoyed by incumbent suppliers. Suppliers that bid have a fair opportunity to win the work.
4. The involvement of an intermediary in the auction process brings valuable experience and facilitates adherence to project milestones.	4. Qualified suppliers may be invited to participate in future online auctions sponsored by their current customer and as such suppliers can grow sales or diversify their customer base, which can reduce expenses related to sales/marketing.
5. The process requires the buyer to evaluate other capable suppliers that they might not otherwise consider under regular business conditions.	5. The suppliers that participate in online auctions are able to see the market price and validate their competitiveness.
6. The process compresses price negotiations from months to hours, thus saving considerable time and effort and reducing the likelihood of significant changes in business conditions that might affect price.	6. Winning suppliers are awarded work that is organized in part or process families.
7. The process leads to a market price. This information is unknown to businesses that are not skilled in cost analysis.	7. Work that is obtained in part or process families enables the supplier to focus on its core competencies.
8. The buyer receives the entire savings upfront, rather than incremental year-over-year reductions.	8. The online auction process usually results in a multi-year long-term agreement.

◆ Review Terms

Attitudes towards information technology
Background review
Business-to-business (B2B) online auctions
Buyer adoption behavior
Communication convenience
Consumption/maintenance/disposal
Continuous replenishment
Cultural factors
Day-to-day purchasing
E-commerce purchasing
E-procurement
Economic factors
Electronic data interchange (EDI)
Fulfillment
Global sourcing
Human resource management
Information gathering
Information management
Information processing
Internet purchase intent
JIT purchasing
Negotiation
Organization
Performance management
Privacy and security
Products and services (P/S)
Purchasing and supply strategy
Purchasing context
Purchasing life cycle
Purchasing management
Renewal
Request for bids (RFB)
Request for information (RFI)
Request for proposals (RFP)
Request for quotes (RFQ)
Socio-demographic characteristics
Sourcing
Supplier contact
Supplier management and development
Supplier selection
Supplier support
Supply chain
Total quality management (TQM)
Value-added chain
Web beliefs and behavior

◆ Discussion Questions

1. How can an organization gain a competitive edge with purchasing management?
2. What is JIT purchasing? Explain JIT purchasing principles.
3. Discuss the new trends of purchasing management.
4. Why is the buyer and supplier relationship so important in JIT purchasing.
5. What are some of the major JIT supplier selection criteria?
6. How do we ensure supply quality in purchasing?
7. What are some of the benefits of JIT purchasing?
8. What is e-commerce purchasing?
9. How do we develop effective strategies for increasing e-commerce purchasing?
10. How can the B2B auction model enhances e-commerce purchasing?

♦ **Questions**

1. Why are the firms that are implementing the JIT purchasing process outperforming non-JIT firms?
2. What are JIT supplier selection criteria? How should they be used?
3. What are the factors that influence decisions of purchasing professionals to utilize the e-commerce purchasing?
4. What is the purchasing life cycle? Why it is important in e-commerce purchasing management?
5. Describe the e-commerce purchasing behavior model.

References

Ansari, A. and Modarress, B., "JIT Purchasing as a Quality and Productivity Center," *International Journal of Production Research*, Vol. 26, No. 1, 1990, pp. 19–26.

Archer, N. and Yuan, Y., "Managing Business-to-business Relationships Throughout the E-commerce Procurement Life Cycle," *Internet Research*, Vol. 10, No. 5, 2000, pp. 385–395.

Banerjee, S. and Sriram, V., "The Impact of Electronic Data Interchange on Purchasing: An Empirical Investigation," *International Journal of Operations & Production Management*, Vol. 15, No. 3, 1995, pp. 29–38.

Beeter-Schmelz, D. R., Bizzari, A. and Graham, R., "Business-to-Business Online Purchasing: Suppliers' Impact on Buyers' Adoption and Usage Intent," *Journal of Supply Chain Management*, Vol. 6, 2001, pp. 4–10.

Cavinato, J. L. and Kauffman, R. G., The Purchasing Handbook: A Guide for the Purchasing and Supply Professional, New York, NY: McGraw-Hill, 1999.

Chapman, S. N. and Carter, P. L., "Supplier/customer Inventory Relationships Under Just-in-time," *Decision Sciences*, Vol. 21, No. 1, 1990, pp. 35–51.

Dong, Y., Carter, C. R. and Dresner, M. E., "JIT Purchasing and Performance: An Exploratory Analysis of Buyer and Supplier Perspectives," *Journal of Operations Management*, Vol. 19, No. 5, 2001, pp. 471–483.

Emiliani, M. L., "Business-to-business Online Auctions: Key Issues for Purchasing Process Improvement," *Supply Chain Management*, Vol. 5, No. 4, 2000, pp. 176–186.

Emmelhainz, M. A., "Strategic Issues of EDI Implementation", *Journal of Business Logistics*, Vol. 9, No. 2, 1988, 55–70.

Emmelhainz, M. A., "Electronic Data Interchange: Does It Change the Purchasing Process?" *Journal of Purchasing and Materials Management*, Vol. 15, 1987, pp. 2–8.

Fung, P., "Managing Purchasing in A Supply Chain Context - Evolution and Resolution," *Logistics Information Management*, Vol. 12, No. 5, 1999, pp. 362–367.

Gattiker, U. E., Perlusz, S. and Bohmann, K., "Using the Internet for B2B Activities: A Review and Future Directions for Research," *Internet Research*, Vol.10, No. 2, 2000, pp. 126–140.

Germain, R. and Droge, C., "The Context, Organizational Design, and Performance of JIT Buying Versus Non-JIT Buying Firms," *International Journal of Purchasing and Materials Management*, 1998, Vol. 24, No. 2, pp. 12–18.

Handfield, R. B., "A Resource Dependence Perspective of Just-in-time Purchasing", *Journal of Operations Management*, Vol.11, No.3, 1993, pp. 289–311.

Hill, S., "B-to-B E-commerce: If You Build It, Will They Come?" *Apparel Industry Magazine*, Vol. 60, No. 8, 1999, pp. 49–55.

Holmstrom, J., "Implementing Vendor-Managed Inventory the Efficient Way: A Case Study of Partnership in the Supply Chain," *Production and Inventory Management Journal*, Vol. 39, 1998, pp. 1–5.

Huang, S., Kwan, I.S.Y. and Hung, Y., "Planning Enterprise Resources by Use of A Reengineering Approach to Build a Global Logistics Management System," *Industrial Management & Data Systems*, Vol. 101, No. 9, 2001, pp. 483–491

Karoway, C., "Superior Supply Chains Pack Plenty of Byte," *Purchasing Today*, Vol. 8, No.11, 1997, pp. 32–35.

Kehoe, D. F. and Boughton, N. J., "New Paradigms in Planning and Control Across Manufacturing Supply chains — The Utilization of Internet Technologies," *International Journal of Operations & Production Management*, Vol. 21, Nos. 5&6, 2001, pp. 582–593.

Lalonde, B. J. and Emmelhainz, M. A., "Electronic Purchase Order Interchange," *Journal of Purchasing and Materials Management*, Vol. 23, 1985, pp. 2–9.

Landry, S., Duguay, C. R., Chausse, S. and Themens, J., "Integrating MRP, Kanban and Bar-coding Systems to Achieve JIT Procurement," *Production and Inventory Management* Journal, 1997, Vol. 38, No.1, pp. 8–13.

Leavy, B., "Two Strategic Perspectives on the Buyer-supplier Relationship," *Production and Inventory Management Journal*, Vol. 35, No. 2, 1994, pp. 47–52.

Lin, B. and Hsieh, C., "Online Procurement: Implementation and Managerial Implications," *Human Systems Management*, Vol. 19, 2000, pp. 105–110.

Lummus, R. R., Vokurka, R. J. and Alber, K. L. "Strategic Supply Chain Planning," *Production and Inventory Management Journal*, Vol. 39, 1998, pp. 49–58.

Mehra, S. and Inman, R. A., "Determining the Critical Elements of Just-in-time Implementation," *Decision Sciences*, Vol. 23, No. 1, 1992, pp. 160–174.

Min, H. and Galle, W. P., "Electronic Commerce Usage in Business-to-Business Purchasing," *International Journal of Operations and Production Management*, Vol. 19, No. 9, 1999, pp. 909–921.

Moe, W. W. and Fader, P. S., "Uncovering Patterns in Cybershopping," *California Management Review*, Vol. 43, No. 4, 2001, pp. 106–117.

Narasimhan, R. and Das, A., "The Impact of Purchasing Integration and Practices on Manufacturing Performance," *Journal of Operations Management*, Vol. 19, No. 5, 2001, pp. 593–609.

Petersen, K. J., Frayer, D. J. and Scannell, T. V., "An Empirical Investigation of Global Sourcing Strategy Effectiveness," *Journal of Supply Chain Management*, Vol. 36, No. 2, pp. 29–38. 2001.

Radstaak, G. and Ketelaar, M. H., *Worldwide Logistics: The Future of Supply chain Services*, Holland International Distribution Council, Hague, The Netherlands, 1998.

Richeson, L., Lackey, C. W. and Starner, J. W., "The Effect of Communication on The Linkage Between Manufacturing," *International Journal of Purchasing and Materials Management*, Vol. 31, No. 1, 1995, pp. 21–30.

Roche, J., "Are You Ready for E-procurement?" *Strategic Finance*, 2001, Vol. 83, No. 1, pp. 56–59.

Romero, B. P., "The Other Side of JIT in Supply Management," *Production and Inventory Management Journal*, Vol. 32, No. 4, 1991, pp. 1–2.

Schniederjans, M. J. and Olson, J. R., *Advanced Topics in Just-In-Time Management*, Westport, CT: Quorum Books, 1999.

Schniederjans, M. J., *Topics in Just-In-Time Management*, Boston: Allyn & Bacon, 1993.

Schonberger, R. J., Japanese Manufacturing Techniques: Nine Hidden Lessons in Simplicity, New York: The Free Press, 1982.

Schorr, J. E. *Purchasing in the 21st Century*, New York: John Wiley & Sons, 1998.

Sunil, B. and Sameer, P., "International Purchasing, Inventory Management and Logistics Research: An Assessment and Agenda," *International Journal of Operations and Production Management*, Vol. 18, No. 1, 1998, pp. 6–38.

Teo, C. P., Ou, J. and Goh, M., "Impact on Inventory Costs with Consolidation of Distribution Centers," *IIE Transactions*, Vol. 23, No. 2, 2001, pp. 99–110.

Turban, E., Lee, J., King, D. and Chung, H.M., *Electronic Commerce: A Managerial Perspective*, Upper Saddleback, NJ: Prentice Hall, 2000.

Vonderembse, M., Tracey, M., Tan, C. L and Bardi, E. J, "Current Purchasing Practices and JIT: Some of the Effects on Inbound Logistics," *International Journal of Physical Distribution & Logistics Management*, Vol. 25, No.3, 1995, pp. 33–48.

Wantuck, K. A., *Just In Time For America, Milwaukee*, WI: The Forum, Ltd., 1989.

Zipkin, P., "Does Manufacturing Need a JIT Revolution?" *Harvard Business Review*, Vol. 69, No. 1, 1991, pp. 40–50.

Chapter 6 E-COMMERCE AND FORECASTING AND SCHEDULING MANAGEMENT

Learning Objectives

After completing this chapter, you should be able to:

Describe and define "forecasting management."

Describe and define "scheduling management."

Explain qualitative and quantitative forecasting methods.

Explain the difference between planning, scheduling, and sequencing.

Describe the objectives in operations scheduling.

List and explain scheduling techniques.

Explain the relationships between Just-in-time (JIT) and forecasting and between JIT and scheduling.

Explain why forecasting and scheduling management is so important in e-commerce era.

Explain why it is important to integrate scheduling into the ERP system and why it is crucial to integrate forecasting into the e-commerce operations.

Describe how to use intelligent agent to enhance scheduling.

Overview of This Chapter

This chapter presents the topics of forecasting and scheduling management in the context of e-commerce. A discussion of the relationships between JIT and forecasting and scheduling management are also presented. The chapter then relates forecasting and scheduling management to e-commerce. The chapter also examines integration issues of forecasting and scheduling management. Finally, the chapter concludes with intelligent agent applications in scheduling.

What is Forecasting and Scheduling Management?

Forecasting Management

Forecasting is a process of predicting what will occur in the future. Forecasts are vital to every business organization and for every significant management decision (Chase *et al.* 2001, pp. 434). However, forecasting is uncertain in natural. In today's dynamic e-commerce business environment customer demands are constantly changing due to the fact that they have more choices and more information on which to base choices. This makes the process of forecasting and the need for improved forecasting accuracy increasingly important. One of the solutions to increase the accuracy of forecasting is to choose the right forecasting method for the right forecasting situation. In general, there are two types of forecasting methods: quantitative forecasting methods and qualitative forecasting methods. Quantitative forecasting methods are based on mathematical formulas, while qualitative forecasting methods are based on judgement, opinion, experience, and other subjective measures. Commonly used quantitative forecasting methods include time series analysis, regression analysis, and simulation. Popular qualitative forecasting methods include Delphi method and market research. [See Reid and Sanders (2002, pp. 205–231) and Gaither and Frazier (2002, pp. 62–97) for a review of these and other basic forecasting methodologies.]

Time series methods are statistical forecasting techniques that use historical data to predict the future. There are many time series methods such as simply moving average, weighted moving average, exponential smoothing, regression analysis, and Box Jenkins technique, just to name a few. *Regression forecast methods* attempt to develop a mathematical relationship between demand and the factors that cause it to behave the way it does. In other words, regression forecast methods try to understand the system underlying and surrounding the time being forecast (Chase *et al..* 2001, pp. 436). *Simulation forecast methods* are used in decision-making (e.g., forecasting) under risks or probabilities. Simulation forecast methods allow the forecaster to make assumptions about the condition of the forecast. *Market research* is a systematic forecast approach using field surveys and/or other research methodologies to determine what products or services customers want and will purchase, and to identify new markets and sources of customers. The *Delphi method* involves obtaining insightful judgment and opinions from a panel of experts using a series of questionnaires to develop a consensus in forecasting.

When to Use What?

To be a useful decision-making tool, forecasting should be fully integrated within the planning context of which it is a part (Wright *et al.* 1986). Which forecasting methods and procedures are followed should depend on the particular planning task. For example, different approaches may be appropriate for different stages of the product life cycle. At the pre-product development stage, the Delphi method, historical analogies and other long-range forecasting techniques may be the most appropriate means of analyzing technological trends (Sanders and Manrodt 1994). At the rapid growth stage, quantitative methods for short-term forecasting (i.e., averaging or exponential smoothing averages) may be appropriate, while the market saturation stage demands the use of regression models to estimate trends and seasonality. When sales forecasts are inputs to decisions about inventory, the forecasting horizon is often short-term and historical in-house data are used. Simple quantitative time series methods may be implemented. In contrast, when a sales forecast is used as input to a capital investment decision in plant or machinery, the forecasting horizon is longer-term and the forecast may be qualitative rather than just quantitative. Managers often utilize a combination of qualitative and quantitative methods in such situations. Explanatory rather than time-series methods may be more suitable. Which methods can be used will depend on the environmental aspects of a decision situation. For example, in some international markets, data availability and local technical expertise may limit forecasting approaches. The forecasting process often involves politics (Mahmoud *et al.* 1992). For instance, sometimes the roles of information provider (i.e., forecaster) and decision maker (i.e., forecast user) are dubious at best. A manager serves an information receiver, an information interpreter, and most critically a measurer of results (Estrin 1990). In such situations, the anticipation of subsequent interpretive tasks would probably affect prior data collection. For example, Fildes and Hastings (1994) reported that product managers biased sales forecasts to benefit their products, budgets, and status.

A survey study by Rice (1997) revealed that despite advances in computer technology, qualitative forecast methods continued to be the preferred methods of forecasters and managers in the multi-national companies. Table 1 shows the results of the forecast methods used by the multi-national firms (worldwide) included in the survey.

Table 1. Popularity of forecast methods worldwide

Forecasting method	Percent use by US firms	Percent use by Third World firms
Executives' assessments	29%	25%
Delphi	24%	9%
Market surveys	17%	12%
Exponential smoothing	16%	1%
Regression	14%	1%
Classical decomposition	9%	2%
Naïve Method	7%	2%
Box-Jenkins	7%	0%

It is interesting but not surprising that the survey results suggest that the most popular and successfully used forecast methods around the world are qualitative forecast methods. The finding of the study is in line with the argument made by Dalrymple (1987), that the continued reliance on subjective techniques suggested that many managers have yet to be convinced that other methods were better.

In summary, forecasting is not merely the result of a technical forecasting process. It is the result of a complex behavioral process influenced by values, goals, and roles of many members of the organization.

Scheduling Management

Scheduling is defined as a plan with reference to the sequence of and time allocated for each item or operation necessary to complete the item (Vollmann *et al.* 1992). In other words, scheduling specifies when labor, equipment, and facilities are needed to produce a product or provide a service. Operations scheduling, a part of the planning and control of production or services, lies at the very heart of organizational performance. The need for efficient scheduling has greatly increased in recent decades thanks to market demands for product quality, flexibility, and order flow times. Objectives in operations scheduling generally include the following: meeting customer due date, minimizing job lateness, minimizing response time, minimizing completion time, minimizing time in the system, minimizing overtime, maximizing machine or labor utilization, minimizing idle time, and minimizing work-in-process (WIP) inventory.

A characteristic that distinguishes one scheduling system from another is "loading" (Chase *et al.* 2001). *Loading* refers to a process of assigning work to limited resources and it can be both "infinite loading" and "finite loading." While *infinite loading* occurs when work is assigned to a work center simply based on what is needed over time, where as a *finite loading* method schedules in detail each resource using the setup and run time required for each order. Scheduling systems can also be differentiated based on different scheduling approaches. *Forward scheduling* refers to the situation in which the system takes an order and then schedules each operation that must be completed forward in time. *Backward scheduling* starts from some data in the future and schedules the required operations backwards. *Level scheduling* refers to maintaining leveled schedules with a specific time interval (Morton and Pentico 1993). Level scheduling handles changes in demand uncertainty level loading by making regular, frequent updates to the schedules. Different scheduling approaches should be applied in different production processes. Table 2 shows types of production processes and scheduling methods.

Table 2. Production processes and scheduling methods

Type of process	Products	Characteristics	Scheduling methods
Continuous	Chemicals, pharmaceuticals, soft drinks, wire and cables, and etc.	Complete automation and facilities dedicated to one product	Finite loading and forward scheduling
Assembly line	Automobiles, computers, fixtures, home electronics, and etc.	Automated equipment and partial automated assembly line	Finite loading and level scheduling, and JIT
Batch production	Industrial parts, high-end consumer goods, and etc.	Group technology cells	Infinite loading, level scheduling, and JIT
Job shop	Custom equipment, specialized instruments, and etc.	Unit production, customized.	Infinite loading, forward scheduling, and MRP

Planning, Scheduling and Sequencing

There is a distinction between planning, scheduling and sequencing. In production planning, for example material requirements planning (MRP), the required level of production in a specified time horizon is determined (Thomas and McClain 1993). Typically, the output of planning consists of material requirements in time. These requirements are then passed to the lower control levels (i.e., scheduling). So, the output of planning (i.e., material requirements in time) is the input of scheduling. Production scheduling focuses on the allocation of limited resources to fulfill material requirements within individual production units. If the schedule is made at the resource level, the production schedule contains a specific "sequence" for that production. Sequencing prioritizes jobs that have been assigned to a resource. Figure 1 depicts the direction of control in the relationship between planning, scheduling and sequencing. The lettered items in Figure 1 are products. According to theory, planning controls the inventory points in the goods flow and gives material requirements to scheduling. The scheduling function then releases jobs to the shop floor. Depending on the need for the leveling of schedules, sequencing decisions are made on the shop floor (Stoop and Wiers 1996).

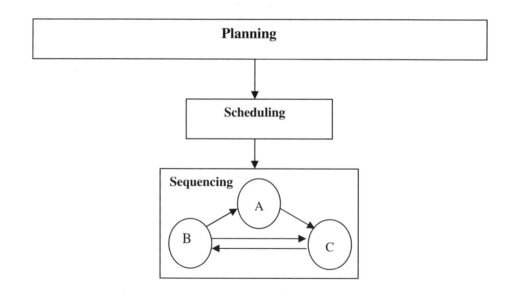

Figure 1. Planning, scheduling, and sequencing

The research in production scheduling has led to many techniques. Some of these techniques are commercially available in software packages. Morton and Pentico (1993) and others (Reid and Sanders 2002, pp. 480–508; Gaither and Frazier 2002, pp. 623–664) provide an overview of some of the more commonly used scheduling techniques listed in Table 3.

Table 3. Scheduling techniques

Techniques	Descriptions
Priority dispatching rules	Priority dispatching rules are usually based on job characteristics (e.g., processing time or due date). Some rules also take the status of the total shop into account (i.e., workload). An example of a dispatching rule is the *shortest processing time* (SPT) rule (i.e., if a job is completed at a work station, the job with the shortest processing time in the queue will be processed next).
Search techniques	These techniques find an optimal schedule by enumerating many (possibly all feasible) schedules and choosing the best one according to a specific performance criterion. For instance, branch-and-bound techniques, and mathematical programming are two commonly used algorithmic-based methods.
Bottleneck methods	These techniques make a distinction between bottleneck and non-bottleneck resources. The bottleneck resource is scheduled first to ensure maximal utilization. Then the critical non-bottleneck resources (i.e., resources preceding the bottleneck) are scheduled to provide the bottleneck continuously with work. A well-known example of a bottleneck technique/software system is *optimized production technology* (OPT).
Knowledge-based techniques	Knowledge-based techniques model the shop floor by means of many hard and soft constraints. These rules are often obtained by eliciting knowledge from experienced schedulers. These techniques are usually aimed at generating feasible schedules.

Of the techniques discussed, *priority dispatching rules* are the most broadly used in practice. Also, these priority rules often belong to implicit scheduling guidelines that schedulers already use, unaware of their meaning in production planning and control theory. However, priority dispatching rules are not very "smart" and they generate schedules that are far from optimal with respect to a specific performance criterion. Most of these rules use local information, which leads to local optimization (i.e., insensitive to the overall state of the production unit). *Mathematical techniques* give the best results if one solely looks at the ability to optimize schedules to conform to one or a combination of performance criteria. *Bottleneck techniques* focus primarily on the utilization of bottlenecks and are not very well suited to optimize schedules to conform to other goals. *Knowledge-based techniques* are not used to optimize schedules, instead they are able to generate a schedule that is feasibly conforms to the many constraints in a knowledge base. However, human factors play critical role in using scheduling techniques. The use of techniques by humans can be improved by making techniques transparent for users. Moreover, a human scheduler can be very pragmatic in using techniques. If they think that it will cost more than can be gained, a technique will probably be ignored.

Forecasting and JIT

JIT is an inventory system where materials and parts are not provided in a production process until they are needed. JIT eliminates or curtails the need for safety stock and as such reduces both waste and inventory costs. Accurate forecasting is crucial for a company that adopts a JIT system. It is especially important for JIT suppliers as they are required to provide materials as needed. A recent trend in supply chain design is continuous replenishment, where continuous updating of data is shared between suppliers and customers. In this system customers are continuously being replenished, daily or even hourly by their suppliers on actual sales. Continuous replenishment, typically managed by the supplier, reduces inventory for the company and speeds customer delivery. Variations of continuous replenishment include quick response (QR), Just-in-time (JIT), vendor-managed inventory (VMI), and zero-inventory. Such systems rely heavily on extremely accurate short-term forecasts, usually on a weekly basis of end-use sales to the ultimate customer. The supplier at one end of a company's supply chain must forecast the company's customer demand at the other end of the supply chain in order to maintain continuous replenishment. The forecast also has to be able to respond to sudden, quick changes in demand. Longer forecasts based on historical sales data for six to twelve months into the future are also generally required to help make weekly forecasts and suggest trend changes.

Using a sample of 130 large US manufacturing firms, Yasin and Wafa (1996) explored the question to what extent did the demand forecasting methods impact the success of JIT. They examined the use of several forecasting methods, including: exponential smoothing models, regression analysis, econometric models, and customer provided forecasts. Based on their results they found there was no significant difference between successful and unsuccessful JIT firms with regard to the type of forecasting models used or the extent of their usage. The accuracy of the forecasting system rather than the model used was the important factor in explaining JIT success. They also found that firms that were satisfied with the accuracy of their forecasting systems were more likely to have had positive JIT experience.

Scheduling and JIT

According to Schniederjans and Olson (1999), in a JIT system the timing of the delivery of parts, materials, and inventories are required to be flawless because the JIT system tries to avoid storage of these items. Detailed JIT principles in production management are summarized in Table 4. As a result, scheduling becomes a daunting process for schedulers in a JIT environment.

Kern and Wei (1996) studied various scheduling methods in a JIT setting. The finding of the study suggested that a level scheduling appeared to be the most viable choice in a JIT production setting due to the fact that the goal of most JIT firms were to create a level production. According to Kelle and Miller (1998) JIT manufacturers use different scheduling and operational tactics to achieve the level scheduling. Some of the popular tactics implemented in a JIT environment include *rate-based scheduling* (i.e., tying production to demand rates), *mixed model scheduling* (i.e., establishing production cells that can handle differing models of the same product to allow production flexibility), frequent revisions to the schedule, and rigid time fences to maintain schedule flexibility.

One of the major goals of JIT scheduling is the proper timing of allocating resources to the shop floor. As such, JIT suppliers need to deliver shipments more frequently and in smaller quantities. To reduce inventory costs, JIT organizations seek to have a shipment size that would permit them to be delivered directly to the shop floor without being stocked in inventory. More frequent delivering and receiving parts and materials in a JIT setting has imposed a tremendous amount of pressure on shipping and receiving department of JIT organizations to perform very efficiently and effectively. Even if JIT suppliers are able to delivery the materials on time, production can be delayed when the shipping/receiving department of JIT buyer is not able to unload the shipment on time. Since most organizations' shipping and receiving departments are fairly limited on space, the scheduling of the unloading of the trucks becomes an important issue for JIT firms. In fact, many organizations have adopted penalties for poor timing of shipments (Dixon 1997; Federgruen and Moshieov 1996; Schniederjans and Olson 1999, pp. 108–110).

Table 4. JIT production management principles

JIT production management principles	Description
Seek uniform daily production scheduling	Producing a fixed amount of inventory every day allows for less waste in production scheduling (i.e., minimizes layoffs or overtime).
Seek production scheduling flexibility	So labor shifts can be made to better match actual customer demand.
Seek a synchronized pull system and eliminate waste	Having a customer order in-hand before the item is produced and there is little need for inventory.
Seek improved flexibility in production setups	Saves labor during product changeovers. Allows for easier reassignment when a lack of specific skills might delay production.
Seek reduced production lot sizes and setup costs	Smaller lot sizes means less WIP inventory and its waste. Smaller lot sizes allows employees to have more opportunity (and be more motivated) to identify and solve production setup problems, thus saving time and costs.
Seek unitary production	Ideally, individual customer demand is "individual" and so single unit production will be the least wasteful.
Seek continuous improvement	Seek to continuously identify and correct all production problems.

The essence of JIT scheduling system is to help JIT organizations to remove the variability embedded in their production systems by adjusting their schedule accordingly based on proper scheduling rules. What is, then, the most effective scheduling rule to be used in a JIT setting? To answer this question, we need to look at studies in JIT scheduling rules. Research in JIT scheduling rules are well-documented (Hum and Lee 1997; Lummus 1995; Duclos, Siha, and Lummos 1995; Shingo 1981).   Lummus (1995) investigated the effects of sequencing rules on the performance of a JIT system with multiple products, and variable setup and processing times.   Table 5 lists the three sequencing rules examined in the study (Lummus 1995; Schniederjans and Olson 1999).   The findings of the study suggest that in most circumstances the demand driven sequencing rule outperforms other sequencing rules in a JIT system with multi-lines.   In other words, JIT firms let demand drive their schedules rather than other sequencing policies.

Table 5. Sequencing rules in a JIT system with multi-lines

Sequencing rules	Descriptions
Toyota production rule	This rule [seeks] to build consistency in a scheduling process by producing the same product on the same day of the each month.
Least changeover rule (LCR)	The LCR minimizes the amount of setups in the process. This can often be found in industries where setups are sequence dependent and poor scheduling leads to a large increase in set-up time.
Demand driven rule	The finished goods that are removed from the production system determine the demand driven sequence. The production sequence is entirely driven by the rate and flow of customer demand.

Another study on JIT scheduling by Hum and Lee (1997) explored the impact of the scheduling rules within a JIT system. Rather than testing a multi-line JIT production system, this study examined a serial line JIT system, where the final assembly station operated on a predetermined schedule based on demand. The results of the study indicated that FCFS, the most widely used scheduling rule, performs the worst under all system conditions, while the SPT, NK, and RK rules perform equally well under any system operation conditions. As the setup times increase, the SPT rule outperforms other scheduling rules. Table 6 shows the four scheduling rules used in this simulation research (Hum and Lee 1997; Schniederjans and Olson 1999).

Table 6. Sequencing rules in a JIT system with a serial line

Sequencing rules	Descriptions
First-come, first-served (FCFS)	The FCFS simply processes jobs as they arrive in the preceding queue. This is the most common scheduling rule used by JIT organizations.
Shortest processing time (SPT)	The SPT chooses those jobs in the queue with the lowest work completion time.
Number of kanbans (NK)	The NK priority to producing the job that has the greatest number of kanbans waiting at the work center.
Ratio of kanbans (RK)	The RK rule is based on the number kanbans waiting for processing relative to the total number of kanbans in the system for that particular part type. The RK rule gives priority to the jobs that have the highest ratio in the system.

Why is Forecasting and Scheduling Management So Important in E-Commerce?

Importance of Forecasting

The Internet is changing the way companies conduct business. It is, however, not the panacea for all the problems in operations management in an e-commerce setting, especially with regard to the need for forecasting. Just because trading partners in a supply chain can communicate faster with the Internet, does not mean volatility and uncertainty will totally go away. Knowing about everything and everyone in a supply chain on an historical and an up-to-the-minute basis does not tell us what will happen in the future with certainty. While the Internet may reduce uncertainty due to enhanced communications, it will not eliminate uncertainty once and for all. As such, the Internet does not eliminate the need for companies to forecast. For instance, Lapide (2000) reported that high tech electronics industry has experienced drastically shortage of components in recent years, although the industry is well known for its sophistication in connecting trading partners electronically to manage the flow of parts and components throughout its supply chain in a JIT system. The primary reason for this problem is attributed to poor forecasting of demand for semiconductor chips and parts, according to Lapide (2000).

Direct Model vs. Forecasting

As discussed in Chapter 3, the "direct model" popularized by Dell Computers, is the most widely used e-commerce business model. In the direct model, as soon as a finished good is consumed or used at its point of consumption, manufacturers, suppliers, distributors, and retailers are immediately notified through the instantaneous propagation of demand signals. These trading partners can use the demand signals to make a replacement product and to replenish inventories in a JIT system. Theoretically under this scenario, products should flow smoothly and consistently throughout a supply chain with virtually no inventory needed and no need to forecast future demand, since all inventories used would be rapidly replaced, on a one-to-one basis. This lets some practitioners to believe that forecasting will no longer be necessary.

However, there are some problems associated with this model. First the direct model of supply chain replenishment cannot react fast enough to future upswings in demand and will lead to lost sales and product shortages. Second, it cannot anticipate downswings in demand, and hence will result in excessive inventories during periods of low demand. As a result, forecasting is still needed even under the direct model scenario in order to plan operations in anticipation of future changes in demand. In particular, demand for most consumer products is subject to the needs of the consumer. Hence by its nature it is random and uncertain. To account for this volatility in demand, safety stock is needed to ensure product availability and adequate customer service levels. To establish adequate inventory safety stocks an estimate of forecast accuracy is needed, in turn meaning a forecast is also necessary.

While the Internet does not totally eliminate the need to do forecasting, the direct model does significantly reduce the need for inventory and diminishes the need to focus as much effort on forecasting processes. Under a model of frequent replenishment and the instantaneous propagation of demand signals along a whole supply chain, order cycle process times are significantly reduced, which leads to all trading partners needing to carry substantially smaller inventories. It can also lead to increased forecasting accuracy because the use of better, fresher, and more detailed information will lead to a greater understanding of supply chain dynamics. In a word, Internet can be viewed as an enabler of business forecasting.

Importance of Scheduling

Scheduling also plays an important role for companies to obtain and sustain competitive edge in an e-commerce setting. Harrington (1999) reported that Heineken, a premier German beer maker, implemented an advanced planning and scheduling system (APS) to determine the optimal flow of products and materials across its supply chain and locate new facilities and keep suppliers. Table 7 summaries how Heineken implements the APS system to achieve effective scheduling.

Table 7. Effective scheduling using APS

APS applications	Descriptions
Demand planning	It provides visibility of near-term demand and develops a forecast for long-range demand.
Supply chain planning	It determines the optimal supply plan to meet current demand.
Transportation planning	It determines the mode of transportation, routing and vehicle loading.
Available to promise (ATP)	It commits product currently in production, in the plan or warehouse, to a customer order.
Capable to promise (CTP)	It inserts an order into the schedule to meet specific customer demand when ATP cannot be performed.
Manufacturing planning	It takes the master schedule and creates a detailed production plan by simultaneously planning materials and plant resources.
Production scheduling	It determines the optimal sequence of orders based on changeover requirements, customer due dates and other constraints.

Fedex also focuses on improving its scheduling process to enhance its business operations and provide better services to its customers (Heizer and Render 2000). For instance, Fedex created a distributed database of shipment information for its enterprise network and the Internet so it and its customers can better track and coordinate orders. In doing so, Fedex has achieved a JIT goal, that is, it delivers materials to customers precisely when and where they are needed for assembly and installation. As a result, it curtails costs because of the reduction of in-transit inventory.

Integrating Forecasting into the E-Commerce Operations

As mentioned previously, forecasting plays a pivotal role in obtaining and maintaining competitive advantage in an e-commerce environment. How to integrate forecasting into the e-commerce operations is a daunting challenge for the managers. There are some innovative practices in the business world to meet this challenge. For example, Wong (2001) suggested that companies started to use an internal e-commerce or intranet approach to develop databases for effectively forecasting environmental costs.

Collaborative Planning, Forecasting, and Replenishment (CPFR) and Internet

Harrington (2000) reported that retailers began to use Internet as a useful tool to facilitate their collaborative planning, forecasting, and replenishment (CPFR) initiatives. According to Harrington (2000), most manufacturers and their retailing counterparts had problems in forecasting accurately the demand and replenishment inventory. Vendor management inventory (VMI) programs such as quick response (QR) and continuous replenishment program (CRP), co-managed inventory (CMI) programs do not render effective forecasting results because the trading partners must still deal with problems in assembling data, forecasting sales, forecasting orders, generating orders, and fulfilling orders. With Internet-based collaborative planning, consumer behavior can be communicated among multiple trading partners in real time. This type of interaction fundamentally changed the nature of relationships and transactions among trading partners. Rather than buyer/supplier relationships, under CPFR, trading partners have collaborative relationships (i.e., collaborative forecasts and replenishment orders). Some of the benefits of CPFR are listed as following: reduced inventory level, reduced transportation and distribution center costs, improved cycle times and customer service, and fewer orders, emergency orders, back orders and returns.

New Product Forecasting and Internet-Based Groupware

New product development is considered to be one of the key factors in a firm's long-term competitiveness. Hence, organizations in various industries are continuously trying to launch new products and services. Besides its importance, new product development is a risky business. Past research suggests that market research activities at the earlier stages of the new product development process tend to increase the chances of a new product's success (Cooper and Kleinschmidt 1993). There are various forecasting methods that can be used to assess the viability of new product concepts at the early stages of their development and one widely used new product evaluation method is "judgmental new product forecasting" (Ozer1999). Judgmental new product forecasting involves asking distributors, executives, experts, product managers, sales managers, and suppliers to make predictions about the market success of a new product. Judgements of groups of people have been widely proven beneficial over individual judgments. For example, compared with individuals, groups make more accurate judgments, group members can discuss and evaluate a wide range of perspectives and assess the sensitivity of the chosen decision to alternative situations (Ozer 1999). Furthermore, group discussions increase the involvement of the group members in the decision-making process and improve their commitments to implement it (Ferrell 1990). There are many ways of conducting group discussions including face-to-face group discussions, the nominal group method, the Delphi method, and computer-aided groups. Because of the speed, convenience, interactivity and worldwide coverage of the Internet, there are also numerous Internet-based technologies that can be used to conduct group discussions.

Traditional *groupware systems* use proprietary software and computer architectures running over *local-area network* (LANs) or *Wide area networks* (WANs), which increases costs and limits the access of potential participants to a group discussion. However, web-based groupware technologies can be used by every potential participant who has Internet access (Dennis 1996). So companies can, for example, easily elicit the opinions of sales people even when they are in different parts of the world. Internet-based groupware can be used with any type of hardware, as it only requires Internet access, and no additional hardware is needed. This is relevant in new product forecasting, especially when suppliers and distributors need to be included in the group discussions. They can have totally different hardware, but still be able to participate in a judgmental new product forecasting process.

Business applications show that companies successfully use web-based discussion tools. For instance, Optical Dynamic Corp., which designs optical lens casting equipment, uses web-based 3-Dimensional collaboration software to design its new products. As a result, everyone in the new product development team has a better understanding of a new design and is less confused about the design intent. Thus, numerous design improvements can be made in the electronic prototype prior to a much more costly physical prototype (Mendoza 1999). Cisco Systems expects to use web-based groupware for 500 sessions a day about initial sales and customer support activities, replacing a less efficient fax-based communication (Mendoza 1999). And Premo LLC, a property company, has been using web-based groupware to collaborate with several diverse parties in different locations. The new system replaced e-mails and overnight couriers, which were cumbersome, slow, and insecure (Dennis 1996).

In conclusion, judgmental new product forecasting requires inputs from a diverse group of individuals including executives, sales people, the members of a supply chain, and experts. With the help of emerging Internet technologies, these individuals can effectively communicate with each other and discuss the future prospects of a new product. Given its ease of use and world-wide free access, it seems that Internet-based group discussion technologies can provide a viable platform for group discussions for judgmental new product forecasting.

Integrating Scheduling into the ERP System

In order to support its global competitiveness and rapid market responsiveness, an individual manufacturing enterprise has to be integrated with its related management systems (e.g., purchasing, orders, design, production, planning and scheduling, control, transport, resources, personnel, materials, quality, etc.), its partners, suppliers and customers via networks (i.e., local networks, the Internet or intranet), which are, in general, heterogeneous software and hardware environments. A manufacturing firm is measured by the cost of the goods it produces, their quality, and the time of their availability relative to the customer's need. The task of shop floor scheduling and control is to deploy resources to produce high-quality goods as inexpensively as possible and when the customer wants them. Decisions such as when/which machines should be used for which products, what order products should be manufactured, when new jobs should be started, what level of inventory should be carried, and when machine maintenance should be performed. To coordinate all of these elements and decisions requires an integration of systems.

Agent-based systems are often used to integrate scheduling into *enterprise resource planning* (ERP) systems (Baker 1998). *Autonomous agents for the Rock Island Arsenal* (AARIA) developed for an Army manufacturing facility, is one of such scheduling systems that provides the fundamental integration of ERP and scheduling functionality in a *multi-agent* (e.g. people, machines, parts) architecture. ERP functionality emerges from the agents (e.g., people, machines, parts) constructed to satisfy the other requirements. Support of the different scheduling modalities provides rich support for planning and finite-capacity scheduling. Table 8 presents some of the AARIA design principles.

Table 8. AARIA design principles

AARIA design principles	Descriptions
Emergent ERP	The aggregate behavior of the agent community subsumes functionality currently provided by manufacturing (ERP systems.
Uniformity	An operation at the boundary of AARIA interacts with external suppliers or customers in the same way that it does with internal ones.
Empowerment	Human stakeholders (including operators, manufacturing engineers, and management) receive the information (both as-is and what-if) they need to do their jobs, with interfaces to let them control the system rather than be controlled by it.
Dynamic Self-configuration	The system configures itself dynamically in response to internal and external changes.
Least Commitment	The customer's statement of demand develops interactively, rather than being specified in detail at the outset. The system plans what it will do only as needed to meet its commitments to customers (advance planning for the sake of advance planning is not supported).
Modality Emergence	Whether a manufacturing capability is advance scheduled, dispatched, or pulled, depends dynamically on its capability, and its dynamic connections to the rest of the factory.
Metamorphosis	The system maintains the continuity between different entities that represent different stages in a common life cycle (for example, an order for a part, the part itself, or its production history).

In summary, agent based approaches provide a natural way to design and implement manufacturing enterprise integration and supply chain management within such environments. Zweben and Fox (1994) may have been the first to propose organizing the supply chain as a network of cooperating, intelligent agents. A similar study has been done by Swaminathan *et al.* (1998) using a multi-agent framework for modeling supply chain dynamics.

Automating to Improve Scheduling

As described in previous sector, scheduling is the process of selecting among alternative plans and assigning resources and times to the set of activities in the plan. These assignments must obey a set of rules or constraints that reflect the temporal relationships between activities and the capacity limitations of a set of shared resources. The assignments also affect the optimality of a schedule with respect to criteria such as cost, tardiness, or throughput. In summary, scheduling is an optimization process where limited resources are allocated over time among both parallel and sequential activities (Zweben and Fox 1994).

Manufacturing scheduling is a difficult problem, particularly when it takes place in an open, dynamic environment. In a manufacturing system, rarely do things go as expected. The set of things to do is generally dynamic. The system may be asked to do additional tasks that were not anticipated, and sometimes is allowed to omit certain tasks. The resources available to perform tasks are subject to change. Certain resources can become unavailable, and additional resources introduced. The beginning time and the processing time of a task are also subject to variation. A task can take more time than anticipated or less time than anticipated, and tasks can arrive early or late. Because of its highly combinatorial aspects, its dynamic nature and its practical interest for manufacturing systems, the scheduling problem is widely studied in the literature by various methods: heuristics, constraint propagation techniques, constraint satisfaction problem formalism, simulated annealing, Taboo search, genetic algorithms, neural networks, etc.

Agent technology has recently been used in attempts to resolve this problem (Choi *et al.* 2000). An *intelligent agent* is defined as a software that learns, infers, and cooperates with other agents or systems to solve given problems autonomously (Choi *et al.* 2000). Table 9 shows the characteristics of an intelligent agent. Choi *et al.* (2000) proposed an intelligent agent, namely a *virtual manufacturing-based sales agent* (VMSA) to support the sales activity for parts manufacturers in an e-commerce environment. Because manufacturability analysis, process planning, and scheduling are key features in development an agent of sales activity for the parts manufacturing business, the proposed VMSA system consists of four agents: a *database* (DB) agent, a manufacturability analysis agent, a process planning agent, and a scheduling agent. Figure 2 shows the architecture of a VMSA system. Table 10 depicts the role of each agent plays in the VMSA system.

Global competition and rapidly changing customer requirements are forcing major changes in the production styles and configuration of manufacturing organizations. Increasingly, traditional centralized and sequential manufacturing planning, scheduling, and control mechanisms are being found insufficiently flexible to respond to changing production styles and highly dynamic variations in product requirements. The traditional approaches limit the expandability and reconfiguration capabilities of the manufacturing systems. The traditional centralized hierarchical organization may also result in much of the system being shut down by a single point of failure, as well as plan fragility and increased response overhead. Agent technology provides a natural way to overcome such problems, and to design and implement distributed intelligent manufacturing environments.

Table 9. Agent characteristics

Characteristics of an agent	Descriptions
Autonomy	The intelligent agent must have the capability to take actions leading to the completion of tasks. There must be an element of independence on the agent.
Communication ability	The intelligent agent will access information from third party sources about the current state of the external environment. This requires an ability to communicate with the repositories of this information.
Capacity for cooperation	An extension of the communication attributes is cooperation. Intelligent agents must be collaborative in their work together.
Capacity for reasoning	The ability to perform reasoning is one of the key aspects of intelligence that distinguishes intelligent agents from other more robotic agents.
Adaptive behavior	To maintain autonomous and reasoning capabilities, the agent must have some mechanism for assessing the current state of its external domain and incorporating this into its decision about future action.
Trustworthiness	Essential to the acceptance of agency is a strong sense of trust that the agent can accurately represent the user and its client.

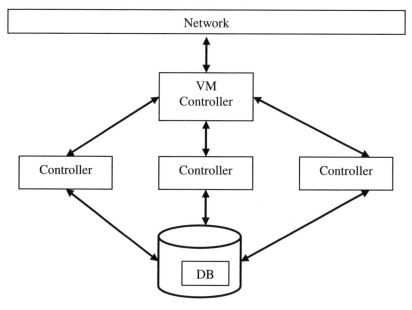

Figure 2. Architecture of VMSA

Table 10. Roles of agents

Agent	Role
VM controller agent	The VM controller does analysis, message routing, mediation, and matchmaking.
Database agent	All information and production environment, such as factory shop models, machining models, and part models are stored in the database.
Manufacturability analysis agent	When a computerized representation of the design and a set of manufacturing resources are received from the sales agent, it determines whether the product design is feasible or not. If it is feasible, the manufacturability analysis agent calculates the manufacturing rating.
Process planning agent	This generates a product feature set and determines the optimal operation sequences.
Scheduling agent	This generates operation schedules based on process planning, taking into account the various manufacturing environments. It calculates the expected finishing date of the order, taking into account the current status of the product line.

Planning vs. Scheduling

Planning is the process of selecting and sequencing activities such that they achieve one or more goals and satisfy a set of domain constraints, while scheduling is the process of selecting among alternative plans and assigning resources and times to the set of activities in the plan. Traditional approaches to planning and scheduling do not consider the constraints of both domains simultaneously. In spite of being sub-optimal these approaches have been in vogue due to the non-availability of a unified framework. Agent-based approaches provide a possible way to integrate planning and scheduling activities through enterprise-level coordination between the product design system and the factory resource scheduling system.

Summary

This chapter first presents basics of forecasting and scheduling management concepts and describes forecasting and scheduling management in the JIT environment. The chapter also explains the importance and uniqueness of the forecasting and scheduling in an e-commerce setting. The chapter also discusses various integration issues of forecasting and scheduling in e-commerce settings. Finally, the chapter illustrates how to use intelligent agent to facilitate forecasting and scheduling management.

♦ Review Terms

Advanced planning and scheduling system (APS)

Agent technology

Autonomous agents for the Rock Island arsenal (AARIA)

Available to promise (ATP)

Backward scheduling

Bottleneck methods

Capable to promise (CTP)

Collaborative planning, forecasting, and replenishment (CPFR)

Co-managed inventory (CMI)

Continuous replenishment program (CRP)

Database agent

Delphi method

Demand driven rule

Enterprise resource planning (ERP)

Finite loading

First-come, first-served (FCFS)

Forecasting

Forward scheduling

Groupware systems

Infinite loading

Intelligent agent

Judgmental new product forecasting

Just-in-time (JIT)

Knowledge-based techniques

Least changeover rule (LCR)
Level scheduling
Loading
Local-area network (LAN)
Manufacturability analysis agent
Market research
Materials requirement planning
(MRP)
Mathematical techniques
(scheduling)
Mixed model scheduling
Multi-agent
Number of kanbans (NK)
Operations scheduling
Optimized production technology
(OPT)
Planning
Priority dispatching rules
Process planning agent
Qualitative forecasting methods
Quantitative forecasting methods

Quick response (QR)
Rate-based scheduling
Ratio of kanbans (RK)
Regression forecast methods
Scheduling
Scheduling agent
Search techniques
Sequencing
Shortest processing time (SPT)
Simulation
Simulation forecasting methods
Time series methods
Toyota production rule
Vendor-managed inventory (VMI)
Virtual manufacturing-based sales
agent (VMSA)
VM controller agent
Wide area networks (WAN)
Work-in-process (WIP)
Zero-inventory

♦ Discussion Questions

1. What is forecasting management and what is scheduling management?
2. What are the objectives of scheduling?
3. What are the differences between planning, scheduling, and sequencing?
4. What are the three scheduling rules examined by (Hum and Lee 1997)
5. What are the four scheduling rules studied by (Lummus 1995)?
6. Why it is important to integrate scheduling into the ERP system?
7. Why it is crucial to integrate forecasting into the e-commerce operations?
8. Describe how to use an intelligent agent to enhance scheduling.

♦ Questions

1. Define quantitative and qualitative forecasting methods. List some of the widely used quantitative and qualitative methods.
2. Describe and compare the following four commonly used scheduling rules: priority dispatching rules, search techniques, bottleneck methods, and knowledge-based techniques.

3. Describe the role of each agent plays in the virtual manufacturing-based sales agent (VMSA) system.
4. Why are forecasting and scheduling management so important in e-commerce era?
5. What are proper forecasting methods for the four different production processes?

References

Baker, A. D., "A Survey of Factory Control Algorithms which Can be Implemented in a Multi-Agent Heterachy: Dispatching, Scheduling, and Pull," *Journal of Manufacturing Systems*, Vol. 17, No. 4, 1998, pp. 297–320.

Chase, R. B., Aquilano, N. J. and Jacobs, F. R., *Operations Management for Competitive Advantage*. 9th ed., Boston, MA: McGraw-Hill/Irwin, 2001.

Choi, H. R., Kim, H. S., Park, Y. J., Kim, K. H., Joo, M. H. and Sohn, H. S., "A Sales Agent for Part Manufacturers: VMSA," *Decision Support Systems*, Vol. 28, No. 4, 2000, pp. 333–346.

Cooper, R. G. and Kleinschmidt, E. J., "Screening New Products for Potential Winners," *Long Range Planning*, Vol. 26, No. 6, 1993, pp. 74–81.

Dalrymple, D. J., "Sales Forecasting Practices from a United States Survey," *International Journal of Forecasting*, Vol. 3, 1987, pp. 379–91.

Dennis, A., Pootheri, S. K. and Hlanatarajan, V. L., "Lessons From the Early Adopters of Web Groupware," *Journal of Management Information Systems*, Vol. 14, No. 4, 1996, pp. 65–86.

Dixon, Lance, "Got a Problem? Get JIT II," *Purchasing*, Vol. 123, 1997, pp. 31–32.

Duclos, L., Siha, S. M. and Lummus, R. R., "JIT in Services: A Review of Current Practices and Future Directions for Research," *International Journal of Service Industry Management*, Vol. 6, 1995, pp. 36–52.

Estrin, T. L., "The Role of Information Providers in Decision Making," *Journal of General Management*, Vol. 15, 1990, pp. 80–95.

Federgruen, A. and Mosheiov, G., "Heuristics for Multimachine Scheduling Problems with Earliness and Tardiness Costs," *Management Science*, Vol. 42, 1996, pp. 1544–1564.

Ferrell, W. R., *Aggregation of Judgments or Judgments of Aggregations?* In N. Moray, WR. Ferrell and WB. Rouse (Eds.) Robotics, Control and Society: Essays in Honor of Thomas B. Sheridan. New York: Taylor and Francis, 1990.

Fildes, R. and Hastings, R., "The Organization and Improvement of Market Forecasting," *Journal of the Operational Research Society*, Vol. 45, 1994, pp. 1–16.

Gaither, N. and Frazier, G., *Operations Management*, 9th ed., South-Western, Cincinnati: Ohio, 2002.

Harrington, L. H., "Better Forecasting Can Improve Your Bottom Line," *Transportation & Distribution*, Vol. 40, No. 7, pp. 21–24.

Harrington, L. H., "Collaborating on the Net," *Transportation & Distribution*, Vol. 41, No. 2, 2000, pp. D8-13.

Hum, S. H. and Lee, C. K., "JIT Scheduling Rules: A Simulation Evaluation," *Omega: International Journal of Management Science*, Vol. 26, 1998, pp. 381–395.

Kelle, Peter and Miller, Pam A., "Transition to Just-In-Time Purchasing: Handling Ounce Deliveries with Vendor-purchaser Co-operation," *International Journal of Operations & Production Management*, Vol. 18, 1998, pp. 53–66.

Kern, G. M. and Wei, J. C., "Master Production Rescheduling Policy in Capacity-Constrained Just-in-time Make-to-stock Environments," *Decision Sciences*, Vol. 27, No. 2, 1996, pp. 365–388.

Lapide, L., "New Developments in Business Forecasting: The Internet Does Not Eliminate the Need to Forecast," *The Journal of Business Forecasting Methods & Systems*, Vol. 19, No. 3, 2000, pp.15–17.

Lummus, R. R., "A Simulation of Sequencing Alternatives for JIT Lines Using Kanbans," *Journal of Operations Management*, Vol. 13, 1995, pp. 183–191.

Mahmoud, E., DeRoeck, R., Brown, R. G. and Rice, G., "Bridging the Gap between Theory and Practice in Forecasting," *International Journal of Forecasting*, Vol. 8, 1992, pp. 251–67.

Memdoza, M., "Collaboration Beyond Engineering," *Computer-aided engineering*, Vol. 18, No. 7, 1999, pp. 24–30.

Morton, T. E. and Pentico, D.W., Heuristic Scheduling Systems with Applications to Production Systems and Project Management, New York:John Wiley & Sons, 1993.

Ozer, M., "The Use of Internet-based Groupware in New Product Forecasting," *Journal of the Market Research Society*, Vol. 41, No. 4, 1999, pp. 425–439.

Reid, R. D. and Sanders, N. R., *Operations Management*, New York: John Wiley & Sons, 2002.

Rice, G., "Forecasting in US Firms: A Role for TQM?" *International Journal of Operations and Production Management*, Vol. 17, No. 2, 1997, pp. 211–220.

Sanders, N. and Manrodt, K., "Forecasting Practices in US Corporations: Survey Results," *Interfaces*, Vol. 24, 1994, pp. 92–100.

Schniederjans, M. J. and Olson, J. R., *Advanced Topics in Just-In-Time Management*, Westport, CT: Quorum Books, 1999.

Shingo, S., Study of "Toyota" Production System from Industrial Engineering Viewpoint. Tokyo: Japan Management Association, 1981.

Stoop, P. and Wiers, V. C. S., "The Complexity of Scheduling in Practice," *International Journal of Operations & Production Management*, Vol.16, No. 10, 1996, pp. 37–53.

Swaminathan, J. M., "Modeling Supply Chain Dynamics: A Multi-agent Approach", *Decision Sciences*, Vol. 29, No. 3, 1998, pp. 607–632.

Thomas, L. J. and McClain, J. O., *An Overview of Production Planning, Logistics of Production and Inventory*, Elsevier Science Publishers, Amsterdam, 1993.

Vollmann, T. E., Berry, W. L., Whybark, D. C., *Manufacturing Planning and Control Systems*, Homewood, IL: Irwin, 1992.

Wong, E.A., "How to Develop a Database for Forecasting Environmental Expenditures?" *Strategic Finance*, Vol. 82, No. 9, 2001, pp. 52–56.

Wright, D. J., Capon, G., Page, R., Quiroga, J., Taseen, A. A. and Tomasini, F., "Evaluation of Forecasting Methods for Decision Support," *International Journal of Forecasting*, Vol. 2, 1986, pp. 139–52.

Yasin, M. and Wafa, M., "An Empirical Examination of Factors Influenced JIT Success," *International Journal of Operations and Production Management*, Vol. 16, No. 1, 1996, pp. 19–26.

Zweben, M. and Fox, M. S., *Intelligent Scheduling*, San Francisco, CA: Morgan Kaufman Publishers, 1994.

Chapter 7   E-COMMERCE AND INVENTORY MANAGEMENT

Learning Objectives

After completing this chapter, you should be able to:

Define and describe "inventory management", its basic purpose and decisions.

Explain the principles of "just-in-time management" as they relate to inventory management.

Explain what characterizes "lean management."

Explain why inventory management is important for e-commerce.

Describe the components of an e-commerce inventory control system.

Explain why it is important to integrate enterprise-wide computer sytems with e-commerce inventory systems.

Explain how using JIT and lean management principles the order picking function of inventory management can best be achieved in e-commerce operations.

Describe e-commerce inventory strategies.

Overview of This Chapter

This chapter presents the subject of inventory management in an e-commerce context. The chapter presents a brief overview of the basics of inventory management as they relate to differing types of business operations. The chapter then explains how e-commerce operations require the use of inventory management principles in the development of e-commerce business strategy. The chapter concludes with a discussion on a series of articles that describe how inventory management is currently conducted to achieve successful e-commerce operations.

What is Inventory Management?

Inventory is physical items that are stored for future use in some type of operation (Swamidass 2000, p. 307). There are two types of inventory: depend demand inventory and independent demand inventory. Dependent demand inventory are inventory items that are used to complete a finished product, like raw materials, supplies, work-in-process (WIP) items. Independent demand inventory are the finished product that final customers will consume.

Inventory management involves the management tasks that are required in the planning and controlling of inventory. These tasks include decision-making on when inventory should be ordered and how much. They can also require related decision-making on storing, order filling or picking, material handling, and inbound and outbound logistics of inventory. The role of the inventory manager is squarely within the domain of *operations management* (OM) and is a primary OM activity that all OM managers are expected to be able to perform. (In this chapter we will use the term "inventory manager" in addition to and as a part of OM management.)

The primary reasons why a business organization undertakes inventory management are two fold: (1) to maximize customer service, and (2) to minimize operations cost. By having inventory available where and when needed a business maximizes their customer service by satisfying customer demand on finished goods. Inventory managers also support the other functional areas such as the marketing of the product by insuring the distribution of finished product to locations that best serve customer demand requirements.

Inventory managers use inventory to reduce inventory costs by taking advantage of quantity discounts by purchasing large order quantities. Having inventory also reduces operation costs that can occur, such as line stoppage that would occur in an inventory stockout situation. Having inventory helps by smoothing manufacturing activity. With a given quantity of inventory production managers can plan level quantity production rates the avoid demand ups and downs, and the subsequent hiring and laying off of production labor that would otherwise have to incur to meet shifting customer demand patterns.

The focus of inventory managers on dealing with cost minimization is a fundamental one that requires a more detailed explanation of what inventory costs are considered and why. While dozens of inventory cost items are relevant, the four that are most commonly suggested in inventory literature are: inventory carrying or holding costs, inventory ordering costs, the cost of the inventory item, and the costs of stockouts (Swamidass 2000, p. 307). In Figure 1 a typical inventory ordering cost curve is presented. This positively skewed curve depicts the fact that as the size of the order quantities for an inventory item increase (assuming total demand of the item is constant); the number of orders, and therefore the ordering costs (i.e., purchasing agent labor, communication costs, checking incoming orders, etc.) will be reduced.

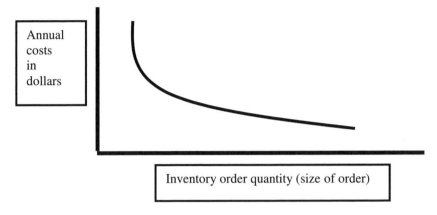

Figure 1. Inventory ordering cost curve

In Figure 2, a typical inventory carrying cost curve is presented. This negatively skewed curve depicts the fact that as you increase the size of the inventory order quantities there will be increases in the holding costs (i.e., taxes, insurance, inventory, accountant, and physical distribution personnel labor, etc.) to maintain and keep tract of the inventory.

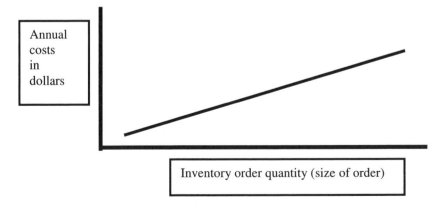

Figure 2. Inventory carrying cost curve

By combining these to opposing cost curves into a model it is possible to calculate an inventory ordering policy with vendors that will minimize total costs. Combining the both cost curves into a single model results in a total cost curve as presented in Figure 3, Curve "A". This traditionally structured u-shaped curve can be entirely shifted up or down when the unit cost of an item is included in the cost curve. In Figure 3, Curve "B" shows a reduction in unit cost depicted by a downward shift in the total cost curve. Once having identified the unique total cost curve for an inventory item, inventory managers seek to find the optimal order quantity (as shown in Figure 3 as Q*) to minimize total costs. The inventory model used to compute these cost curves has traditionally been referred to as the *economic order quantity* (EOQ) model. For a mathematical presentation on the mechanics of the various EOQ models see Chase *et al.* (2001, pp. 517–527), Heizer and Render (2001, pp. 479–500), and Gaither and Frazier (2002, pp. 540–561).

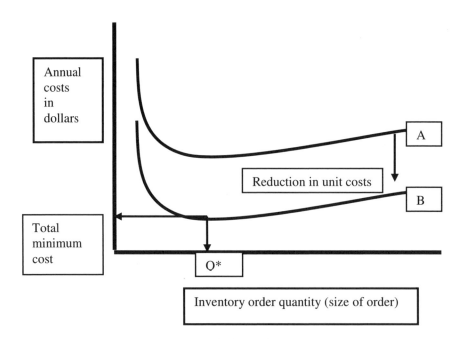

Figure 3. Total ordering and carrying cost curves

The inventory models that have been used to generate the cost curves presented in Figures 1, 2, and 3 require a number of simplifying assumptions (e.g., constant, even customer demand rate) that frankly are rare to be found in actual practice. So a wide range of additional costs components have added to bring reality into these simple inventory models. One important cost component that can be added is that of stockout costs. *Stockout costs* are the costs of not having inventory available when customers demand it. Companies not only lose the profit that they would have received but can lose all the profit from future purchases if the customer no longer does business with the firm.   The mathematical treatment of stockout costs is to include still more inventory in the ordering policy based on some probabilistically generated demand function. For a review of the mathematical basics of stockout computation see Chase *et al.* (2001, pp. 519–529).

Unfortunately, the narrowness of considering only a hand full of cost factors in determining order quantities has lead most firms to abandoning the use of such cost models for purposes of inventory planning. Instead today, inventories "philosophies" are chiefly used to guide the planning and control of inventory. Two such philosophies are "just-in-time management" and "lean management."

Just-in-time (JIT) *management* (as presented in other chapters) is an OM philosophical strategy for minimizing waste in production operations (Schniederjans and Olson 1999, p. 3). Its original principle-driven philosophy in inventory management applies to all areas within e-commerce operations. Some of the these JIT inventory management principles are presented in Table 1.

As stated in prior chapters, *lean management*, is an outgrowth of the JIT principles (Heizer and Render 2001, p. 530; Swamidass 2000, pp. 346–352). In the area of inventory lean management seeks to eliminate all supplies, raw materials, WIP, and finish goods inventory except those that are needed for efficient production operations. It also advocates the use JIT inventory principles.

Both JIT management and lean management seek to avoid waste in production operations, reduce operating costs, and permit flexibility for change to meet altering customer demands. In doing so, these currently popular philosophies of inventory management are ideal to for e-commerce operations. As will be seen in the following sections, e-commerce operations are implementing these very principles to achieve business performance success.

A Measurement of Employee-Inventory Value Added

In the labor intensive environment of an e-commerce operation there needs to be a quick means of measuring the *value added* (i.e., a producer's perceived utility by the customer) by employees as it relates to inventory items or their cost. One measure that can be used for comparison purposes is the *employee value added ratio* (Schniederjans 1993, p. 94):

Table 1. JIT inventory management principles

JIT inventory principle	Description
Seek zero finished goods inventory	While it is not possible for all e-commerce operations to completely eliminate all inventory, the goal of zero inventory is viewed as a target that firms should continually strive to achieve. Reducing the size of inventories to just equal daily production requirements, reduces average inventory and the waste of capital investment in inventory.
Seek zero buffer WIP inventory	Reducing all WIP and parts inventory at work stations saves space in the production or service areas of a facility. This savings can reduce facility costs. While not all operations can completely eliminate WIP inventory it should be reduced to no more than one or two units as backups.
Seek reduced batch lot-sizes	In operations that produce batch lot-sized production runs, the frequency of batches should be increased while decreasing the lot size. This permits greater flexibility in amounts of inventory produced to meet changes in demand. In the longer-term it helps to reduce finished goods inventory and provide greater ability to meet changes in demand.
Seek smaller order sizes	By reducing the order size of incoming inventory, there is a saving of space to stage the incoming inventory, less material handling and auditing will be needed at one time (saving labor and equipment), and it will reduce average inventory and its costs.
Seek improved inventory handling	Minimize all handling by layout design changes to minimize inventory movement within the production facility. Specifically, more arrival points of inventory closer to production usage to save moving distance. Reducing the travel distance of inventory often frees up space that permits a reduction in the size of physical facilities and saves handling, labor, and physical space costs.
Seek continuous improvement in inventory management	Maintain a culture that invites the identification and willingness of employees to change processes and systems to reduce waste.

Employee value added = (Dollar sales) – (Inventory purchase costs)
                       Number of employees

Ideally, under a JIT or lean management program, inventory purchase costs in the formula above should be low, resulting in a very large dollar sales-to-employee ratio. This ratio can be computed for any time period and is used on a comparative basis to show improvement over time or as a benchmarking measure of performance. For example, if a company has a monthly average of $10.5 million in total dollar sales, a monthly average of $2.5 million in inventory purchase costs, and has 100 employees working for them, the resulting employee value added ratio is:

Employee value added = ($10,500,000) – ($2,500,000) = $80,000 per employee
                         100

The larger the employee value added ratio is the better.

Another approach to the same type of measure is with the *employee cost value added ratio* as shown below:

Employee cost value added = (Dollar sales) – (Inventory purchase costs)
                            Total cost of employees

Ideally, under a JIT or lean management program, both inventory purchase costs and the total cost of employees in the formula above should be low, resulting in a very large dollar sales-to-dollar cost of employee ratio. As stated for the other ratio, this ratio can be computed for any time period and is used on a comparative basis to show improvement over time or as a benchmarking measure of performance. For example, if a company has a monthly average of $10.5 million in total dollar sales, a monthly average of $2.5 million in inventory purchase costs, and has a monthly average total cost of employees working for them of $250,000, the resulting employee value added ratio is:

Employee cost value added = ($10,500,000) – ($2,500,000) = $32
                            $250,000

The $32 in the ratio above means that for every dollar of cost allocated to employees brings $32 in net sales after inventory costs have been netted out. As with the previous ratio, the larger this ratio is the better.

Why is Inventory Management So Important for E-Commerce?

The magnitude of potential benefits that a successful inventory management strategy can have on an e-commerce operation is dependent on the type of e-commerce operation. While not all organizations have tangible finished inventory items, they all at least use supplies that need to be managed. Referring back to the e-commerce business models introduced in Chapter 1, Table 2 indicates the potential magnitude of benefits a successful inventory management strategy can have to the various types of e-commerce operations.

Table 2. Impact of benefits of inventory management on e-commerce operations

Type of e-commerce business model	Description	Magnitude of potential benefits from successful inventory management
Advertiser	Company makes money by selling advertising space on their Web site.	Low
Service	Company creates a Web site that offers customers a service or range of services.	Medium
Virtual mall	Company offers a wide range of differing manufactured products on a Web site.	High
E-retailing	Company can offer a single customized or non-customized products like brand-name appliances.	High
Information disseminator	Company offers up-to-date source of information of a specific nature.	Low
Sales facilitator	Company connects buyers with sellers on a Web site.	Low
E-procurement	Company provides efficient and cost reducing linkages between buyers and sellers of industrial organizations.	High

E-commerce experienced a major setback in its infancy which had to do with inventory failures. In the holiday season in the later part of 1999, the major forecasting organizations, like Forrester Research Inc. where estimating revenues for e-retailers to increase by 33 percent from the prior year of 1998 (Culbertson *et al.* 2001). That was an estimated US market of $4 billion. Many inventory managers used this total sales estimate to plan their inventory demand. Many inexperienced e-commerce inventory managers did not plan for contingencies and potential stockout situations. The actual demand in 1999 turned out to be $12 billion, and many e-commerce operations failed to deliver their customer products in a timely manner. Large e-commerce organizations like Toysrus.com were reported to have failed to deliver on as much as 5 percent of their 1999 customer orders. They later gave each of their customers a $100 apology gift and this stockout situation in turn negatively impacted Toys R Us's stock price by 16 percent. Also, as a result of the inventory failure of the 1999 a Web shoppers survey reported customer satisfaction levels were only at the 52 percent. That means that 48 percent of the Web customers were not satisfied with their experience in shopping and possibly one in two customers might not return to the Web for their consumer purchases. Culbertson *et al.* (2001) quoted the Jupiter Communication organization as having estimated the cost of attracting each customers to e-commerce purchasing anywhere from $30 to $200. So the cost of losing e-commerce customers to any one business or the industry as a whole can be sizable. One solution to avoid losing customers is to have good inventory management and that is why, for many firms, inventory management is a critical success factor for business success.

Fortunately the inventory issues of the late 90's and early 2000's are not very prevalent today. With the inventory planning and execution leadership of firms like Amazon, e-commerce firms understand that consumers will not tolerate inventory shortages because of demand spikes. E-Retailers notify customers that items are either out of stock or will take additional days for delivery.

In the sections that follow a series of suggested inventory management practices and strategies are offered based on current e-commerce research. Collectively they cover most e-business models and provide a basis for the development of a comprehensive and successful e-commerce inventory management strategy.

A Control System Approach to E-Commerce Inventory Management

Inventory is pulled through supply chains from suppliers to retailers. Retailers place orders with wholesales, wholesalers place orders with manufacturers, and manufacturers place orders with raw material and component part suppliers. As demand grows in size it creates great fluctuations at the raw material end of the ordering supply chain (i.e., the Bullwhip effect from Chapter 3). As explained by Culbertson *et al.* (2001) e-commerce demand is for most of the e-businesses relatively stable since it is at the retailing end of the supply chain (albeit, e-purchasing is an exception). This means the e-commerce operations don't have to worry much about long lead times because they can quickly restock from wholesalers or manufacturers (i.e., not having to wait for the products to be produced). Also, the short outbound lead times to the final customer can be achieved by using express mail, FedEx, or other speed delivery systems currently available world-wide. This permits e-commerce operations to avoid having to invest large amounts of their capital in maintaining inventory. Yet in many e-commerce organizations, there is a need to maintain some inventory. What Culbertson *et al.* (2001) suggests to carefully determine this unique e-commerce demand and the subsequent inventory levels using a computer-based inventory control system.

The inventory management control system reported by Culbertson *et al.* (2001) is designed around a series of algorithmic components. The use of these components depends on the specific type of e-commerce operation but basically includes the following:

Tracking changes in demand but not overreacting to sudden changes or demand spikes (i.e., extremely high or low points of demand).
Define and incorporate indications of demand trends in forecasts.
Continuously adjust reorder rates to maintain target inventory levels.
Continuously recalculate inventory target levels to match changes (e.g., trend changes).
Apply the same logic to all inventory stock items.

To implement this system a combination of statistical techniques are employed to generate a forecast for the expect unit demand. To know what you need to reorder in units of inventory you need to know what you can expect in terms of demand. Under this system actual demand (for a day, week, or month depending on the cycle for placing orders) is smoothed. Culbertson *et al.* (2001) reported that a simple moving average, an exponential-weighted moving average, and trend analysis statistical methods are all used to smooth actual demand and arrive at a forecast. These forecasting methods are fundamental to all inventory managers, and can be found in most any basic operations management textbook. For an excellent review see Gaither and Frazier (2002, pp. 82–92). As we can see in Figure 4, the relatively volatile actual demand can be converted into a much smoother non-linear forecast demand function.

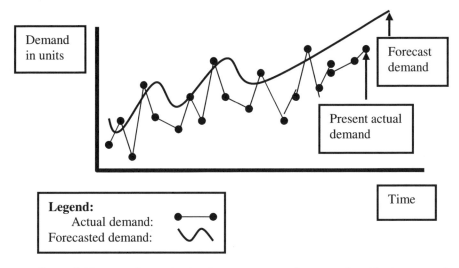

Figure 4. Forecast demand using inventory control system algorithmic approach

One of the features of exponential smoothing models is that they are capable of projecting a forecast into the future by only one time period. That is how this approach allows forecasters to plan the future inventory reorders. By using the forecast from the model, the next time period's demand and therefore the inventory order quantity is accurately anticipated. Because of customer demand surges (a very important factor in e-retailing) there is usually a *safety stock* established, which is a extra amount of inventory that an organization must carry in order to cover unexpected demand surges. For a review of the basics on the calculations of safety stock and how it can be incorporated into a reorder system see Gaither and Frazier (2002, pp. 553–557), Heizer and Render (2001, pp. 487–489 and pp. 495–500), and Chase *et al.* (2001, pp. 519–525).

A company must also establish a *target inventory level* that is based in part on the safety stock level and a minimum amount of inventory that is normally tied up in WIP. This target inventory level can also be viewed as *reorder point* (i.e., an inventory level in units where an order is placed to replenish inventory levels during the time from when an order is placed to when it is delivered) to let the inventory manager know when it is time to place the next order. Once demand is determined for the future period from the smoothed demand, it can be subtracted from the current available inventory stock, allowing the purchasing agent or inventory manager to identify the shortage (or surplus) in inventory and place the appropriate replishment reorder size.

As the Culbertson *et al.* (2001) algorithmic approach is continually used over time, the difference between the actual demand and the forecast demand improves, resulting in less variability and greater control in achieving desired inventory target levels. This reduction in the variability inventory target levels, as shown in Figure 5 will allow inventory managers an opportunity to revisit safety stock and inventory target levels to see if less inventory can be safely used to reduce inventory costs. As an "adaptive" approach this system requires inventory managers to constantly recomputed the inventory target levels and avoid unnecessary inventory stock.

Figure 5. Supply of inventory available to service customer demand

Culbertson *et al.* (2001) reported that their inventory control system applied at Hewlett-Packard was quite successful. Once implemented the company experience zero stockouts, an inventory reduction of 40 percent, and the ability to reduce purchasing staff by more than 90 percent. Moreover, the system being computer-based, allowed for direct ties into other computer systems to support the overall enterprise-wide computing system. Other human resource benefits were also reported including less stress and less purchasing agent turnover.

One final comment on this inventory control system relates to its relationship with the JIT and lean manufacturing philosophies. The same JIT and lean management principles of reducing inventory, seeking flexibility in ordering, continuous improvement in inventory management (e.g., recalculating inventory target levels), and reducing inventory costs are a part of the Culbertson *et al.* (2001) inventory control system. Moreover, the JIT and lean management ideas of making the purchasing job more challenging (because it now requires constant recalculation of inventory target levels), seek to reduce purchasing costs (by reducing the number of purchasing agents), seek inventory ordering flexibility (to allow for rapid changes during the recalculation of inventory target levels), seek timely communications (necessary to make daily or weekly changes), and maintain a close relationship with suppliers (necessary for permitting rapid changes). Clearly this e-commerce inventory control system is both complimentary and supportive of the JIT and lean management principles.

Integration of E-Commerce Inventory Management with Enterprise-Wide Systems

Not all companies think of themselves as being large enough to afford enterprise-wide information systems. But for those organizations who have such large-scale systems or who are planning such systems, may be able to achieve a competitive advantage by integrating them to better serve their customer demands.

Early in the development of e-commerce operations it was clear to many businesses that merging their Internet or e-commerce business with their enterprise-wide business system computers was essential to achieve unique critical success in inventory management. In a survey of the e-commerce forest products industry by Vlosky (1999) a number of critical success factors were identified. One of which was the necessity to bring a company's Internet resources into a broader-based system that included *intranets* (i.e., the use of Internet technology within a company for proprietary reasons and represented by the circled area in Figure 6) and *extranets* (i.e., a network that uses the Internet to link intranets with select business partners, like external suppliers and transportation organizations). What we are talking about here is not just linking these systems together but linking them to provide value to the customer. Specifically, to provide customers with the ability to reach into the workings of the business to identify inventory, both in-stock and other planned orders that will determine the availability of inventory for a given time period. Currently, many extranets and intranets have security systems (sometimes called *firewalls*) to prevent access by Internet customers. What is being proposed here does not mean the elimination of firewalls, but rather that they be less limiting to customer inquiries. That is, customers should be given relevant information on inventory, including current status of inventory levels and other inventory risk-related information that might delay delivery of inventory.

In organizations that use *material requirements planning* (MRP) software (i.e., software used to keep tract of incoming and outgoing inventory and production scheduling in manufacturing operations), this might mean to open access to customers so they can continuously check in real-time the status of all inventory availability, not just their current orders. Since this information is freely available in MRP systems, there are no additional costs in its collection, only a matter of relinquishing control over the information to customers. This is particularly important for construction companies, who are the primary customers of the forest products industry. The forest products industry's longer-lead times (i.e., from forest to finished inventory) can be a critical factor in the construction industry where demand timeliness in delivery can add substantially to construction costs and that industry's successfulness.

What does this type of open system mean to an e-commerce operation? Vlosky's (1999) survey identified a number of benefits by utilizing e-commerce in the forest products industry related to inventory. Some of the benefits related to e-commerce inventory management are listed in Table 3.

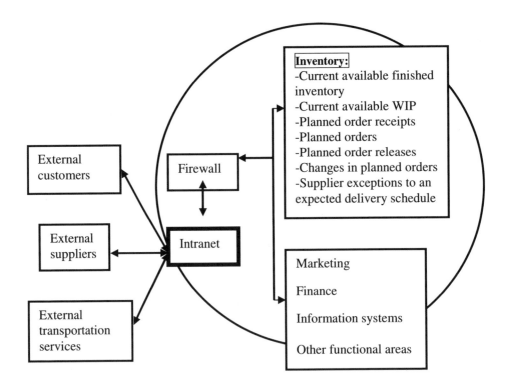

Figure 6. Intranet and extranet

In contrast to the e-retailers who have short replishment cycles, the forest products industry is one where inventory supply acquisition can take time to be acquired. By maintaining and integrating all information systems (i.e., Internets, intranets, and extranets) the disadvantage of a longer-term procurement system can be over come by providing timely information that inventory managers and their customers can use to identify company-wide available and planned resource acquisition of forest products. This is another JIT and lean management advocacy where internal inventory managers and customers are being empowered with inventory information so they can make better informed inventory decisions. The implications here are particularly important for e-commerce businesses like e-procurement where suppliers might have to wait until manufacturers produce items over a longer time period.

Table 3. Benefits of integrated e-commerce inventory system

Inventory area	Description
Customer Service	Internet access permitted faster access to information on availability of inventory, which in turn permits a faster response, which in turn generates greater sales reducing inventory.
Distribution	Online access to shipment information permits access to external transportation partners (i.e., commercial trucking lines), which reduces work associated with communicating and helps to identify bad planning and loading internally.
Human resources	Internet access permits customers to check order status online, reducing phone call representative labor time in dealing with customer requests.
Inventory control	Improved inventory control due to improved information on inbound inventory locations and estimated arrival times.
Inventory planning	Permits automatic reordering of high rotation spare parts inventory saving labor time of purchasing agents and stockout costs.
Inventory reduction	Reduction in inventory possible by eliminating the unknown availability to customers who know they will not face a possible stockout situation.
Warehousing	Internet integration allowed the creation of inventory system in customer's warehouse, permitting faster flow of demand information from customers and more accurate forecasting of e-procurement needs.

As a further extension of the integration theme, Smaros and Holmstrom (2000) explain how the integration of information systems in e-commerce necessitates the use of technologies that allow inventory data collection in a timely manner and that *vendor managed inventory* (VMI) (i.e., where suppliers and vendors maintain their own inventory in their customers facilities so as to be near the point of demand) are successful strategies for inventory management in e-commerce grocery operations, called *e-grocery* stores. In the demand environment of a grocery store, regardless of whether it is a brick-and-mortar or e-grocery operation, customer demand is immediate and highly volatile. By having a VMI operation, most of the burdens of inventory management are passed onto the vendor, who, having a larger number of customers can balance daily shifts in demand volatility more easily because of the collective fluctuations in their broader market.

For capital intensive e-commerce operations that have an immediate and volatile customer demand, the VMI approach can save much needed investment capital for other investment in technologies that assist in other inventory activities. One of the technologies that Smaros and Holmstrom (2000) recommend is *radio frequency identification* (RFID) technology, which is based on antennas and radio signals. Basically, inventory items will be tagged with a radio frequency transponder that is integrated with other data acquisition computer technology, like *Universal Product Code* (UPC) electronic scanners that read bar code on products from labels. As customers consume the inventory items the transponders can send radio signals to an integrated computer system to collect, match additional vendor information, and automatically contact vendors and suppliers of inventory stock usage and needs as depicted in Figure 7. In addition, the collected data can be further utilized to develop profiles of customer buying habits to develop consumer behavior models that can be factored into forecasting efforts to better plan inventory purchases. These patterns, for example can be used to identify inventory *purchase choice variants* (i.e., why one customer might purchase one set of products and then purchase a different or new product in a subsequent purchase). By knowing the buyer behavior e-grocery inventory managers can anticipate when customers might run out of a product and thereby, plan their purchases to meet the anticipated customer demand. Achieving what JIT and lean management philosophy call "synchronized pull demand" and minimizing the time the stock lays around in inventory.

Maximizing Order Picking Inventory Activities

One of the non-value-added inventory management activities required in most e-commerce e-retailing operations is "order picking." When a customer places an order for inventory items, the person or technology that picks the items from inventory and places them where the can be packed and shipped is performing the inventory activity called order picking. By reducing the amount of effort, labor, and time necessary to perform the order picking task while accomplishing the same amount of work, an e-commerce operation achieves the JIT and lean management goal of improving productivity through the reduction of non-value-added activities.

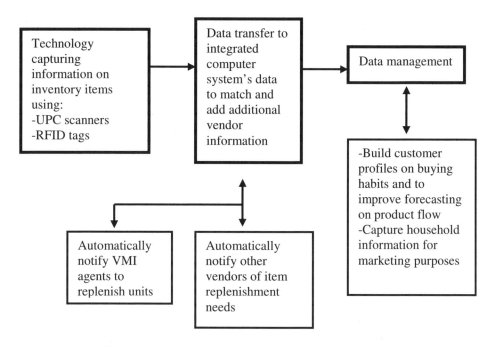

Figure 7. Integrated technology-based inventory system

Kamarainen *et al.* (2001) suggested that by applying JIT and lean management principles to e-grocery operations it is possible to reduce material handling and waste in the order picking functions of inventory management. To accomplish this they identified the faster and slower moving products and regrouped them in the layout of distribution centers where the inventory is stored. They avoided putting the slower-moving products from being in the way of the faster moving products, while keeping in mind the product group characteristics (i.e., some products are sold as a normal grouping so these would logically be placed together). They also took frequency of occurrence information in order picking into consideration consistent with Smaros *et al.* (2000) e-grocery inventory terms of types of demand: continuous demand (i.e., high frequency and stable demand items), occasional demand (i.e., low frequency demand items), and single purchase demand (i.e., rarely purchased items). From those types of demand, Kamarainen *et al.* (2001) developed a set of recommendations on the application of JIT and lean management strategies for positioning inventory items as presented in Table 4. While it is recognized that other layout factors (e.g., temperature, sound, light, etc.) can and should be included in a layout analysis, minimizing wasted distance as a function of the frequency of demand should be a critical factor in designing a final layout for inventory storage in picking areas.

Table 4. Types of demand and JIT/lean strategies

Type of demand	JIT and lean management recommended strategies
Continuous	To minimize material handling place picking area close to docks near shipping department. Avoid storing items by moving them directly on pallets to shipping for a quick break down on incoming orders. Move inbound and outbound areas near one another to minimize movement of these inventory items.
Occasional	This inventory should be unpacked from pallets but left in wholesale modules or in smaller units. Items should be stored on *flow racks* (i.e., shelves that have rollers that move inventory automatically or mechanically) or in open shelves for ease of picking. *Picking cells* (i.e., grouping of inventory that share common order picking characteristics) as presented in Figure 8 can be developed to improve picking efficiency by grouping compatible products.
Single purchase	Picking cells are not necessary for these items and these items may be positioned in the facility at some distance or as fillers in shelving areas where space permits. The most important factor for these inventory items is to minimize stockouts to avoid partially unfilled orders.

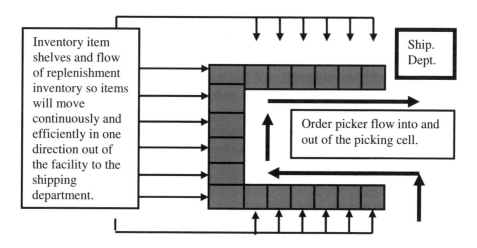

Figure 8. Order picking cell based on JIT and lean management principles

E-Commerce Inventory Strategies

When you acquire a Dell Computer via their Internet ordering system, they construct it using a "make-to-order" inventory strategy. That is, a make-to-order strategy is one where the customer order is in-hand before production of the finish unit begins. This permits them to provide their customers with a customized product if desired or one of their standardized models with a fixed set of features. For the customized products component parts and some subassembly inventory are available through a JIT system where orders can be place with suppliers on a daily basis. This permits an almost zero inventory JIT principle to be achieved and clearly is a demand pull system, where the customer's order pulls the inventory through the system, rather than being pushed by a forecast schedule of production. The more standardized computer products allow Dell to group standardized production tasks together to improve production efficiency. This again allows JIT ordering of inventory just in time for its use in a batch product run of specific computer model.

For e-retailers who do not manufacture what they sell, the idea of waiting for a customer order to be in-hand can in some situations be tolerated with out a loss of customer service, due in part to improved delivery systems like United Parcel Service (UPS) and FedEx whose faster outbound deliveries make up the time for slow inbound deliveries to the e-retailer. In cases where delays caused by internal production problems (e.g., strikes, labor problems, equipment failure, etc.) the Internet allows inventory shortage information to be shared quickly and inexpensively with customers to ease the uncertainty customer have when stated order delivery time periods are known to be extensive or sudden shortages necessitates a delay in delivery. In cases where back-ordering is permitted to allow for delivery from suppliers to e-retailers (again in an effort to achieve a JIT zero inventory level), the Internet can be used to update delivery information and permit even transportation information updates. For example, Godiva.com is a retailer of chocolate, a perishable product. They notify their e-commerce customers by e-mail of the receipt of their orders. Another e-mail is sent at the completion of the order processing in their distribution facility and shipping information with a Web link to their transportation partners is also provided so additional customer order tracking can take place. One of their transporters, FedEx, has a computer monitored delivery system that permits Godiva's customers to gain access to FedEx's distribution computer tracing system and allows customers to actually know the route, and routing status of where their package is located. For customers who are distantly located from Godiva's distribution facilities, the fact that the routing status allows them to see their product move from city-to-city, ever nearer the destination, provides a unique customer assurance of delivery.

Summary

This chapter begins with a description of the basic ideas and principles that are used in inventory management, including those of JIT and lean management. A number of suggestions from research studies for conducting inventory management in e-commerce operations are also described. These suggestions include an inventory control system, computer integration, an order picking system, and strategies for inventory management in e-commerce settings.

One observation that can be made about this chapter's content is the fact that existing inventory management philosophies, specifically JIT and lean management, that were designed to handle the brick-and-mortar operations, can and should be used in e-commerce operations. Indeed, the rapid pace of change that is a predominate characteristic of e-commerce operations management is fully supported by the very nature of the JIT and lean management philosophies. While the research on the causes of e-commerce failure are antidotal at this time, like Culbertson et al. (2001), it is clear from the factual accounts of bad customer service (which is a primary responsibility of OM managers,) that inventory management must be continually improved. Some of the basic ideas of JIT and lean management proposed decades ago by Schonberger (1982; 1986) and others

(Monden 1983, 1993; Ohno 1988; Womack and Jones 1996) are as critical today for establishing a competitive advantage as they were years ago. (For a basic review of JIT principles see Schniederjans (1993) and for a review of more advanced JIT topics see Schniederjans and Olson (1999).)

◆ Review Terms

Demand spikes
Demand pull system
Dependent demand inventory
Economic order quantity (EOQ)
E-grocery
Employee cost value added ratio
Employee value added ratio
Extranets
Firewalls
Flow racks
Independent demand inventory
Intranets
Inventory management
Just-in-time (JIT) management
Lean management
Lean manufacturing
Make-to-order

Material requirements planning (MRP)
Operations management (OM)
Order picking
Picking cells
Production cells
Purchase choice variants
Radio frequency identification (RFID)
Reorder point
Safety stock
Stockout costs
Universal product code (UPC)
Value added
Vendor managed inventory (VMI)
Work-in-process (WIP)

◆ Discussion Questions

1. What are the two different types of "inventory" and how are they different?
2. Explain the difference between "just-in-time management" and "lean management"?
3. If you had to reduce the advocacy of JIT and lean management down into a couple of words, which would you use?
4. Why do you think the impact of inventory management is fairly low for the Information Disseminator and Sales Facilitator types of e-business models?
5. Why is it so important to integrate e-commerce operations with enterprise-wide information systems?
6. How should a "picking cell" be structured to maximize efficiency and minimize costs?

♦ Questions

1. What are the primary reasons why an organization has inventory?
2. What are the principles of "just-in-time management"?
3. What are the characteristics of "lean management"?
4. Why is inventory management important to e-commerce operations? Cite examples.
5. What are the basic components of the proposed e-commerce inventory control system proposed in this chapter?
6. What are some of the benefits of merging Internet systems of e-commerce with enterprise-wide computer systems?
7. What is VMI? Explain.
8. What types of JIT and lean management strategies can be used to handle the differing types of e-commerce customer demand?
9. What is the "make-to-order" e-commerce inventory strategy?
10. How does a "demand pull system" help management inventory in e-commerce operations?

♦ Problems

1. If a company has a monthly average of $75 million in total dollar sales, a monthly average of $45 million in inventory purchase costs, and has 350 employees working for them, what is the resulting "employee value added ratio"? If a company has generated a $158 million in total dollar sales, has incurred $62 million in inventory purchase costs, and has incurred total cost of employees working for them of $10, what is the resulting "employee cost value added ratio"?

2. An e-retailing operation wants to see how well it is doing in its industry on generating sales per employee. If the benchmark for the industry is a "employee value added ratio" of $75,000, how well is the retailing operation doing if the company's last year's total sales were $40 million, its total inventory purchase costs for the year is $45, and the average number of employees per year was 1,250? Compute the "employee value added ratio" and explain your conclusion.

3. An e-commerce operation has been required to achieve an "employee cost value added ratio" benchmark for their industry by their corporation parent. The benchmark "employee cost value added ratio" for the industry is $150. Did the e-commerce operation achieve its benchmark if the company's last

year's total sales were $110 million, its total inventory purchase costs for the year was $65 million, and the total cost of employees for the year was $150,000? Compute the "employee cost value added ratio" and explain your conclusion.

4. An e-retailing store has a yearly "employee value added ratio" of 12,693, $262,666 in monthly sales, and $2.2 million in inventory purchase costs per year. How many employees does the company have?

References

Chase, R. B., Aquilano, N. J. and Jacobs, F. R., *Operations Management for Competitive Advantage.* 9th ed., Boston, MA: McGraw-Hill/Irwin, 2001.

Culbertson, S., Burruss, J. and Buddress, L., "Control System Approach to E-commerce Fulfillment: Hewlett-Packard's Experience," *The Journal of Business Forecasting*, Winter 2001, pp. 10–16.

Gaither, N. and Grazier, G., *Operations Management.* 9th ed., Cincinnati, OH: South-Western, 2002.

Heizer, J. and Render, B., *Operations Management*, 6th ed., Upper Saddle River, NJ: Prentice Hall, 2001.

Kamarainen, V., Samaros, J., Jaakola, T. and Holmstrom, J., "Cost-effectiveness in the E-grocery Business," *International Journal of Retail and Distribution Management*, Vol. 29, No. 1, 2001, pp. 41–48.

Monden, Y., The Toyota Management System: Linking the Seven Key Functional Areas, Cambridge, MA: Productivity Press, 1993.

Monden, Y., *The Toyota Production System: Practical Approach to Production Management*, Atlanta, GA: Industrial Engineering and Management Press, 1983.

Ohno, T., Toyota Production System: Beyond Large-Scale Production, Cambridge, MA: Productivity Press, 1988.

Schniederjans, M. J., *Topics in Just-In-Time Management*, Needham Heights, MA: Allyn and Bacon, 1993.

Schniederjans, M. J. and Olson, J. R., *Advanced Topics in Just-In-Time Management*, Westport, CT: Quorum Books, 1999.

Schonberger, R. J., Japanese Manufacturing Techniques: Nine Hiddent Lessons in Simplicity, New York: The Free Press, 1982.

Schonberger, R. J., World Class Manufacturing: The Lessons of Simplicity Applied, New York: The Free Press, 1986.

Smaros, J. and Holmstrom, J., "Viewpoint: Reaching the Consumer Through E-grocery VMI," *International Journal of Retail and Distribution Management*, Vol. 28, No. 2, 2000, pp. 55–61.

Swamidass, P. M. ed., *Encyclopedia of Production and Manufacturing Management*, Boston, MA: Kluwer Academic Publishers, 2000.

Vlosky, R., "E-business in the Forest Products Industry," *Forest Products Journal*, Vol. 49, No. 10, 1999, pp. 12–22.

Womack, J. and Jones, D., Lean Thinking: Banish Waste and Create Wealth in Your Corporation, New York: Simon and Schuster, 1996.

Chapter 8   E-COMMERCE AND QUALITY MANAGEMENT

Learning Objectives

After completing this chapter, you should be able to:

Define and describe quality management, its basic purpose, philosophies, and methodologies.

Explain what "Pareto Analysis" seeks to achieve in quality management.

Explain how a "Cause and Effect Chart" and an "SPC Chart" helps in quality management.

Describe JIT quality management principles.

Describe lean management attributes on quality.

Explain why quality management is important for e-commerce operations.

Explain how "benchmarking" can be implemented in e-commerce operations.

Explain why it is important that e-commerce information technology be integrated to support quality management activities.

Describe the determinates of service quality and how the "value chain" can be used to support quality management activities.

Describe a procedure for implementing a quality management program in service operations.

Overview of This Chapter

This chapter presents the subject of quality management in an e-commerce context. The chapter presents a brief overview of the basics of quality management as they are applied in both service and manufacturing operations. The chapter then explains why quality management principles are important for e-commerce business operations. Finally, the chapter concludes with a discussion on a series of research articles that describe how quality management research should be used to achieve successful e-commerce operations.

What is Quality Management?

The concept of quality means different things to different people. Quality can be user-based focusing on what the consumer sees and feels they are receiving when they consume a product. Quality can also be product-based focusing on measurable standards and attributes of what a product should deliver to its consumer.

Quality standards (sometimes referred to as *quality targets*) are the stated quality goals that managers seek to achieve in manufactured and service products. Quality standards are derived from "quality specifications." *Quality specifications* can be defined as the range of acceptability in product variation that consumers expect of products and that producers set as quality targets that they will achieve in a cost efficient manner. Quality specifications are derived from a product's "design quality" and "conformance quality." *Design quality* is the inherent value of the product to the consumer in the market place, which includes such product dimensions as durability, response, aesthetics, features, performance, reputation, and reliability. *Conformance quality* is the degree to which product design specifications are achieved. For example, how close a soup manufacturer comes in filling a 12 ounce can with exactly 12 ounces of soup is a conformance quality measurable standard. Insuring design quality and conformance quality is what "quality management" is all about.

Quality management, also called *total quality management*, is a combined philosophical and methodological approach to insure that the products and services an organization offers satisfies its customer's expectations by meeting or exceeding quality standards. Some of the many currently used philosophical components of quality management are listed and briefly described in Table 1 and methodological components of quality management are listed in Table 2.

As illustrated by the Taguchi methods, quality management no longer uses static standards or specifications for quality but dynamic ones that are constantly improving and increasing the level of quality standards to meet the higher expectations of today's e-commerce consumers. Embodying the dynamic nature of modern management, *Just-In-Time* (JIT) principles and *lean management* are ideal philosophical approaches to quality management. As previously discussed in prior chapters *JIT management* is an OM philosophical strategy for minimizing waste in production operations (Schniederjans and Olson 1999, p. 3). Its original principle-driven philosophy in quality management focus on the shop-floor level of operations is no longer limited to any particular area within e-commerce operations but can be applied to the entire e-business operation. Some of these JIT quality management principles are presented in Table 3.

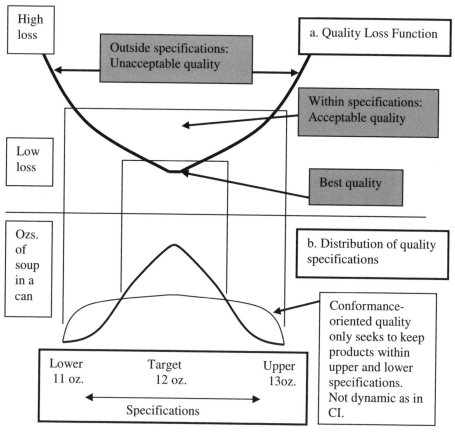

Figure 1. Taguchi quality loss function

Table 1. Philosophical components of quality management

Philosophical component	Description
Continuous improvement (CI)	CI advocates a never-ending process of continuous improvement in employees, equipment, inventory, suppliers, and procedures. The objective is product and service perfection, and is based on the notion that every aspect of the organization can be improved. The Japanese calls CI programs *kaizen*, others call it *zero-defects* and *six sigma* programs. Here quality management is a process of setting and achieving ever-higher goals.

(Continued)

Table 1. (Continued)

Philosophical component	Description
Quality at the source	The concept requires all partners in business supply chain and production processing (i.e., vendors, employees, distributors, etc.) to take responsibility for insuring that output meets or exceeds quality specifications. Ideally this helps the organization achieve zero defects throughout the production process.
Employee empowerment	This philosophic advocates the delegation of responsibility and authority for quality to all employees. The logic here is that employees are nearest to the product or service being delivered and are in a better position to identify and correct quality problems if they have the authority and responsibility to do so. One approach to accomplishing this is through *quality circles* (i.e., a group of employees who meet regularly with a facilitator to study, identify, and resolve quality related problems).
Benchmarking	This approach involves selecting a best performance quality standard for products, services, costs, or practices that represents what the best organization in an industry has achieved. This "best performance" is then used by other organizations as a targeted quality goal or benchmark to achieve.
Taguchi quality concepts	These concepts are focused on the identification and elimination of variance in production processes that lead to poor quality. Taguchi proposed a relationship of quality conformance to quality loss of profit due to poor quality. The idea of a Taguchi *quality loss function* (in Figure 1a) is based on the logic that the less the quality the more the producer stands to lose (i.e., lost customers, rework, scrap, etc.). As shown in Figure 1b, quality targets and specifications once stated in a conformance-oriented organization focuses on conforming to upper and lower limits. This does not motivate improvement in quality, it only encourages consistently to a stated acceptable level of quality. Taguchi methods seek the dynamic elimination of variation from the target specification. This results in continuous improvement (CI) and in the longer-term better product quality results.
International quality standards	The International Standards Organization (ISO) developed the ISO9000 and ISO14000 certification process that certifies a consistency in the way quality is measured and reported for manufacturers and service organizations. This system is used to help international organizations better compare one countries product quality from another. The attainment of the ISO certification insures consumers with a consistency of quality measures that can be easily compared from one country's manufacturing or service operation to another.

Table 1. (Continued)

Philosophical component	Description
Shingo system	This approach involves the designing of systems to insure a fail-safe procedure is in place. Sometimes called *poka-yoke systems*, this philosophy seeks to build into the operating systems safe guards that prevent poor quality. That might mean equipment with automatic switches that shut down if poor quality is detected, component parts engineered so they can only be assembled in the right way by employees, and kitting parts together in sets so assembly is insured of correct quantities.
Quality function deployment (QFD)	QFD involves the use of *inter-functional teams* that combines employees from manufacturing, design engineering, and marketing to incorporate what the customer feels is important in terms of product quality. The customer information is translated by marketing into engineering and manufacturing goals that produce a product that maximizes customer expectations.

Table 2. Quality management methodologies

Methodology	Description
Statistical quality control (SQC)	• Sampling plans used to screen incoming and outgoing product quality. Sampling plans are often used in situations where the volume of goods is so great that 100 percent inspections are impractical. • *Statistical process control* (SPC) charts used to monitor ongoing processing quality. There are many different types of control charts but all have the basic characteristics as those presented in Figure 2 (See Kim and Schniederjans 2000).
Check sheets	As shown in Figure 3, a check sheet can be used to tally the observed defects found in people, products, or processes. Check sheets can also be used to insure quality by listing the items that must be included in a service product and require employees to check them off. An example of this is pilots using check sheets for each take-off and landing to insure that all the steps in delivering these critical service products are achieved.
Pareto analysis	As shown in Figure 4, this type of analysis requires the identification of quality problems and their frequency of occurrence. In the figure the defects are listed (as A, B, C, D) and their frequency of occurrence is shown as a distribution. Pareto logic suggests that the more frequent the occurrence of the problem, the more effort should be devoted to its resolution. So Pareto analysis seeks to prioritize the effort to resolving the more frequently occurring problems first, the second more frequent will be solved second, and so on.

(Continued)

Table 2. (Continued)

Cause and effect diagrams	As shown in Figure 5, this graphic aid lists possible causes of quality problems in a diagram that is developed for each production process or product. Over time when quality problems are observed, the diagram can be used to tract back through the five possible contributing factors of materials, methods, environment, human resources, and technology to more easily fine the possible causes of the observed poor quality. These diagrams are also referred to as *Ishikawa diagrams* and *fish-bone charts*.

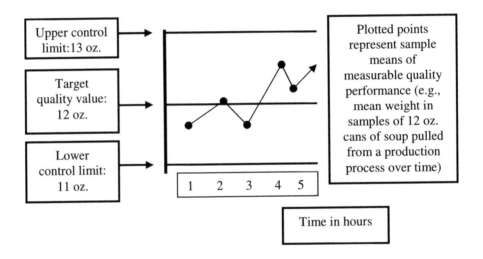

Figure 2. Quality methodologies: Statistical process control chart

Service product defective	Agent 1	Agent 2	Agent 3	Agent 4
Did not greet customer	//	////	/	/
Failed to explain services	/	///	////	
Failed to offer expected service	//	//	/	/
Etc.				

Figure 3. Quality methodologies: Check sheet

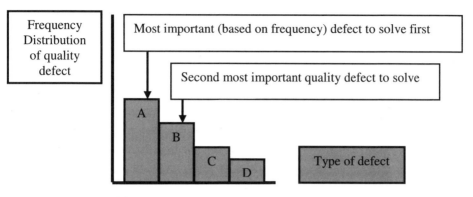

Figure 4. Quality methodologies: Pareto chart

CAUSES: Numerous causal factors to poor quality are identified over time and listed in the diagram below as represented by arrows in each of the five areas. These can then be reviewed each time poor quality is observed as possible causal factors in any particular product or service quality problem.

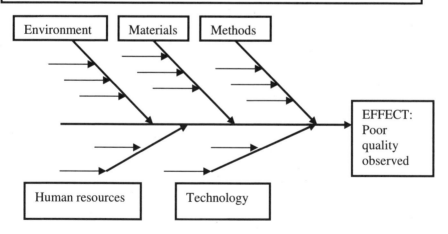

Figure 5. Quality methodologies: Causes and effect diagram

Table 3. JIT Quality management principles

JIT quality principle	Description
Use fail-safe automated technology	Where automated technology can be cost-justified, it should be employed to insure consistency in product or service quality. Also, equipment usage (i.e., the right wrench for the right bolt) and design elements (i.e., the right bolts for the right screw) should be engineered into the product to prevent employee error.
Seek to empower employees	Give personnel to be responsible and have the authority to control production quality. Encourage them to suggest and fix quality problems that they identify. Install warning systems (i.e., buzzers, lights, etc.) to permit employees to bring to the attention of management quality problems when observed.
Maintain 100 percent quality inspection	During the production process, at the various stages of WIP, have employees perform quality checks to identify defects early in the production process, saving later wasted effort in scrap and labor in final product inspection. The result will be that all products (i.e., 100 percent) will be inspected in this way even if a final quality check is not required.
Use statistical quality control	Use SQC charts to monitor quality during the production process. Use the charts to anticipate and identify problems rather than just for quality conformance goals. The goal here is to eliminate sources of product process variation to continually reduce them and in turn continually improve product quality consistency.
Visibility management	Areas of visibility management in quality include: simplification (keep only what is needed at work stations and remove seldom used equipment making it easier to do the right thing), organization (designate specific locations for everything in work areas to avoid losing equipment and using the wrong tool), and cleanliness (keep everything clean to avoid soiling or damaging products). You also want to keep quality performance information available for all employees to see.
Maintain technology	Give all operators of technology the responsibility for maintaining and reporting on equipment performance. Require operators to perform some of the routine and preventative maintenance on technology.

Table 3. (Continued)

JIT quality principle	Description
Seek to continuously identify and correct all quality related problems	One of the reasons why continuous improvement (CI) programs exist today is because of JIT quality principles. By empowering employees to continuously identify and suggest solutions for quality problems in products, processes, and materials, a company's finished product will continuously improve in quality.

As stated in prior chapters, *lean management*, is an outgrowth of the JIT principles (Swamidass 2000, pp. 346–352). Some of the attributes credited to lean management related to quality management are listed in Table 4 (Heizer and Render 2001, p. 530; Swamidass 2000, p. 351).

Table 4. Lean management attributes on quality

Related area	Attribute
Quality	Build systems to reduce quality errors in production processing. Seek to produce a perfect product every time. Use statistical processing charts and all quality control methods to monitor and identify areas where quality can be improved. Use JIT quality management principles.
Visual management	Make quality very easy to observe using charting methods to display and monitor quality performance.
Production processes	Seek to minimize or eliminate all non-value added activities including labor and scrap related to poor quality parts or materials, and labor and scrap related to returned goods because of poor quality. Seek to continuously improve all production systems to produce increased quality products.
Human resources	Seek to empower all employees by education on quality principles and methodologies.

Both JIT management and lean management are ideal philosophies for quality management in e-commerce operations. As will be seen in the following sections, e-commerce operations are implementing these very principles to achieve business performance success.

Why is Quality Management So Important for E-Commerce?

In one of the first theoretical papers on the development of e-commerce activities in manufacturing, Nembhard *et al.* (2000) outline a framework for all subsequent research in e-commerce. Included in this framework is quality engineering, which involves the application of quality management principles and methodologies, previously discussed in this chapter. Similarly in a study by Bhatt and Emdad (2001) the authors outline a model for e-commerce that allows the application of JIT and lean management philosophies and methods to eliminate waste and improve product value to customers. Both studies clearly show the critical success role that quality plays in present and future e-commerce.

Fortunately e-commerce operations are uniquely positioned to more easily perform quality management tasks. Finch (1999) demonstrated how manufacturers could dip into customer Internet conversations during e-commerce activities to obtain valuable product and service quality information. Chang and Visser (1998) also demonstrated how customers could be involved in product quality decisions while the manufacturing of ordered products is being planned and produced, and even after production in a vendor's warehousing facility.

To legitimize the application of JIT and lean management there has to be a clear opportunity to improve in e-commerce operations. The opportunities to reduce the costs of quality include (Chase *et al.* 2001, pp. 268–270; Heizer and Render 2001, pp. 172–173):

1. Internal organization failure costs: these are the costs incurred during the transformation process of goods while they are WIP, including scrap, rework from customer returns, and repair of items returned.

2. External organization failure costs: these are the costs incurred as a result of poor quality reaching the customer, including the labor to handle complaints, warranty replacements, lost customers due to poor quality, and the loss of goodwill.

3. Prevention costs: these are the costs that are associated with reducing the opportunity or potential for poor quality, including the costs of running quality training programs, quality improvement programs, and quality consultants.

4. Appraisal costs: these are the costs related to evaluating and identifying products, processes, services, and component parts for possible poor quality, including inspection quality labor costs (i.e., employees or staff that perform quality inspections), materials testing costs, and product reliability testing costs.

Depending on the type of e-commerce operation (i.e., service or manufacturing), these costs can be considerable. Developing a strategy of quality improvement through the use of JIT and lean management principles can reduce these quality-related costs. This reduction in costs can in turn help an organization achieve a competitive advantage, and by lowering product costs to the consumer in the longer-term due to the quality cost reductions a larger market share is the logical outcome.

Benchmarking for E-Commerce Business Operations and Supply Chain Quality

A very important critical success factor (CSF) in e-commerce operations is an organization's supply chain (as discussed in Chapter 3). Using JIT or lean management approaches to reducing waste in a supply chain can have substantial benefits and lead to a competitive advantage, if and only if, a firm can identify specific areas in their supply chain in which improvement by waste reduction can take place. Shah and Singh (2001) and Heizer and Render (2001, pp. 449–450) suggest that benchmarking can be used to improve supply chain performance. A suggested procedure for benchmarking includes the following steps (Shah and Singh, 2001; Heizer and Render 2001, pp. 176–177; Chase *et al.*, 2001, pp. 271–273):

1. Establish a benchmarking team to oversee the implementation of the benchmarking process. Often a part of a continuous improvement (CI) program, benchmarking requires oversight to insure success. The team should be guided by supervisors and contain employees from the same areas where process change will take place. This might mean that supply chain partners (inside and outside of the firm) and internal organization distribution and transportation personnel should be a part of the team. The teams should also include technical specialists (i.e., industrial management or quality engineers) who can help to plan the implementation of the processes that will be changed.

2. Identify the processes requiring improvement. One of the best ways to do this step is by using process performance measures for business operations, like those presented in Table 5. Measuring an organization's supply chain can require unique formulas. Some internal organization supply chain measures of management efficiency can include those presented in Table 6. These formulas provide a quick comparative set of measures on operations and supply chain process performance.

3. Identify "best performance" process measures. Benchmarking requires the identification of a company whose process performance is the "best" in the industry. Some of these firms can be identified by reviewing research reports in the literature (i.e., journal publications, trade magazines, association publications, etc.). There are hundreds of sources for this information online (see www.bettermanagement.com or www.industryweek.com).

4. Collect data on current operations and supply chain activities and perform comparative analysis. Using the formulas in Tables 5 and 6, as well as other measures a current status measurement should be made. These measures can then be compared with those "best performance" benchmarks from an industry leader for differences. The amount of difference defines the Pareto Analysis ranking of importance (i.e., the greater the difference, the important that process performance area is to be improved).

5. Establish a set of recommended process changes. Long-term and short-term changes should be defined and multiple strategies suggested for there implementation.

6. Follow-up. To insure the successfulness of this type of program, visual management techniques should be employed. Performance measures that helped to identify operations problems, both current and proposed should be posted where related personnel can see them. As progress is may toward the stated benchmark goals management should communicate the progress and continue to offer suggestions on approaches to improvement. Also, updating of "best performance" measures should take place periodically as quality standards change over time.

A benchmarking program is not a one-time process improvement activity, but is meant as a long-term program of CI. It is a program of incremental improvement toward meeting, and perhaps beating, quality expectations of e-commerce customers.

Integration Strategy for E-Commerce Technology and Quality Management

In a study by Dewhurst *et al.* (1999) and another by Zsidisin *et al.* (2000) the connection between information technology (IT) investments to support e-commerce and quality management was investigated. What both studies showed was that a strategy for the integration of all IT was necessary to successfully support a quality management program.

Table 5. Operations process performance measures

Related process area	Formula
Operation time	Setup time (i.e., time required to set a job or a service up) + Run time (i.e., time it takes to complete a job or a service)
	Example: An e-commerce manufacturer needs to setup cells for each batch of products they produce. To arrange tools and equipment at a workstation requires a setup time for Product A of 10 minutes. If a batch of 10 units of Product A takes 65 minutes of production time, the operation time for the batch is 75 minutes (i.e., 65+10). The smaller this time measure the better.
Throughput time	Average time for a unit of product to move through a system or average time to deliver a service product (This includes both processing time and time spent waiting in the system for processing.)
	Example: An e-commerce insurance company must process insurance forms. An insurance form must be processed by three separate individuals, one at time, taking an average of 4 minutes each for processing each form. It also takes a total of 3 additional minutes of transmittal time to move the form between the three offices. So the throughput time is 15 minutes (i.e., 4+4+4+3). The smaller this time measure the better.
Velocity	Throughout time/Value-added time (i.e., time for only those activities that add value to the finished product)
	Example: In the insurance form example above the value added time is just the 12 minutes the staff is performing their tasks. So the velocity is 1.25 (i.e., 15/12). The closer this ratio is to 1 the better.
Efficiency	Actual output/Standard output (i.e., number of units of product expected or demanded by management)
	Example: An e-retailer expects to sell 500 units per hour of operation. During one day the average actual output per hour was 525 units. So the efficiency ratio is 1.05 (i.e., 525/500). The larger this ratio is the better.

(Continued)

Table 5. (Continued)

Related process area	Formula
Productivity	Output (in any economic measure, including units, time, or dollars) /Input (in any economic measure, including units, time, or dollars) Example: An e-lawyer agency delivered 1,000 hours of billable service to its clients in a single day. The actual labor hours spent in delivering those billable hours were only 900 hours. So the productivity ratio is 1.11 (i.e., 1,000/900). The larger this ratio is the better.
Utilization	Actual time in use/Total time available Example: An e-travel agency is open 40 hours a weeks to do business. In one particular week only 30 hours of the time clients where actually being processed. So the utilization ratio is only 0.75 (i.e., 30/40). The larger this ratio is the better.
Cycle time	Average time between successive completions of a product Example: An e-travel agency takes on average 17 minutes to process a typical customer's travel airline bookings online. So the cycle time for an individual customer is 17 minutes. The smaller this value is the better.

Table 6. Supply chain performance measures

Related process area	Formula
Cost of holding inventory (CHI)	$CHI = I * ICC$ Where: I is total cost of inventory (including raw materials, WIP, and finished goods); ICC is the inventory holding cost percentage or the percentage of costs allocated to carrying inventory in stock. Example: A e-commerce manufacturing company has a total investment of $1.2 million in all of its inventory throughout its supply chain. The company estimates that the costs of carrying or holding this inventory represents 5 percent of its total cost per year. So, the CHI is $60,000 (i.e., 1.2*0.05). The smaller this value the better managed the supply chain.

Table 6. (Continued)

Related process area	Formula
Internal supply chain management costs (ISCMC)	$ISCMC = DC * CHI$ Where: *DC* is the total distribution costs per year. These costs can include transportation and material handling expenses. Example: Suppose in the e-commerce example above the manufacturer incurs a per year $50,000 distribution costs that include transporting, loading, unloading, and warehousing. So, the ISCMC would be $110,000 (i.e., 50,000+60,000). The smaller this value the better managed the supply chain.
Internal supply chain inefficiency ratio (ISCIR)	$ISCIR = ISCMC/NS$ Where: *NS* is the net sales per year. Example: Suppose in the e-commerce example above the manufacturer has had $12 million is net sales for the year. So, the ISCIR is 0.009 (i.e., 110,000/12,000,000). The smaller this value the better managed the supply chain.

To develop such a strategy Dewhurst *et al.* (1999) explained that prior research had consistently revealed the need for several organization change dimensions to be in place. These dimensions included:

The need for top management support in making the IT changes.
A culture of change for customers, suppliers, and the workforce to support the IT changes.
Employee involvement and empowerment present to make the changes possible.
The use of product design processes that could absorb the changes.

In addition a number of quality management related issues were also reported as necessary in the integration process. These quality issues included:

1. Quality data and reporting capacities
2. Benchmarking
3. The use of statistical process control (SPC) methods

4. Clearly defined role for the quality department
5. Quality improvement rewards for employees
6. Supplier focus on quality
7. Statistical measurement and feedback
8. Employee involvement in quality programs

Dewhurst *et al.* (1999) felt that these quality management issues could be supported by IT and were related to its successfulness in supporting the organization as a whole. Similarly Zsidisin *et al.* (2000) looked at the same relationships but for an e-commerce application in a service industry. They found that investments in Web-based IT to support the service quality substantially enhanced quality dimensions including competence, reliability, responsiveness, access, credibility, and security. They also found that by integrating their data base system into the Web e-commerce activities they were able to capture quality information that could be used for CI programs. This was particularly important in OM activities of redesigning Web sites, delivering their service products online to their customers, in forecasting future customer e-commerce demand, and improving the perceived reputation of the service organization.

E-commerce Value Chain and Quality Management

As Bhatt and Emdad (2001) suggest a value chain for e-commerce or any operation provides a structure that links the activities an organization performs to create value for customers and profits for the firm. The core activities in any value chain includes: inbound logistics, operations, outbound logistics, marketing and sales, and service. While most manufacturing organizations deal with tangible products, many e-commerce organizations are more in the business of providing a service information product or the location and delivery service of a tangible product. As such, most e-commerce operations are more focused on service quality. And as noted by Liao *et al.* (2001) service quality is a critical factor in e-commerce success.

To enhance e-commerce service quality we must know what determines service quality. What are the determinates of service quality? Depending on the type of e-commerce operations service quality can have several determinates as presented in Table 7. As noted in Table 7 there are a number of OM quality considerations that should be examined in light of improving the quality of service products. It should be noted that e-commerce has both limitations and advantages over traditional brick-and-mortar operations in selling products. For example, the sensorial appeal quality determinate in a brick-and-mortar operation allows for additional considerations that may play an important factor in products such as "odor" in helping to sell chocolate or "feel" to help sell soft clothing. Yet, successful e-commerce operations can exploit other unique characteristics of the e-commerce shopping experience to help make a sale. The ability of just pointing and clicking online to purchase, package, and deliver chocolates from firms like www.Godiva.com the chocolatier adds substantially to the convenience quality of the e-commerce transaction. Also, for example, 3-dimensional software imaging allows universities to display their campuses in the most ideal way to help motivate perspective students to experience a tour that physically might be unreasonably long when undertaken in a more traditional manner. This illustrates the idea of finding points in the value chain that e-commerce can uniquely exploit and use them to over come other areas in the chain where value can not be enhanced or is at a disadvantage to the brick-and-mortar operation.

Table 7. Determinates of service quality

Determinate	Description	OM quality consideration
Conveni-ence	Ease of access to service.	Insuring little or no downtime of online operations. Maintaining technology and personnel at all times to process customer orders and requests.
Credibility	Trustworthiness and honesty in product.	Long-term consistency of service product delivery. Service quality follow-up in cases of failure and warranty compliance.
Competence	Possessing the skills and knowledge to deliver the product.	Quality training and testing of personnel.
Communi-cation	Keeping customers informed in style, language, and capacity they can understand. Can involve the ability to convey the nature of the service, its costs, and the ability to deal with cognitive dissonance in Web presentation.	Optimum design of Web site to attract and impart information for to the customer. The ability to permit different versions to accommodate differences in age, cultural, and language uses.

(Continued)

Table 7. (Continued)

Determinate	Description	OM quality consideration
Responsive-ness	Timeliness of service.	Staffing to permit prompt access and forecasting personnel scheduling needs to deal with service variation over time.
Reliability	Consistency and dependability of service performance.	Quality control conformance on employee delivery of service product.
Courtesy	Respect, consideration, and friendliness of service provider.	Quality training and personnel screening to insure quality conformance.
Security/Safety	Avoidance of risk as perceived by the customer.	Design of Web site to assure user of security on online transactions. Software acquisition and implementation that protects users in online transactions. Implementation of firewalls where necessary to protect customer data.
Sensorial appeal	The ability of the product or service to be perceived as meeting a customer's need.	Providing quality appearance and sound information to customers, which might require special imaging and sound conveyance software.
Flexibility	The ability to meet customization requirements of customers.	Building flexibility in equipment and technology to permit variety of production capabilities. Diverse training of personnel to enhance their capabilities to provide varied services as requested.

To operationalize a quality service program requires a careful examination of all aspects of an organization's value chain in an effort to develop a quality competitive advantage. A procedural framework for this program is presented in Figure 6. The outcome of such a program is usually the development of a quality competitive advantage.

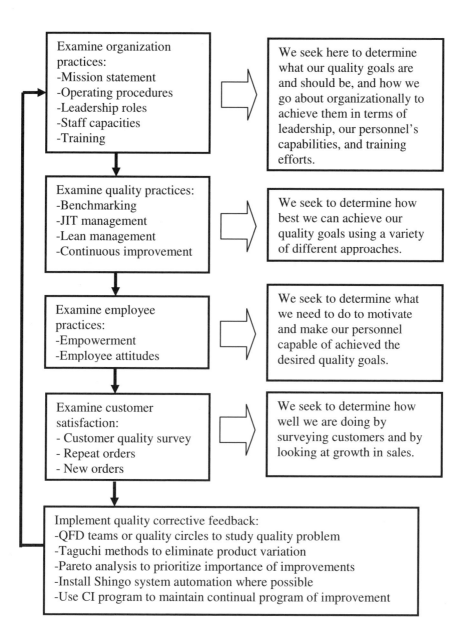

Figure 6. A procedural framework for a service quality program

Summary

This chapter begins with a description of the basic ideas and principles that are used in quality management, including those of JIT and lean management. A number of suggestions from research studies for conducting quality management in e-commerce operations are also described. These suggestions include benchmarking, computer integration, and value chain management in e-commerce settings.

Some of the basic ideas of JIT and lean management proposed decades ago by Schonberger (1982, 1986) and others (Monden 1983, 1993; Ohno 1988; Womack and Jones 1996) are as critical today for establishing a competitive advantage in quality as they were years ago. (For a basic review of JIT principles see Schniederjans (1993) and for a review of more advanced JIT topics see Schniederjans and Olson (1999).)

◆ Review Terms

Appraisal costs
Benchmarking
Cause and effect diagrams
Check sheets
Conformance quality
Continuous improvement (CI)
Cost of holding inventory (CHI)
Critical success factor (CSF)
Cycle time
Design quality
Efficiency
Employee empowerment
External organization failure costs
Fish-bone charts
Information technology (IT)
Inter-functional teams
Internal organization failure costs
Internal supply chain inefficiency ratio (ISCIR)
Internal supply chain management costs (ISCMC)
International quality standards

International standards organization (ISO)
Ishikawa diagrams
JIT management
Just-in-time (JIT)
Kaizen
Lean management
Operation time
Pareto analysis
Prevention costs
Poka-yoke systems
Process performance measures
Productivity
Quality
Quality at the source
Quality circles
Quality engineering
Quality function deployment (QFD)
Quality loss function
Quality management
Quality specifications
Quality standards

Quality targets	Statistical quality control (SQC)
Taguchi quality methods	Total quality management
Throughput time	Utilization
Six sigma	Value chain
Shingo system	Velocity
Statistical process control (SPC)	Zero-defect

♦ Discussion Questions

1. How are "design quality" and "conformance quality" related to "quality specifications"?
2. What are the philosophical components of "quality management"?
3. What is CI? How is important in quality management?
4. What is "quality at the source"?
5. How is the Taguchi "quality loss function" related to "conformance quality"?
6. What does a "Pareto Analysis" do to help a quality management program?
7. What are the "JIT quality principles"?
8. What are the "lean management" attributes associated with quality management?
9. Why is "quality management" important in e-commerce?
10. What steps might you take to implement a "benchmarking" program in e-commerce?
11. What change dimensions are necessary for an integrated e-commerce technology strategy?
12. What are the determinates of "service quality"?

♦ Questions

1. Why is quality so important to e-commerce operations?
2. List three philosophical components of quality management. How do they actually help improve product quality?
3. If one quality problem occurs three times a week and another quality problem occurs only once a month, which problem would we address first under Pareto logic? Why?
4. In reference to Figure 1, why does Taguchi quality management find "acceptable quality" unacceptable? Explain?
5. Could the quality method of "check sheets" be used to monitor quality for a baseball player in their game performance (i.e., hits, runs, errors)? Explain.

6. How is the philosophical component "Shingo System" related to the JIT quality principle of "Using Fail-safe Automated Technology"? Explain.
7. Which of the JIT quality principles are pretty much the same as the lean management attributes related to quality management?
8. What is the difference in the Operations Process Performance Measure ratios of "Efficiency" and "Productivity"?
9. What quality related management issues have to be in place in order to support a successful IT integration of e-commerce technology?
10. List three determinates of service quality. What OM quality considerations must be made to seek improved service quality?

♦ **Problems**

1. Units of product can be produced in batches of 200 economically. What is the "operation time" for the e-commerce manufacturer if it takes 2.5 hours to setup the equipment in production cells for each batch and it takes 80 minutes of production time to complete the batch? The manufacturer installs a CI program and can now achieve an operation time of 75 minutes for the batch of 200 products. If the benchmark time is only 50 minutes, is the manufacturing improving or not? Explain.
2. An e-retailer takes orders online. An order taker first takes the order from the e-mail and converts it into an order form. An order picker picks and packs each order. A shipping clerk weighs and ships the item. The average time the order takes is 3.8 minutes. The order picker takes an average of 7 minutes to pick up the order and the supper takes an average of 3.6 minutes to process the order for shipping. What is the "throughput time" for orders? If the benchmark for this throughput time is 20 minutes, how is e-retailer doing in terms of throughput time? Due to a warehouse configuration change, the order picker's average time increased by 18%. What is the new throughput and how does it compare to the benchmark?
3. In an e-procurement organization, purchasing agents spend 5.3 hours a day doing tasks related to acquiring goods and 1.2 hours a day looking up phone numbers. What is the "velocity" of this job? Is it good? Explain.
4. An information facilitator e-commerce operation for automobiles has an expected 45,000 e-mail hits a day from customers wanting to learn the location of where automobiles are for sale. During one day the actual number of customers seeking information was 77,337. What is the efficiency

ratio of this operation? Can you say if the resulting ratio is good or not? Explain.

5. The line items in an e-commerce warehouse order picking operation are 10,000 per day. Today the order pickers picked 13,225 line items. What is the productivity ratio for this day's order pickers? In general, is the resulting ratio a good or bad productivity measures result? Explain.

6. If it takes an average of 3 minutes to process an online customer order and 2 more minutes on average to have an automated warehouse process the order, what is the "cycle time" for completely processing the order? If the benchmark time for this type of business is only 15 minutes, can we say if they are improving or not? Explain.

7. A small e-retailer who distributes goods out of their home incurs total shipping bill from a U.S. post office, UPS and Federal Express of $12,000. The total cost of inventory is $58,000 a year and the inventory holding cost percentage is 1%. What is this e-retailers ISCMC? If the benchmark cost for this size of business is only $12,000 per year, are they improving or not? Explain.

8. If an e-commerce operation has an ISCMC of $2.8 million and net sales of $55 million, what is their ISCIR? If the benchmark ratio for this type of business is only 0.09, can we say if they are improving or not? Explain.

9. Given the following data, which wine company has the best internal supply chain inefficiency ratio?

Measure	e-Booze	e-Buzz	e-Wine
Cycle Time	38 minutes	415 minutes	52 minutes
Cost of Inventory	$92,000	$1.5 m	$172,385
Utilization	.75	.98	1.3
% of costs allocated to carrying inventory in stock	.05	.09	.13
Productivity	1.11	.75	3.25
Total distribution cost	$8,000	$23,998	$13,226
Net Sales	$1.75 m	$32 m	$8.21 m
Velocity	1.08	.98	.55

References

Bhatt, G. and Emdad, A., "An Analysis of the Virtual Value Chain in Electronic Commerce," *Logistics Information Management*, Vol. 14, Nos. 1-2, 2001, pp. 78–84.

Chang, S. and Visser, J., "A Framework of Distributed Quality Control," *Industrial Engineering*, Vol. 35, Nos. 1-2, 1998, pp. 181–184.

Chase, R. B., Aquilano, N. J. and Jacobs, F. R., *Operations Management for Competitive Advantage*. 9th ed., Boston, MA: McGraw-Hill/Irwin, 2001.

Dewhurst, F., Lorente, A. and Dale, B., "Total Quality Management and Information Technologies: An Exploration of the Issues," *International Journal of Quality an Reliability Management*, Vol. 16, No. 4, 1999, pp. 395–405.

Finch, B., "Internet Discussions as a Source for Consumer Product Customer Involvement and Quality Information: An Exploratory Study," *Journal of Operations Management*, Vol. 17, No. 5, 1999, pp. 535–557.

Heizer, J. and Render, B., *Operations Management*, 6th ed., Upper Saddle River, NJ: Prentice Hall, 2001.

Kim, G. and Schniederjans, M. J., "Use of Short-run Statistical Process Control Techniques: A Comparison of US and Japanese Manufacturing," *Mid-American Journal of Business*, Vol. 15, No. 1, 2000, pp. 21–30.

Liao, Z. and Cheung, M., "Internet-based E-shopping and Consumer Attitudes: An Empirical Study," *Information and Management*, Vol. 3, 2001, pp. 299–306.

Monden, Y., The Toyota Management System: Linking the Seven Key Functional Areas, Cambridge, MA: Productivity Press, 1993.

Monden, Y., *The Toyota Production System: Practical Approach to Production Management*, Atlanta, GA: Industrial Engineering and Management Press, 1983.

Nembhard, H., Shi, L. and Park, C., "Real Option Models for Managing Manufacturing System Changes in the New Economy," *The Engineering Economist*, Vol. 45, No. 3, 2000, pp. 232–257.

Ohno, T., Toyota Production System: Beyond Large-Scale Production, Cambridge, MA: Productivity Press, 1988.

Schniederjans, M. J., *Topics in Just-In-Time Management*, Needham Heights, MA: Allyn and Bacon, 1993.

Schniederjans, M. J. and Olson, J. R., *Advanced Topics in Just-In-Time Management*, Westport, CT: Quorum Books, 1999.

Schonberger, R. J., Japanese Manufacturing Techniques: Nine Hiddent Lessons in Simplicity, New York: The Free Press, 1982.

Schonberger, R. J., World Class Manufacturing: The Lessons of Simplicity Applied, New York: The Free Press, 1986.

Shah, J. and Singh, N., "Benchmarking Internal Supply Chain Performance: Development of a Framework," *The Journal of Supply Chain Management*, Winter 2001, pp. 37–47.

Swamidass, P. M. ed., *Encyclopedia of Production and Manufacturing Management*, Boston, MA: Kluwer Academic Publishers, 2000.

Womack, J. and Jones, D., Lean Thinking: Banish Waste and Create Wealth in Your Corporation, New York: Simon and Schuster, 1996.

Zsidisin, G.A., Jun, M. and Adams, L.L., "The Relationship Between Information Technology and Service Quality in the Dual-direction Supply Chain," *International Journal of Service Industry Management*, Vol. 11, No. 4, 2000, pp. 312–328.

Chapter 9   E-COMMERCE AND HUMAN RESOURCE MANAGEMENT

Learning Objectives

After completing this chapter, you should be able to:

Describe and define "human resource management".

Describe and explain the relationship between Just-in-time and human resource management.

Understand the human resource management in business process reengineering.

Explain how human resource management influences globalization.

Explain why human resource management is so important in e-commerce era.

Describe how to overcome complexity in e-commerce operations.

Describe human resource strategy for e-commerce operations.

Understand global e-commerce concept and some of its barriers to success.

Explain the concept of "virtual teamwork" and its impact on e-commerce.

Overview of This Chapter

This chapter presents the topic of human resource management (HRM) in an e-commerce setting. The chapter explains the relationships between HRM and Just-in-time management, HRM and business process reengineering, HRM and globalization. Why HRM is so important in the context of e-commerce is also discussed. Finally, the chapter concludes with the impact of virtual teamwork on e-commerce operations.

What is Human Resource Management?

Human resource management is an attempt to resolve the failures of personnel management, human relations, and industrial relations and to provide direction as to how organizations should handle people so that organizational effectiveness and individual satisfaction will be maximized (Marciano 1995). Luthans (1998) defined the *human resource management* (HRM) as the collection of activities of attracting, developing, and retaining people with the necessary knowledge and skills to achieve an organization's objectives. According to (Huselid 1997), HRM involves designing and implementing a set of internally consistent policies and practices that ensure a firm's human capital (employees' collective knowledge, skills, and abilities) contributes to the achievement of its business objectives. It is evident that people provide organizations with an important source of sustainable competitive advantage and that the effective management of human capital, not physical capital, is the ultimate determinant of organizational performance (Wright *et al.* 1994).

HRM practices comprise the many activities through which firms create human capital that meet these conditions. Specifically, firms can use technical HRM activities to select high-ability employees, whose talent is rare by definition, and to train employees so they have the unique skills. Strategic HRM activities, on the other hand, help a firm to ensure that its human resources are not easily imitated. Because of the social complexity and causal ambiguity inherent in strategic HRM practices such as team-based designs, empowerment, and the development of talent for the long term, competitors can neither easily copy these practices nor readily replicate the unique pool of human capital that such practices help to create.

Impact of JIT on HRM

The notion that Just-in-time (JIT) systems positively affect HRM practices is well documented in the literature (Power and Sohal 2000; Yasin *et al.* 1997; Deshpande and Golhar 1995). Schniederjans and Olson (1999) summarized top 10 ranked HRM activities of JIT manufacturing firms from a survey study by Deshpande and Golhar (1995) by combining union and non-union HRM manager rankings (see Table 1).

A recent HRM study by (Power and Sohal 2000) examined the extent and emphasis of particular HRM strategies in Australian JIT companies through an empirical survey research. The results of the study indicated that HRM in Australian JIT environments could be characterized by a stronger emphasis on a number of factors including change management, participative decision making, flexibility and multi-skilled workforce, and open and effective communication processes. What was particularly striking from this analysis was the evidence gained not only of the added emphasis on these issues in the JIT companies, but of the potential for "adding value" through combining management strategies. Table 2 shows some of the findings of this and other HRM studies.

Table 1. Important JIT workforce characteristics and rankings

Workforce characteristics	Overall ranking by HRM managers
Concern for organization's success	1
Ability to inspect work	2
Ability to work in teams	3
Worker flexibility	4
Self-disciplined	5
Communication skills	6
Multi-skilled workforce	7

Table 2. JIT HRM factors

JIT HRM factors	Results of the study
Change management	Change management plays an important rule within an organization for the success of JIT. Further analysis and comparison of this factor indicated a need for senior management to be either managing or driving this process.
Participative decision making	JIT companies were likely to be involving their workforce in the decision-making processes of the firm.
Flexibility and multi-skilled workforce	JIT firms are significantly associated with job flexibility and a multi-skilled workforce.
Open and effective communication processes	JIT companies are more inclined toward using ideas from production operators, more likely to have effective "top down" and "bottom up" communication processes and be actively working to eliminate barriers between individuals and departments.
Empowerment	It is indicated the factor of empowerment to be an important determinant within the JIT companies.

(Continued)

Table 2. (Continued)

JIT HRM factors	Results of the study
Employee development and training	JIT firms devote more resources in employee training.
Work/production teams	The contribution of team work is shown to improve operational performance in the JIT companies.
Synergies created through combined strategies	There was evidence to suggest that the combination of particular factors could significantly affect the competitive position of JIT companies. This finding supports earlier work in the auto industry identifying the need to integrate human resource systems and production strategies by using groups of interrelated and internally consistent human resource practices (MacDuffie 1995).

Drawing upon the HRM literature, Schniederjans and Olson (1999, pp. 126–133) discussed several current studies focused on HRM issues in JIT operations. Table 3 summarizes the issues discussed in their book including *teamship* (e.g., absenteeism and legal limitations), learning, empowerment, labor relations, and layout design.

Table 3. Advanced issues involving JIT and HRM

JIT HRM issues	Descriptions
JIT and *Teamship*	A well recognized characteristic of JIT operations is the use of teams of people on the shop floor (Heeley 1991). Teams encourage employee participation, help to empower employees to overcome work restrictions, help to motivate new ideas that improve production, and improve the quality of work life.
Absenteeism	Since the JIT teams were made up of full-time employees, it was also observed that they generated more team cohesion and a reduction in overall absenteeism (Conti 1996).

(Continued)

Table 3. (Continued)

JIT HRM issues	Descriptions
Legal limitations	There are certain legal ramifications (e.g., violation of work rules, etc.) in self-directed work teams in JIT production planning and control (Abraham and Spencer 1998).
JIT and Learning	Ocana and Zemel (1996) proposed a conceptual framework to address JIT learning issues. They concluded that all the JIT training in the world is useless unless learning takes place, that if the old system is working, don't fix it, that performance criteria used to judge JIT systems should be changed periodically to insure constant change taking place, and that firms sometimes adopt characteristics of JIT operations without adopting other JIT characteristics that inherently lead to sequential improvement in the operating systems.
JIT and Empowerment	Empowering employees is one of the JIT basic principles. Mullarkey et al. (1995) claimed that organizations that should take a HRM developmental approach to introducing JIT by providing the multi-skilled training and JIT education before reducing inventory will result in a better social climate for acceptance and use of JIT principles.
JIT and Labor Relations	According to Inman and Mehra (1989), US firms face the possibility of resistance by labor unions. JIT seeks the avoidance of waste, while labor unions are concerned with job security. While unions may be opposed to cross training of employees, JIT-spawned workforce reductions and an increase in productivity. Communication channels must be kept open to facilitate the flow of ideas between management and labor. Dahlem et al. (1995) observed the differences in the ways dealing with labor relations between Japan and Swedish JIT firms and recommended US firms to do whatever it took to effectively deal with labor relations.
JIT and Layout Design	The issue of visualization in JIT layout design is one of the basic principles required in JIT operations (Moden 1998). In JIT firms there are two types of visualization: immediate and long-range (Dahlem et al. 1995). Immediate visualization utilizes technologies to prominently give the current status of production line activities. These visual displays are used to allow employees to see how well their performance is matching up against the production quotes or expectations in quality. Long-range visualization involves the display of statistics, diagrams, and matrices to depict longer-term production standards and on-going production line activities, like down-time expectations and actual downtime behavior.

Business Process Reengineering (BPR) and HRM

One of the main reasons presented for the difficulty in successfully implementing business process reengineering (BPR) projects is an apparent lack of consideration towards the HRM issues (Aghassi 1994). Zucchi and Edwards (1999) examined HRM practices and some related issues facing organizations seeking to implement BPR projects. Their study included HRM issues such as the organizational structure and culture, role of managers, training, and reward systems discussed below.

1. *Organizational Structure and Culture*: BPR typically produces a flatter organization and a flatter organization means that people are given more responsibility, increased decision making capability, autonomy, and flexibility. It also permits managers to be closer to customers and have a first-hand perception of the reality of the business (Hammer and Champy 1993). The importance of organizational culture in the management of change is well documented in the literature (Grint 1997; Schein 1992). Changing values and beliefs are important aspects in any serious attempt to transform business performance. Structure and culture are closely interrelated, and so both must be considered at the same time. Changing structure without paying enough attention to an organization's values and beliefs can result in an expensive and ineffective exercise if the organizational culture does not match the different organization.

2. *The Role of Managers*: Previous studies suggest that managers in organizations that have been through a BPR project see their role as being changed, especially middle managers (Grint 1994; Hammer and Champy 1993). One of the difficulties for managers in fitting into a process orientated organization is to define exactly what they have to do in a wider and more generalist role, where they have their own performance measured with respect to how well they run a process rather than how well they run a department (Stein 1995).

3. *Team Working*: Teams are considered an important element in order to achieve all the benefits of a process-orientated organization (Davenport 1993). Davenport (1993) also stated that another benefit deriving from the use of teams is related to the improvement of the quality of the work life due to the increased possibility of social interaction.

4. *Reward system*: Both Davenport (1993) and Hammer and Champy (1993) stressed the need to compensate both workers and managers on the basis of their performance in creating value, rather than for the time they pass on the job. Hammer and Champy (1993) also emphasized the need to stop using career advancement as a reward for performance in the current job.

Table 4 summarizes the typical pattern for human resource practices in re-engineered organizations based on a study by Zucchi and Edwards (2000).

Table 4. HRM in reengineered organizations

HRM in BPR	Descriptions
Organizational structure and culture	The change has been carried out with attention to the human factor in terms of training and information given, and the creation of a system to monitor employees' behavior and attitude.
The role of managers	Managerial attitude towards BPR was favorable. The re-engineering involved a change in the managerial role towards an increased focus on performance and responsibility, managers were more accountable and more visible and at the same time they had more authority and autonomy in their job. They had to delegate more and they had to become facilitators of others' work. They had to be trained for their new role.
Team working	The re-engineered organization had instituted a training system aimed at creating a multi-skilled workforce, the use of cross-functional teams and team autonomy, but does not have a job rotation policy. The teams do not go through dedicated training, nor are there team-based financial rewards.
Reward system	In a re-engineered organization, the reward system is changed, and is more focused on performance. In addition, the career path is changed and is more a function of the skills acquired.

HRM and Globalization

HRM is evolving from solely that of a support function, characterized by compliance with external regulation regarding selection, termination, compensation, benefits administration, and labor relations to one of strategic importance which is increasingly being asked to assume important new roles that pertain to globalization (Kerr and Von Glinow 1997). These new roles include international extensions of more traditional HRM support functions such as providing country-specific knowledge of union and labor policies, legal and regulatory requirements, compensation, and benefits practices. They include preparing people for international assignments and reentry after those assignments are completed (Teagarden and Gordon 1994). HRM can be used to enhance organizational learning and to help the company build a world-class workforce (Barney 1991). Perhaps most importantly, HRM is becoming a strategic vehicle which allows firms to balance headquarters demands for global coordination or integration with subsidiary level demands for adaptation or local responsiveness (Bartlett and Ghoshal 1989). This balancing act can be seen whether the organization in question is a joint venture or some other strategic alliance, positioned off-shore or even a large domestic firm.

Teagarden and Von Glinow (1997) suggested some *international human resource management* (IHRM) best practices as following:

1. IHRM practices often vary within companies from business unit to business unit.

2. Non-cultural contextual variation inhibits the transferability of HRM practices across national boundaries.

3. Host country-specific HRM practices often vary from home country practices.

4. Country-specific practices vary based on the home country of the multi-national enterprise. Many specific HRM practices are culturally bound and thus represent culture specific phenomenon not meaningfully generalized nor benchmarked.

Why is HR Management So Important in an E-Commerce Setting?

Business organizations are in the midst of a fundamental restructuring in an e-commerce era. Old recipes for success are failing, and new ones often produce surprising results. The rules that determined value and performance in the past have changed, and leaders are struggling to guide their firms in this uncertain environment (Luftman 1999). Three main forces are driving how firms evolve. They are the application and evolution of information and communication technologies, the globalization of markets, and the development and deployment of advanced manufacturing and logistical technologies, often supported by information technologies. These interdependent forces pose formidable challenges and will radically alter the work organization in the coming decade. Technologies, such as Internet-based desktop video conferencing, application sharing, collaborative communications software, and intranets/extranets collectively are changing the way that organization members work and interact.

These and other advanced applications of information technologies (IT) are creating a rich infrastructure that is both empowering and at times overwhelming (Lucas 1999). Consider that employees can communicate more efficiently, with more individuals, across larger distances, on more complex topics, share more information, manipulate more data, and use a wider variety of media choices than ever before.

The primary way that IT has changed how employees collaborate is by facilitating richer and more complex computer-mediated interactions (Lucas 1999). For example, *desktop video conferencing* (DVC) systems provide a broader range of communications media (i.e., voice, video, and text) than either e-mail or telephones. In addition, the use of a video interface allows nonverbal cues in these interactions. These systems also provide the infrastructure to allow real-time application sharing so that participants can collaboratively view, edit, and create information. When DVC is combined with intranets/extranets and collaborative software (e.g., Lotus Notes), employees are able to work, archive, and schedule future work sessions entirely online. The end result is the recreation of the dynamics of face-to-face communication and simultaneous participation in online collaboration, using sophisticated tools to achieve this collaboration. Thus, online interactions actually provide new ways for people to collaborate beyond traditional face-to-face business meetings, telephone conferencing, and e-mail (Townsend *et al.* 1998).

This rich infrastructure allows people to collaborate effectively on complex projects even when they are not located in the same geographical area. Connection to the electronic infrastructure allows meaningful interaction across geographic distances that would have once restricted a group's interaction, or even prohibited it altogether. As such, organizational leaders have been encouraged to experiment with new structures that require geographically dispersed members to work cooperatively on a regular basis. A major outcome of connecting employees in this manner is the increasing prevalence of "virtual teams." *Virtual teams* (i.e., teams involving people who are not physically collocated) present many advantages to organizations primarily by increasing the potential talent pool for problem solving or to serve on projects, regardless of their location. At the same time, use of virtual teams eliminates the downtime and costs associated with travel to team meetings. Thus, advances in IT have changed virtual teams from a concept with limited real-world application, to a highly effective and increasingly common form of employee interaction. Finally, because *virtual teamwork* eliminates much of the downtime associated with travel and effectively increases employees' productive capacity, employees will be more likely to participate in multiple team assignments than before.

Hansen and Deimler (2001) proposed an e-commerce HRM model, namely the *business-to-employee* (B2E) model. They argued that B2E management let companies satisfy employees' needs while streamlining formerly time/labor-intensive processes and that by reducing organizational barriers, B2E enabled people to interact more along lines of work than along lines of command. A comprehensive B2E program has three components: online business processes, online people management, and online services to the workplace community (Hansen and Deimler 2001). Table 5 illustrates how to reap the benefits of B2E model. Each of the three components of B2E management offers benefits to both employees and the company. The drivers of those benefits are easier interactions and more employee self-service, mass customization and *work-life bundling* (i.e., blending work life and personal life). In general, a reduction in interaction efforts has the most influence on the business-process component, self-service and mass customization affect the people-management component, and work-life bundling affects the community-services component.

Table 5. Benefits of B2E

Facets of B2E	Benefits of B2E
Online business processes	B2E applications reduce the cost and effort associated with employees' interactions and information searches.
Online people management	Improving people management B2E gives greater freedom to employees through self-service and mass customization. Self-managed training is one example of self-service.
Online services to the workplace community	Both employees and organizations benefit from online self-service. Employees find dealing with human-resource matters online less stressful and bureaucratic than handling them in person.

Improving Organization Structure to Overcome Complexity in E-Commerce Operations

Sones (2001) stated that the explosion of Internet technology had created an e-commerce era, which old business paradigms collapsed frequently due to the complexity in e-commerce operations. For instance, systems integration in the e-commerce increases the system complexity tremendously. He argued that a long-term resolution required the ability to enhance the gains of integration while mitigating the risks of complexity. Modeling after object-oriented systems analysis and design (OOSAD) paradigm, Sones (2001) proposed an objective corporation framework to deal with the complexity issue in e-commerce operations. Figure 1 depicts the objective organization model. A bureaucracy type of organization structure is shown on the left, while the left side shows the objective organization structure comprising of a broker and administrator. The broker in the community of objective corporations fulfills many of the responsibilities delegated to the executives and senior management of a bureaucracy. The responsibilities of a broker include fostering new firms, assisting closure of obsolete firms, landing jobs, identifying and mitigating risks, dissecting tasks and assigning firms, evaluating opportunities for the community, and shepherding collaboration. The major responsibility of the administrator, as with bureaucratic middle management, is the tactical supervision of the workforce in the accomplishing of a certain task such as resolving job-related disputes, allocating resources, and synthesizing the final product. Sones (2001) claimed that objective organization model could help companies to alleviate the complexity of e-operations via the radical reengineering of organizational structuring to reap benefits of the Internet technologies.

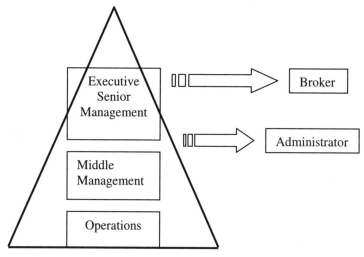

Figure 1. Objective organization model

Marchewka and Towell (2000) examined the organizational structure and strategy issues by comparing two different network relationships: hierarchical network vs. market network in an e-commerce setting based on a case study research of Amazon.com and Wallace Computing Services. Table 6 shows the market and hierarchical network strategy comparison.

Table 6. Market vs. hierarchical networks

Dimension	Market network	Hierarchy network
Network	Open network (e.g., Internet)	Closed network (e.g., proprietary)
Locus of control	Many buyers and sellers	Single seller and many buyers
Transactions	Buyers selects sellers on transaction-by-transaction basis	Buyer and seller have tightly coupled relationship
Complexity of goods or services	Low – would be difficult to communicate good's features in marketplace to adequately match needs	High – buyer familiar with goods or services of seller
Attributes of products and services	Determined by open market	Prices, quality standards, and delivery schedules are set
Relationship	Ephemeral	Based on long-term or preexisting relationship
Search and monitoring costs	On-going – must occur for each transaction	Predetermined – in-place or negotiated before hand
Loyalty	Low	High
Value	Can be different for buyers and sellers	Similar for buyers and sellers
Focus of concern	Security of transactions	Mitigation of opportunistic behaviors
Value chain	Seller involved indirectly with the value chain of the supplier	Seller involved directly with the value chain of the buyer
Switching costs	Low	High
Effect	Brokerage	Integration
Strategy	Low price	Differentiation

A Human Resource Strategy for E-Commerce

The environment facing e-commerce firms can be characterized by unpredictable and high-velocity change, where speed is one of the most important competitive advantages. The competitive environment faced by e-commerce companies requires a much more compressed time line. Hamel (1998) stated that, when time was a major resource, a firm and even an entire industry could become obsolete in six months. The rate of innovation in developing products, managing the supply chain, or building quality into products has reduced dramatically. Obviously, in such an environment, traditional strategies, cultures, and time orientation are no longer relevant.

Saltzman and Luthans (2001) explored the strategy, culture, and time orientation that influenced the speed and timing needed by companies to be successful in an e-commerce era. Speed which accounts for competitive advantage dramatically changing environment today, has completely altered the very essence of strategy, organizational culture, and time orientation. D'Aveni (1995) stated that timing is everything. Timing is characterized by rapidly escalating competition based on price-quality positioning, competition to create new know-how and establish a first mover advantage, competition to protect or invade established product or geographic markets, and competition based on deep pocket alliances.

According to Brown and Eisenhardt (1998), three strategic concepts: edge of chaos, edge of time, and time pacing become particularly relevant for firms to succeed in an e-commerce environment. Table 7 lists and describes the three strategic concepts.

Saltzman and Luthans (2001) also examined how to cope with the edge of time and time pacing through organizational culture. They argued that in order to create the flow of existing and changing competitive advantages, successful organizations develop an adaptive, flexible culture that involves participative decision making, empowerment, knowledge sharing across the boundary-less organization, team sharing of ideas, and visionary leadership. Since e-commerce is characterized by unprecedented speed, new ideas, products, and services their high-velocity, hyper-competitive environments have changed the rules of the game for high-tech firms. Organizations that successfully compete on the edge need to create an adaptable and flexible organizational culture. However, building on past experiences for established and new firms is also fundamental to creating competitive advantage. Organizational cultures based on decision-making that involves all employees who will be affected, and is especially based

Table 7. Three e-commerce strategic concepts

Strategic concept	Description
Edge of chaos	Edge of chaos is applicable to organizations that are partially structured. If an organization's structure can be characterized on one extreme as totally chaotic, then change is unlikely to happen in an uncoordinated environment. On the other hand, an organization structure that can be characterized as too settled prevents change. The middle-position environment seems the most flexible and adaptable for the appropriate level of change.
Edge of time	Edge of time is relevant to organizations that balance the need to learn from the lessons of the past, the need to carry out the operations of the present, and the need to look optimistically to the future. There are important lessons from the past, but too much reliance on the past doesn't allow the perspective of the future to take form. By the same token, too much focus on the future ignores the day-to-day operations and prevents current implementation and execution of strategies. However, keeping future perspectives in mind is necessary to envision and create change rather than just reacting to it.
Time pacing	Time pacing, is one of the most important strategies for leading in fast-changing and unstable markets of e-commerce. Time pacing is the creation of new services or the capturing of new markets in a regular, rhythmic, and proactive manner. In a company where speed and intensity are synchronized, time pacing secures a reliable rhythm for change.

on shared information and knowledge, can gain an advantage through the edge-of-time strategy.

Organizations with high variety and many opportunities to learn, and especially those with diverse teams having a variety of viewpoints, will benefit from the wide array of perspectives generated in order to create a vision (Saltzman and Luthans 2001). Companies with leaders emphasizing team goals, idea exchange, and working as a team will neither get locked on a single plan concerning the development of business nor allow the firm to play a simple reactive role to the moves of a competitor.

How E-Commerce is Altering International Service Industries

Global e-commerce (GEC) represents the real image of the free market and free traders. It means access to larger markets, mobility, and flexibility to employ workers and manufacture products anywhere using the Internet technology (Turban *et al.* 2000). The potential future for GEC's is an inevitability, however contraints exist due to language barriers, local government regulations, access limitations. Table 8 shows some to the major barriers of global e-commerce.

Table 8. Barriers of global e-commerce

Barriers to GEC	Description
Legal issues	Legal issues involve jurisdiction issues, export/import regulations and compliance, intellectual property, security, contracts, authentication procedures, privacy protection, and user technology limitations.
Market access issues	Market access is very crucial to GEC organizations. Building an IT infrastructure capable of accommodating all users and all types of data is in greatly needed.
Financial issues	Financial issues in GEC include customs and taxation, electronic payment systems, and money exchange.
Language	The language barrier between countries and regions presents a complicated challenge. The primary problems with this level of language customization are cost and speed due to translation.

Wymbs (2001) studied how e-commerce was transforming the global service industries, more specifically, explored how emerging information-centric business models are replacing legacy systems, examined how e-commerce is changing the process of services industries, and provided insights on how a new type of strategic planning was required for services in a knowledge-based economy. Table 9 summarizes some of the results of the global service industries research by Wymbs (2001).

Virtual Teamwork to Improve Operations

With video conferences, e-mail, the Internet, corporate intranets, and sophisticated groupware, it is possible for people to work together no matter

Table 9. Analyses of global service industries

Analyses of global service Industries	Description
Information centric services	The most significant effect of the Internet is to cut the cost of interaction (i.e., the search, coordinating, and monitoring that customers and companies must do when they exchange goods and services). The Internet enhances the ability to generate better ideas more swiftly and increases the speed associated with the dynamic changing nature of the global service industry.
Process change	E-commerce is changing the way global service industries do business. For instance, the Internet is a potential gateway to low-cost international banking through a virtual presence. The economics of the Internet-based brokerage model are quite intriguing. E-business information services, such as management consulting are a necessary complement to transactions involving goods and services.
New business strategies	Hamel (1999) provided several business strategies for the global service industry as following: business has reached the end of increment change stage and catching-up is not enough, strategy needs to be created for the future, and business and government are more likely to be aspiration constrained than resource-constrained.

where they are geographically based (Lipnack and Stamps 1997). Many people work in virtual teams that transcend distance, time zones, and even organizational boundaries. While the use of teams may indeed be on the rise, the face-to-face aspect of normal working relationships is changing dramatically. Virtual teamwork has become an everyday reality for employees in both big and small companies. Although technology creates business opportunities and enables us to communicate with partners in faraway places, we cannot rely on technology alone to create a sense of commitment or teamwork. Human relations and interaction remain paramount. Effective teamwork is difficult in the best of times and conditions. Teamwork depends in part on members' ability to trust one another. Technology cannot substitute for the relationships that foster trust. Successful teams, of all nature, must pay a great deal of attention to building the foundations of sound teamwork. Virtual teams must work even harder to compensate for many of the elements that are inevitably lost when teams work together, yet apart. Virtual teams must include elements that are timeless and enduring in all successful groups. They also must include features that are cutting edge. The challenge today is to invent and improve virtual teams while retaining the benefits and characteristics of effective teams from previous organizational forms.

Virtual team is defined as a group of people who interact through interdependent task guided by common purpose and work across space, time, and organizational boundaries through the Internet or other networks (Lipnack and Stamps 1997). Table 10 summarizes characteristics of virtual teams (Bal and Teo 2000). Table 11 lists types of virtual teams proposed by Duarte and Snyder (1999).

However, unlike traditional face-to-face teams, virtual teams routinely cross boundaries through an array of interactive electronic technologies (Kezsbom 2000). Socially, however, they lag behind everyday reality. There are no by chance encounters or meetings, no getting together casually for lunch, passing each other in the hallway, or dropping by one another's office. A major reason why many of today's more traditional teams are ineffective is that they overlook the strong implications of the seemingly obvious. Imagine, in the boundary-less virtual team, what occurs when team members ignore how really different they are. Virtual teams must adjust to the new realities of their situations.

Table 10. Characteristics of virtual teams

Characteristics of virtual teams	Description
Four common criteria	• Geographically dispersed • Driven by common purpose • Enabled by communication technologies • Involved in cross-boundary collaboration
Other characters	• It is not a permanent team • Members solve problems and make decisions jointly and are mutually accountable for team results • Small team size • Inconsistent membership • Team members are knowledge workers

Table 11. Types of virtual team

Type of virtual teams	Description
Networked teams	Consist of individuals who collaborate to achieve common purpose.
Parallel teams	Carry out special assignments, tasks, or functions that regular organization does not want or is equipped to perform.
Project/product development teams	Team members conduct projects for customers for a defined period of time.
Work/production teams	Perform regular and ongoing work.
Service teams	Service teams are now to be distributed across distance and time.
Management teams	Management teams can be separated by distance and time.
Action teams	They offer immediate responses and in emergency situations.

Global Virtual Teams

Working in multinational, global virtual teams pose certain challenges not usually encountered when a group of people work together in the same building or city. Some of these challenging differences may be quite obvious, as when a group of people are working in different time zones, all over the world. Many companies use time differences to their advantage by transacting business virtually around the clock, but for people other than bond traders time differences can be frustrating (Schniederjans 1998, pp. 108–113).

Other problems encountered by global virtual teams whose work literally spans the globe may be more subtle, yet equally as important. Nonverbal communication can account for as much as 60 percent of the message an individual conveys. This can entail a suggestive glance, a reddening neck, or twitching face-clues that often convey a plethora of important emotions. Team members who are in separate locations are deprived of these clues that indicate their colleagues' opinions, attitudes, and emotions. Even in the best videoconferencing, facial expressions can be difficult to pick up if the transmission is poor, if someone is off camera, or when the mute button is pressed.

In a global virtual team members often do not have the opportunity to know the people with whom they are assigned or expected to work. Extracurricular activities can do more to cement a team than a number of teambuilding sessions. When all participants are in the same place, dinners and outings serve as an invaluable means of breaking the ice. When social contact is replaced by e-mail or videoconferences, team members lose the chance to socialize with their colleagues, form a more realistic opinion of them, and bond.

Completing projects through groupware means that team members are isolated from one another, which increases the chances for misinterpretation. Groupware allows information about a project to be fed into a huge structured database that can be accessed by all team members. When databases fail to contain the newest information, one can sometimes assume that the virtual team is not working well together. People then tend to hoard what they know or share only within their discipline or function, rather than share with all team members. Table 12 lists the solutions to some of the challenges faced by global virtual teamwork (Kezsbom 2000).

Table 12. Solutions to global virtual teamwork

Solutions	Descriptions
Concentrate on building credibility and trust	When team members have few opportunities to get to know each other, trust and credibility are naturally in limited supply.
Create time together	Team processes are expedited by spending more time on the front-end and in reaching consensus in developing procedures.
Stress cooperative goals	Cooperation generates positive feelings of family, community, and a sense of good will that is necessary for the team's future.
Keep communication constant	A groupware system that offers sophisticated e-mail, conferencing, newsletters, and bulletin board services may encourage more frequent online communication.

Summary

This chapter first presents the concepts of HRM and discusses the relationship between them and JIT operating environments. The chapter then explains the importance HRM in an e-commerce setting. The chapter also discusses how to use HRM strategies to cope with the drastic changes in e-commerce. Finally, the chapter explores the issue of using virtual teamwork to improve operations in the context of e-commerce.

♦ Review Terms

Action teams
Administrator
Broker
Business process reengineering (BPR)
Business-to-employee (B2E)
Change management
Desktop video conferencing (DVC)
Edge of chaos
Edge of time
Employee development and training
Empowerment
Flexibility and multi-skilled workforce
Global e-commerce (GEC)
Global virtual team
Human resource management
Information centric services
Information technology (IT)
International Human Resource Management (IHRM)
Just-in-time (JIT)

Management teams
Networked teams
New business strategies
Objective organization model
Object-oriented systems analysis and design (OOSAD)
Open and effective communication processes
Organizational culture
Parallel teams
Participative decision-making
Process change
Project/product development teams
Service teams
Teamship
Teamworking
Time pacing
Virtual team
Virtual teamwork
Work/production teams
Work-life bundling

♦ Discussion Questions

1. How can an organization gain a competitive edge with HRM?
2. What is the relationship between JIT and HRM?
3. Discuss JIT human resource management factors.

4. How does BPR impact on HRM?
5. How does human resources cope with the globalization?
6. What is IHRM? Discuss some of the best practices of IHRM.
7. What is HRM so important in an e-commerce environment?
8. What is business-to-employee (B2E) model? Explain how B2E enhances e-commerce operations.
9. What causes the complexity of e-commerce? How can we deal with and overcome the complexity issues in e-commerce operations?
10. What is the "objective organization model"? How can it improve e-commerce operations?

◆ Questions

1. What is market network and hierarchy network? Explain the relationship between the two.
2. How does human resource strategy facilitate e-commerce operations?
3. What are "edge of time and "time pacing"? How do we cope with them through organizational culture?
4. What is "virtual teamwork"? How can a virtual teamwork improve e-commerce operations?
5. What is a global virtual teamwork? Discuss some of the barriers of the global virtual teamwork?

References

Abraham, S. E. and Spencer, M. S. "The Legal Limitations to Self-Directed Work Teams in Production Planning and Control," *Production and Inventory Management Journal*, Vol. 39, 1998, pp. 41–45.

Aghassi, H., "Organizational Structures, People and Technology," in Coulson-Thomas, C. (ed.), *Business Process Re-engineering Myth and Reality*, 1994, Kogan Page, London, pp. 192–200.

Bal, J. and Teo, P. K., "Implementing Virtual Team-working. Part 1: A Literature Review of Best Practice," *Logistics Information Management*, Vol. 13, No. 6, 2000, pp. 346–352.

Bartlett, C. A. and Ghoshal, S., *Managing Across Borders: The Transnational Solution*, Boston: Harvard Business School Press, 1989.

Brown, S. L. and Eisenhardt, K. M., *Competing On the Edge: Strategy As a Structured Chaos*, Boston: Harvard Business School Press, 1998.

Conti, R. F., "Variable Manning JIT: An Innovative Answer to Team Absenteeism," *Production and Inventory Management Journal*, Vol. 37, 1996, pp. 24–27.

Dahlem, P., Ericsson, J. and Fujii, H., "Labor Stability and Flexibility-Conditions to Reach Just-In-Time," *International Journal of Operations and Production Management*, Vol. 15, 1995, pp. 26–44.

D'Aveni, R. A., *Hyper-competitive Rivalries*, New York: The Free Press, 1995.

Davenport, T. H., Process Innovation, Reengineering Work through Information Technology, Boston: Harvard Business School Press, 1993.

Deshpande, S. P. and Golhar, D. Y. "HRM Practices in Unionized and Non-unionized Canadian JIT Manufacturing," *Production and Inventory Management Journal*, Vol. 36, 1995, pp. 15–19.

Duarte, D. L. and Snyder, N.T., *Mastering Virtual Teams*, San Francisco, CA: Jossey-Bass Publishers, 1999.

Grint, K., "Reengineering History: Social Resonances and Business Process Reengineering," *Organization*, Vol. 1, No. 1, 1994, pp. 179–201.

Hamel, G., "Strategy Innovation and the Quest for Value," *Sloan Management Review*, Vol. 39, No. 2, 1998, pp. 7–15.

Hammer, M. and Champy, J., Re-engineering the Corporation: A Manifesto for Business Revolution, London: Nicholas Brealey, 1993.

Hansen, M. T. and Deimler, M. S., "Cutting Costs While Improving Morale with B2E Management," *Sloan Management Review*, Vol. 43, No. 1, 2001, pp. 96–100.

Heeley, C. B. *The Human Side of Just-In-Time*, New York: American Management Association, 1991.

Huselid, M. A, Jackson, S. E. and Schuler, R. S., "Technical and Strategic Human Resource Management Effectiveness as Determinants of Firm Performance," *Academy of Management Journal*, Vol. 40, No.1, 1997, pp. 171–188.

Inman, R. A. and Mehra, S., "Potential Union Conflict In JIT Implementation?" *Production and Inventory Management Journal*, Vol. 30, No. 4, 1989, pp. 19–22.

Kerr, S. and Von Glinow, M. A., "The Future of Human Resource Management," *Human Resource Management*, Vol. 36, 1997, pp. 115–120.

Kezsbom, D. S., "Creating Teamwork in Virtual Teams," *Cost Engineering*, Vol. 42, No. 10, 2000, pp. 33–36.

Lipnack, J. and Stamps, J., Virtual Teams: Reaching Across Space, Time, and Organizations with Technology, New York: John Wiley & Sons, 1997.

Lucas, H. C., *Information Technology and the Productivity Paradox*, New York: Oxford University Press, 1999.

Luftman, Jerry N., ed. *Competing in the Information Age.* New York: Oxford University Press, 1999.

Luthans, F. *Organizational Behavior*, 8th ed. Boston: Irwin and McGraw-Hill, 1998.

MacDuffie, J. P., "Human Resource Bundles and Manufacturing Performance: Flexible Production Systems in the World Auto Industry," *Industrial and Labor Relations Review*, Vol. 48, No. 2, 1995, pp. 197–221.

Marchewka, J. T. and Towell, E. R., "A Comparison of Structure and Strategy in Electronic Commerce, *Information Technology & People*, Vol. 13, No. 2, 2000, pp. 137–149.

Marciano, V. M., "The Origins and Development of Human Resource Management," *Academy of Management Journal,* Best Papers Proceedings, 1995, pp. 223–228.

Moden, Y., Toyota *Production System: An Integrated Approach to Just-In-Time, 3 rd ed.,* New York: Engineering and Management Press, 1998.

Mullarkey, S., Jackson, P. R. and Parker, S. K., "Employee Reactions to JIT Manufacturing Practices: A Two-phase Investigation," *International Journal of Operations and Production Management*, Vol.15, 1995, pp. 62–80.

Ocana, C. and Zemel, E., "Learning from Mistakes: A Note on Just-In-Time Systems," *Operations Research*, Vol. 44, 1996, pp. 206–214.

Power, D. and Sohal, A. S., "An Empirical Study of Human Resource Management Strategies and Practices in Australian Just-In-Time Environments," *International Journal of Operations & Production Management*, Vol. 20, No. 8, 2000, pp. 932–958.

Saltzman, L. and Luthans, F., "After the Bubble Burst: How Small High-tech Firms Can Keep in Front of the Wave," *Academy of Management Executive*, Vol. 15, No. 3, 2001, pp. 114–124

Schein, E. H., *Organizational Culture and Leadership*, 2nd ed, San Francisco, CA: Jossey-Bass, 1992.

Schniederjans, M. J., *Operations Management in a Global Context*, Westport, CT: Quorum Books, 1998.

Schniederjans, M. J. and Olson, J. R., *Advanced Topics in Just-In-Time Management*, Westport, CT: Quorum Books, 1999.

Sones, R., "Resolving the Complexity Dilemma in E-commerce Firms Through Objective Organization," *Logistics Information Management*, Vol.14, No. 1, 2001, pp. 107–119.

Stein, A., "Re-engineering the Executive: The 4th Generation of EIS: A Case Study," *Information and Management*, Vol. 29, 1995, pp. 55–62.

Teagarden, M. B. and Gordon, G. G., *Global Human Resource Management: Corporate Selection Strategies and the Success of International Managers*, in Selmer, J. (ed.), Expatriate Management: New Ideas for Business, New York: Quorum Press 1994, pp. 17–36.

Teagarden, M. B. and Glinow, M., "Human Resource Management in Cross-cultural Contexts: Emic Practices versus Etic Philosophies," *Management International Review*, Vol.37, No. 1, 1997, pp. 7–20.

Townsend, A. M., DeMarie, S.M. and Hendrickson, A. R., "Virtual Teams: Technology and the Workplace of the Future," *Academy of Management Executive*, Vol.12, 1998, pp. 17–29.

Turban E., Lee, J., King, D. and Chung, H. M., *Electronic Commerce: A Managerial Perspective*, Upper Saddle River, NJ: Prentice Hall, 2000.

Wright, P. M., McMahan, G. C. and Mc Williams, A., "Human Resources and Sustained Competitive Advantage: A Resource-Based Perspective," *International Journal of Human Resources Management*, Vol. 5, 1994, pp. 301–326.

Wymbs, C., "How E-commerce is Transforming and Internationalizing Service Industries," *Journal of Services Marketing*, Vol. 4, No. 6, 2000, pp. 463–477.

Yasin, M. M., Small, M. and Wafa, M. A., "An Empirical Investigation of JIT Effectiveness: An Organizational Perspective," *Omega*, Vol. 25, 1997, pp. 461–471.

Zucchi, F. and Edwards, J. E., "How Similar are Human Resource Management Practices in Reengineered Organizations?" *Business Process Management Journal*, Vol. 6, No. 3, 2001, pp. 214–220.

Zucchi, F. and Edwards, J. E., "Human Resource Management Aspects of Business Process Reengineering: A Survey," *Business Process Management Journal*, Vol. 5, No. 4, 1999, pp. 325–333.

Chapter 10   E-COMMERCE AND REENGINEERING AND CONSULTING MANAGEMENT

Learning Objectives

After completing this chapter, you should be able to:

Define and describe "reengineering management".

Explain the relationship between "reengineering" and "continuous improvement."

Explain the "reengineering life cycle."

Explain how to conduct a reengineering program.

Define and describe "consulting management."

Explain why reengineering and consulting management are necessary in e-commerce operations.

Describe a methodology that can be used to determine if reengineering or consulting should take place in an e-commerce operation.

Describe how "business process reengineering" can be implemented using the Internet.

Describe how reengineering an e-commerce supply chain can benefit an organization.

Overview of This Chapter

This chapter presents the subjects of reengineering and consulting management in an e-commerce context. The chapter presents a brief overview of the basics of these approaches to change management. The chapter then explains why reengineering and consulting management is important for e-commerce business operations. Finally, the chapter concludes with a discussion on a series of research articles that describe how reengineering should be used to achieve successful e-commerce operations.

What is Reengineering Management?

A famed U.S. economist, Joseph Schumpeter, viewed progress coming from "gales of creative destruction." Basically, this view holds that an organization's success is mostly a function of its ability to embrace disturbance such as dislocation, difficulty, and ambiguity. Starting in the 1990's and continuing to this day, one of the greatest contributors to organizational disturbance is "reengineering." Reengineering is a process of drastically or radically changing people, processes, and the organization itself, through the use of modern technologies and methodologies, to achieve organizational objectives such as improved efficiency, quality, and competitiveness (Chase *et al.* 2001, pp. 655–658; Hanna and Newman 2001, pp. 295–302). Reengineering management also called business process reengineering (BPR) or process reengineering are the activities that are involved in the managing of the restructuring of production processes in an effort to improve efficiency.

Many organizations have sought to use a reengineering management program as a means to rapidly enhance product quality in an effort to develop a competitive advantage. Many of the same organizations have used the *quality management* principle of *continuous improvement* (CI) to more gradually achieve enhanced product quality. (See Chapter 8 for a review on quality management and CI.) The results of using the more radical reengineering approach verses the more gradual continuous improvement approach is sometimes mixed. For example, AT&T's Universal Card Services division won the *Malcolm Baldrige National Quality Award* in 1992 and yet found itself in the same year losing market share because it's CI program had not kept pace with the quality of its competitors. To meet the competitive challenge, AT&T reengineered its service delivery procedures and technology. The result was a rapid and direct improvement in quality that continues to exceed industry quality benchmarks (Harrar 1994).

CI in quality or productivity is usually viewed as an incrementally increasing linear function or non-linear function as presented in Figure 1. Yet improvements in quality can be quite dramatic and inconsistent with those represented in Figure 1. The introduction of a reengineered new technology or a new reengineered production process can cause a quantum leap of improvement in quality or productivity more characteristic of the discontinuous function in Figure 2. The difference between the assumed linear or nonlinear continuous, and actual discontinuous behavior of a quality or productivity function can lead to organizational disturbance. For example, the Kodak Corporation is just one of many major US organizations that have experienced a disturbance between a CI

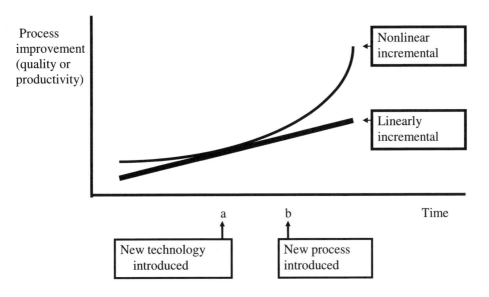

Figure 1. Expected improvement in quality or productivity under a CI program

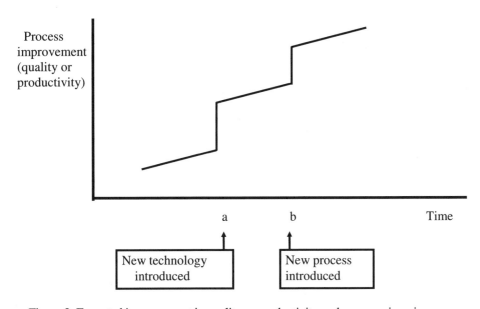

Figure 2. Expected improvement in quality or productivity under a reengineering program

program and a reengineering program. In the early 1980's, Kodak embarked on a company wide campaign to enhance quality through quality management principles (Grant *et al.* 1994). Kodak management used CI as a means to guide and document their quality progress. While considerable improvements in operational and competitive performance were observed, Kodak management in the early 1990's felt that their continuous, incremental improvement was not financially significant or sufficient on a comparative basis with competitors. Thus, Kodak in 1991 undertook a $1.6 billion restructuring effort. This restructuring entailed substantial reengineering of their organization in the hopes of a quick and dramatic improvement in lowering costs to allow their products and financial situation to be more competitive. The results were that by 1993 little longer-term savings in operating costs were achieved. Indeed, the impact in the short-term caused most of the top executives that undertook the reengineering efforts to be dislocated from Kodak.

One might conclude that the true relationship between the successful application of the CI and reengineering is inversely related. Researchers feel that in some cases there is insufficient time between reengineering programs to allow for the product quality systems to stabilize under a previous and ongoing successful CI program. As Ciampa (1993) warned, the organization instability caused by reengineering programs needs to be anticipated and a time period allowed for readjustment to settle down the changes in the climate of the organization. Also as Plenert (1994) points out, a failure not to take into account the upheaval of a reengineering program and permit a steadying down period using quality management principles like CI will probability result in a failure of the reengineering program to achieve improvement in product quality or productivity.

What emerges from experiences at Kodak and other organizations reported in the literature which have experienced less than successful results with reengineering and CI programs is a timing conflict between the long-term nature of CI and the short-term nature of reengineering. Grant *et al.* (1994) made the point that organizations that are focused on the long-term goals of quality management principles will not be successful if they are driven by short-term measurement goals like quarterly profit reports as Kodak did in the 1990's. There is a philosophical difference between those managers who think reengineering can be used to achieve overnight improvements in quality or productivity and the managers who use CI methods over a longer-term to achieve small, incremental improvements in quality. Both types of managers must be able to work together to merge their respective short-term and long-term approaches to quality or productivity enhancements as a combined approach with both short-term and long-term benefits.

Unfortunately managers who operate under the CI principle of quality management and whose organizations ignore reengineering run the risk of losing great potential quality improvements. In Figure 3 the possible opportunity loss (i.e., either OL1 or OL1+OL2) risk that managers run by not capitalizing on the enhanced product quality or productivity brought about by reengineering efforts can be quite substantial. Specifically, managers' risk can include losing out on sales from underestimated true product quality, incurring waste in the use of human resources unneeded because of the more streamlined work processes and enhanced quality product, and a failure to take advantage of a reduced response time in meeting customer needs. Clearly, managers who do not recognize in a timely manner the benefits that can be brought about by reengineering can be lead to mistakenly conclude that reengineering has not substantially helped product quality, when in fact it has. In other words, these managers can help cause the failure of reengineering if they do not consider the discontinuous quality improvement behavior inherent in a combined short-term reengineering program and longer-term quality management programs like CI.

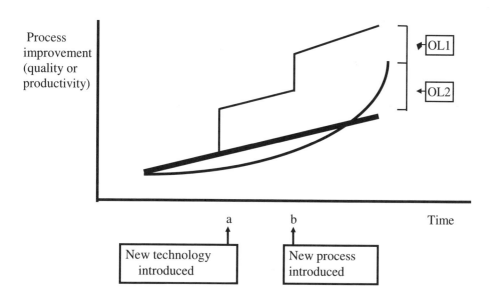

Figure 3. Opportunity loss of quality under discontinuous improvement

To understand a combined reengineering and CI program we must carefully examine the timing characteristics of these two organization change agents. Reengineering is a short-term detour in the life of a long-term continuous improvement program. As Plenert (1994) suggests, reengineering detours can lead to the end of the life of some organizations. As a short-term detour in life for organizations, each reengineering program must have a beginning and an end, or a "reengineering life cycle."

The *reengineering life cycle* of a program includes all necessary organization change efforts from the time reengineering is begun to when the organizational disturbance impact of the change have been smoothed by smaller, more incremental changes like those experienced in a CI program. The life cycle of a reengineering program would include the total time from point **a** to point **b** in Figure 4. The inclusion of the smoothed CI time period, with a much steeper slope, as a part of the reengineering program can be interpreted as the necessary time that should be allowed to permit the organization to stabilize their processes.

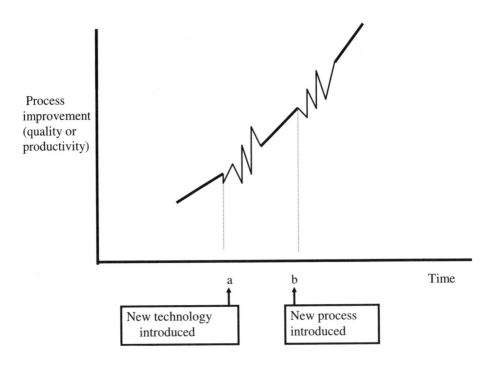

Figure 4. Reengineering life cycle

Since e-commerce operations are more change oriented than traditional brick-and-mortar operations, reengineering management offers a strategy for organizational change that permits as rapid a change as is necessary to keep up with technology and competition changes. The key to use this management approach successfully is to balance the "gales of creative destruction" with a managerial understanding of human, technology, and system limitations in a short-term fixed period of time.

A Procedure for Conducting a Reengineering Program

In Figure 5 a procedure for conducting a reengineering program is presented (Hammer 1997; White 1996). As shown in Figure 5, Step 1, either a customer objective emerges (usually from an analysis of customer complaint e-mails to the organization) that convinces e-commerce operations management (OM) managers that change is necessary or the organization might just have decided to set new strategic objective to achieve. In either case, change is called for. In identifying the goals and particularly the specifications for change a number of sources of information may be called for in Step 2. For example, benchmarking (see Chapter 8) might be a source of goals and specific specifications to improve production processes. Other technical methodologies can also be employed, such as "gap analysis." (We will be discussing "gap analysis" later in this chapter.)

In Step 3 the current process (and "process" here can mean a very large set of interrelated tasks, departments, and organizations) must be mapped or described. One of the primary methodologies to do this is with a *process map*, also called a *process flowchart* which is a simple graphic aid used to define each of the elements that make up a process. They allow OM managers to see how materials or customers flow through a process so opportunities for improvement can be identified and implemented during the reengineering of the process. An example of a process flowchart for an internal organization request for inventory from a manufacturing department is presented in Figure 6. As can be seen in Figure 6A (before reengineering is applied) the requisition for inventory is made to an inventory department where the inventory is stored. A decision must be made if they have the inventory that is requested. If they have what is requested, it is sent directly to the manufacturing department. If they do not have what is requested, they must acquire it through a supplier and have it delivered to a receiving department, which in turn would send it to the inventory department so it can eventually be sent to the manufacturing department. The decision and the steps all take staff time and an investment of capital in inventory.

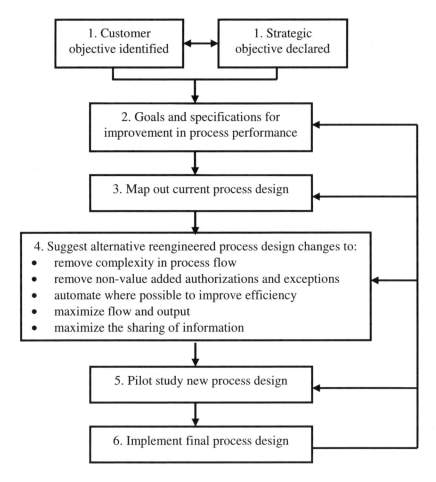

Figure 5. Reengineering procedure

Moving to Step 4 in the reengineering procedure in Figure 5 we would apply some possible changes in the inventory requisition process to reduce the complexity of the process and reduce time and wasted effort. While many strategies and guidelines can be employed to redesign changes in the process, the repeatedly recommended strategy for reducing waste in processes in prior chapters has been through the use of *Just-In-Time* (JIT) and *lean management* principles. In this inventory situation, one way to reduce complexity and inventory is to employ the JIT principle of eliminating inventory by allowing the supplier to maintain and supply all inventory requirements. (See Chapter 7 on inventory management.) This would result in eliminating the inventory department and the capital investment in inventory. We might also require our supplier to deliver the inventory directly to the point of need within the manufacturing facility as suggested in JIT material handling principles. This would eliminate the need for a receiving department. As a result of these changes in the role of the supplier, the resulting reengineered inventory requisition process would look like the process flowchart in Figure 6B. This would constitute the temporary design that would, in Step 5 of the Figure 5 reengineering procedure have to be pilot tested to see if would be feasible. This pilot testing can in some situations be tested by creating simulation models and running them on computers. In other situations a small-scale version of the system is tested prior to its adoption company-wide.

A. Process Flowchart before Reengineering

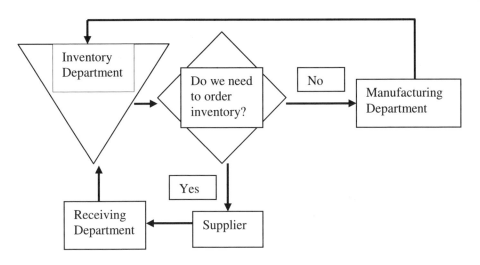

B. Process Flowchart After Reengineering

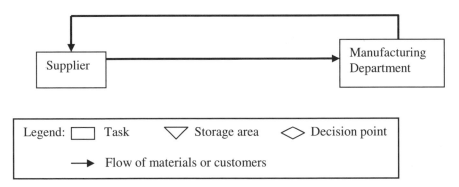

Figure 6. Process flowchart of a reengineered inventory requisition process

This pilot-testing phase also allows for minor revisions in the process design to take place. Eventually the reengineered process design can be fully implemented in the final Step 6. Like all CI processes, there is always a need for corrective feedback to take place and revision be made throughout the reengineering procedure to adjust and make as perfect as possible the process to achieve its desired goals.

What is Consulting Management?

Consulting involves activities required to impart knowledge and information. Consulting activities can be performed by internal organization experts or outside experts. Many firms, like Accenture (www.accenture.com) offer a full range of consulting services for all types of operations. The areas where consultants tend to be used the most include those in Table 1. Many of the types of decisions on Table 1, like locating plants, tend to be rare. The fact is that maintaining internal organization personnel to make this infrequent and timely decision might not be cost effective. Moreover, specialized consulting organizations can focus their resources (i.e., training, technology, software, etc.) on these very limited domains of knowledge and expertise, making them far more capable in those specialized areas than an e-commerce operation might would choose to be. Consultants can aid in the various aspects of making changes in organizations, which is often a difficult task and challenge for managers who must at the same time be running the organization. Some of the common organizational change activities that consultant perform are presented in Table 2.

Table 1. Areas where consulting is commonly used

Area	Examples of types of consulting decisions
Products, parts, materials	Supplier selection; selection of inventory planning and control systems; Make or buy decisions
Facilities	Design or redesign of plants; Adding, selling, or locating plants; Site selection
Human resources	Selecting personnel; Recruitment of specialized personnel
Processes	Technology acquisition; Process improvement; BPR and reengineering

Table 2. Activities consultants perform for their clients

Consulting activity	Description
Team building	Helping to form teams and enhance team performance. This might include helping team members to redesign work tasks, work methods, decision-making processes, and improve communication. This can also include techniques and strategies for resolving differences between teams, where consultants can act as a peacemaker to resolve dysfunctional conflicts and build cooperation with behavioral modification techniques.
Survey	Consultants can help in data collecting, disseminating, and reporting survey information collected on customers, benchmarking competitors, and internal operations. This would include data collection means of questionnaires, interviewing, group meetings, as well as evaluating individual, group, and organizational effectiveness.
Technological interfacing	Consultants can help to define work tasks, improve skills, and restructure management systems so personnel can work more efficiently and effectively in using the e-commerce technology.
Diagnostic	Consultant can help identify problems and help create solutions to solve them.
Training and education	This is the most common form of consulting. Consulting seminars aimed at changing organization culture and social problems, improving leadership skills and managing stress. This would also include the development of reengineering and quality programs that would be self-sustaining after the consults have completed their jobs.

Consulting management involves managing consulting activities to provide expertise from either internal or external organization sources in an effort to solve problems and make informed decisions. Consulting management is, therefore a management of organizational change. A procedure for implementing organizational change that consultants have used as a general guideline in performing their tasks is presented in Figure 7. The nature and subject of consulting management is so diverse there is no way to actually characterize all aspects of field, particularly as they relate to e-commerce operations. Unfortunately, there are no journal empirical research publications on e-commerce and consulting at this time, but by the dynamic nature of e-commerce it is clear that consulting should be commonly used and is essential to successful operations. Chase *et al.* (2001, p. 327) includes consulting as an important area of application in e-commerce operations. Greiner and Savich (1998) suggest that consulting is one of the best and most costless approaches to organization change. For some e-commerce organizations that can afford consulting expertise but not the investment in permanent staffers, consulting can be a *critical success factor* (CSF) in the acquisition of an essential competitive advantage.

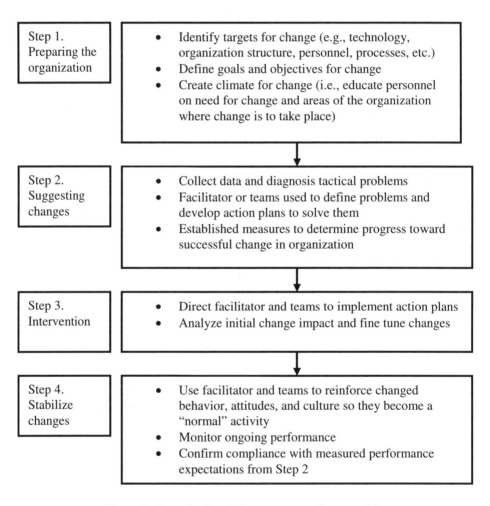

Figure 7. Organizational change process for consulting

Why are Reengineering and Consulting Management So Important for E-Commerce?

Unique to e-commerce operations (as compared to brick-and-mortar operations) is the fast pace of action. For example, e-commerce operations are considerable shaped by the developments in computer hardware, software, and networking technologies. As these technologies change, so must the e-commerce operations to take full advantage of the competitive advantages they bring. Since these technologies are themselves dramatically changing, the decision-making opportunities to adopt, use, and replace them require fast-paced implementation environments. The task is further complicated by the fact that most people working in e-commerce operations have had to unlearn inappropriate lessons from their brick-and-mortar environments.

Consultants can bring a culture of change to the organization. They can initiate reengineering programs and help manage them. Most importantly, they can act as agents of change, bringing with them experience in the process of change to permit improvements in operations that could not otherwise be possible without them. Since e-commerce operations must by necessity under go continuous revision to meet with their uniquely volatile markets, consultants can continually help advise on how best to make the ongoing changes. One of the areas that consultants have been most successful in implementing is the use of JIT management techniques to eliminate waste in production operations (Chase *et al.* 2001, pp. 268–270; Heizer and Render 2001, pp. 172–173). Examples of areas where waste reduction is possible and the types of consultants are needed include those presented in Table 3. (For a basic review of JIT principles see Schniederjans (1993) and for a review of more advanced JIT topics see Schniederjans and Olson (1999).)

It comes down to this: making changes in an organization is risky and can be very costly. E-commerce operations require more change than conventional brick-and-mortar operations. To avoid the wastes that can occur during the many and necessary changes that will take place in an e-commerce operation it makes "JIT sense" to avoid the wasted effort and hire the best change agents available. For most e-commerce operations, the change agents are external organization consultants.

Table 3. Areas where consultants can improve e-commerce operations

Target of waste elimination	Description	Type of consultant needed
Waiting	Time wasted by staff and equipment when workload is unbalanced. E-commerce areas where time can be wasted include online order taking, order filling, and purchasing activities. The goal here is to make the workload even between workstations and work areas to minimize time for customers and product to be waiting for processing.	Industrial engineers, process engineers
Transporting	Time wasted by needless traveling of customers or product during delivery. E-commerce examples can include Web site design defects that cause unneeded time for processing customer orders, and the delivery time from when the order is placed to when it arrives at the customer's destination. The goal is to minimize all wasted time in all areas from when the customer places the order to its delivery.	Logistic specialists, material handling specialists, industrial engineers
Motion and effort	Work effort wasted by staff because of inefficient or unnecessary human resource movement. E-commerce examples include unnecessary steps in order taking (i.e., too many Web windows to go through in taking a customer order), too many steps in processing an order, and too many steps in collecting and organizing customer data retrieval. The goal here is to improve productivity by making the various jobs more efficient by reducing non-necessary procedural steps in processes and where possible mechanization and automation.	Industrial engineers, time-study experts, motion-study experts, mechanical engineers, Web design engineers
Defective quality	Work effort wasted by poor quality. E-commerce examples include wasted scrap materials, wasted staff time in processing customer order returns, and rework labor from returned products. The goal here is to eliminate all product and service defects and in doing so, eliminate all wasted time and materials used to process returns.	Quality engineers, quality control experts

A Methodology to Determine if Reengineering or Consulting is Needed in E-Commerce Operations

Many e-commerce operations are characterized as having a very flat, small number of managers or owners in their start-up phase. Even when large organizations create an e-commerce division there has usually been a very small number of managers running the division. This smaller-type of leadership bureaucracy tends to lead some managers in feeling a degree of propriety ownership. There is nothing wrong with that type of feeling as it usually associated with individuals who are self-motivated and hard working. Unfortunately, it can lead managers to try and take care of problems themselves when in fact other outside experts and specialists might be better able to solve serious e-commerce problems.

To know when it is time to call in a consultant or launch a reengineering effort a problem must first be detected. In some situations the problem is as easy to see as a lost sale or a major equipment failure. In many e-commerce situations, problems happen so fast that a company can be out of business before they even know they have a problem. For this reason, e-commerce operations must be continuously pro-active in looking for problems. Indeed, welcoming an active search for problems to resolve is one of the previously mentioned principles of JIT and lean management (see Chapter 4).

It is sometimes difficult for managers of e-commerce operations to know when they have a serious problem and then ask for help to solve it. To help managers to identify problems and know its time to ask for help a graphical aid called "gap analysis" can be used. *Gap analysis* allows members of an organization to evaluate their performance in achieving success on critical success factors (CSFs). For e-commerce operations the most serious problems will be those related to their CSFs (though any type of criteria can be used). Building on the JIT principle of *visual management* a *gap chart* can be developed that compares an organization's CSFs on the basis of where they are (i.e., an actual status of an operation) and where they desire themselves to be (i.e., a benchmark or competitor desired status level).

This gap chart can be developed in a number of ways, one of which is to use judgmentally generated measures on CSFs. By taking questions, like those in Table 4, two surveys can be conducted. One survey will be given to the e-commerce operation's customers who will be asked to evaluate the operation's product or service for select CSF measures on a 1 (i.e., poor rating) to a 10 (i.e., perfect rating) scale. This survey will establish the "actual" status of the operation. A second survey can be given to same customers to evaluate a benchmark competitor or to managers of the e-commerce operation to evaluate

Table 4. Typical survey questions for a gap analysis

CSF	Survey question									
Quality	How would you rate our product/service quality?									
	Poor				Average					Perfect
	1	2	3	4	5	6	7	8	9	10
Product/service design	How would you rate our product/service design?									
	Poor				Average					Perfect
	1	2	3	4	5	6	7	8	9	10
Purchasing	How would you rate our purchasing department service?									
	Poor				Average					Perfect
	1	2	3	4	5	6	7	8	9	10
Human resources	How would you rate our personnel?									
	Poor				Average					Perfect
	1	2	3	4	5	6	7	8	9	10
Supply chain	How would you rate our supply chain service?									
	Poor				Average					Perfect
	1	2	3	4	5	6	7	8	9	10

the status of a successful competitor. This survey will establish the "desired" status of each CSF or where the organization would like to be. By then taking the mean of the individual's scores of each survey, points can be plotted on a gap chart as presented in Figure 8. The difference between the plotted actual and desired points on the chart represents the "gap" between where an organization is and where they want to be. The greater the gap, the greater the necessity of a consultant or reengineering program to be used to bring the CSF back toward a desired range of performance.

As we can see in Figure 8 the gaps between the CSFs of product/service design, human resources, and supply chain are very minor, indicating that in these areas the organization appears to be providing a level of expected or desired service performance to the customer. The wider gaps between the CSFs of quality and purchasing clearly indicate that help is needed in these areas. That help can take the form of either a reengineering program undertaken by the e-commerce organization or by bringing in the necessary consulting expertise to lesson the gap.

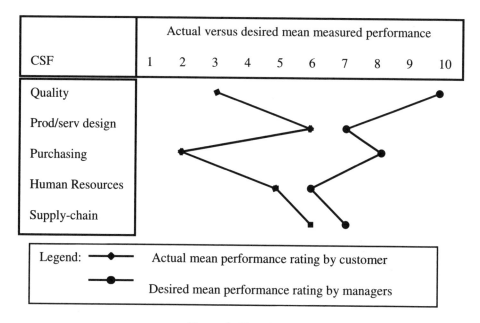

Figure 8. Gap chart

Like most performance related approaches, gap analysis should be a part of a CI program. Periodic changes in perceptions may necessitate an occasional reengineering effort and as previously stated, the relationship between CI and reengineering must be taken into consideration for a successful application of both OM approaches. Gap analysis supports the continuous nature of a CI program in that surveys can be initiated routinely to check ongoing performance.

Implementing Business Process Reengineering Using the Internet

E-commerce operations are based on Internet technology. This Internet technology provides managers with unique opportunities to enhance their BPR efforts. Grover and Malhotra (1997) found that information technology (IT) was a critical success factor for BPR implementation. Parker (1996) had previously found that the Internet was an IT enabler that allowed organizations to create an environment of accessible communication networks. What this means is that e-commerce operations are uniquely positioned to better achieve success in a BPR program than less Internet-intensive organizations. Wells (2000) sited several reasons why the Internet can and should be used to implement BPR programs. Some of these reasons are stated in Table 5.

Table 5. Reasons for using the Internet with BPR

Reason why Internet should be used in BPR	Explanation
Cost	The basic cost of placing a business online is under $40 saving the e-commerce organization from having to use major resources to motivate users to acquire this technology. Since the Internet connects virtually all businesses, their suppliers, and their customers, it can support a wide reach in BPR program applications enabling change to more easily be changed
Return on investment (ROI)	Between the low-cost of Internet technology (i.e., PCs, software, etc.) and its ability to reach new and very distant markets, the ROI is usually in a matter of days, rather than the typical investment in terms of years. This makes a BPR program cheaper to implement and quicker to achieve a ROI in the BPR program investment.
Ease of use	With Internet technology currently reaching over 100 million users in the US alone and every type of business using it, there is no wasted time needed by an e-commerce organization to train users. Since the success of BPR chiefly rests with individuals and their ability to communicate with each other, the Internet is a primary empowerment tool for BPR.
Information efficiency	The Internet can provide timely information to BPR participants. When compared to printed materials, the Internet provides a means by which the rapid changes in processes, procedures, and operations can be communicated to all BPR participants in a timely fashion. The Internet also allows for timely feedback information for waste avoiding (e.g., scrap in WIP) and for corrective control to take place when BPR changes are not working as expected.
Knowledge efficiency	The Internet allows for rapid storage and sharing of information of all types (e.g., video, voice, photos, graphics, text, etc.). The permits expertise to be spread throughout an organization with more effective multimedia approaches. BPR changes in training manuals and procedures can be updated and quickly dispensed to help educate personnel.
Knowledge acquisition	The Internet connects managers to a wealth of new knowledge through the *World-Wide-Web* (WWW). This new knowledge is very necessary to perform BPR to provide ideas for the changes that will take place.
Technology independence	Different departments in a single e-commerce organization can have many different computer technologies. The Internet allows these differing computer technologies to share information regardless of the brand name of the computer manufacturer or Internet browser used. This independence helps the necessary cross-functional partnering necessary for BPR programs to be successful.

Wells (2000) also examined a number of research constructs in successful BPR implementation. What was found was that the amount of management resources and employee resistance to BPR were not very significant CSFs in BPR implementation. What were critical were "organizational culture" and the use of "change management." *Organization culture* is how the organization supports cooperation, co-ordination, and the empowerment of their employees (Schermerhorn 2001, p. 38). Wells (2000) research found that the "Egalitarian culture" was significantly related to successful BPR programs. The *Egalitarian culture* is characterized by the managerial features presented in Table 6. E-commerce operations managers should seek to install and enhance these features in their organizations in order to achieve an organizational culture that will help improve the successfulness of BRP programs.

Table 6. Features of an Egalitarian organization culture

Managerial feature	Relationship with Internet
Shared organizational vision and information	The Internet permits a constant means of updating and sharing information on an organization's mission statement, where its visionary goals in that statement are derived and how successful the organization is in achieving those goals. As the organization becomes successful, informed personnel will increasingly accept and "buy into" the vision. In doing so, it helps BPR to be accepted as a strategy of change to modify and improve the means by which visionary goals will be achieved.
Employee decision-making empowerment	The Internet provides a link with all of an organization's decision-making technology and methodology. It empowers all employees to have access to the best decision making tools the organization has to participate in BPR decision-making processes.
Open communications	The Internet provides the greatest means of verbal, written, and visual communication capabilities that has ever been afforded employees. This helps to maximize participant contributions by all employees to BPR programs.
Strong leadership	The Internet and the various Internet technologies allow managers to stay in touch with their subordinates more closely than ever before. It allows leaders to better issue timely commands that improve BPR results.

Change management is a procedural means of implementing change in an organization (Schermerhorn 2001, pp. 382–390). Changes in an organization can be either planned changes (i.e., a result of specific and planned efforts at change with direction by a change leader) or unplanned changes (i.e., spontaneous changes, without direction of a change leader). The targets for change can include any and all of those listed in Table 7. Having an organization that is comfortable with "change" and use to it as a means to successful operations (including what employees do for a job) will help to make BPR successful in e-commerce operations where constant change is necessary for business success.

Table 7. Organizational targets of change

Organizational targets for change	Description
Technology	All operations and information system technology used in the design and workflow that integrate employees and equipment into operating systems.
Culture	The values and norms of the individuals and groups that make up the organization.
Organization structure	The organizational lines of authority and communication.
Personnel	All human resources including attitudes and skills.
Tasks	The job design, specifications, and descriptions that employees perform, and their objectives and goals.

Reengineering E-Commerce Supply Chain Buyer-Supplier Interface

Competitive pressures in e-commerce continually force successful organizations to reduce costs and compress the time required to deliver products or services to customers. This involves a CI process throughout an organization's supply chain to streamline operations. (See Chapter 3 for review of supply chain management.) Internet-based e-commerce operations are uniquely positioned to reduce cost by integrating customers and their suppliers through electronic networks (Roberts and Mackay 1998).

Table 8. Benefits of reengineering e-commerce supply chain operations

Type of benefit	Explanation
Network efficiency	By focusing on building supplier-business-customer networks, reengineering and BPR efforts in isolated areas within the organization will be made easier to accomplish. It's like making an investment in information infrastructure that will later help in improving information flow related to reengineering or BPR efforts.
Reduced procurement costs in making customer sales	By investing in automation (i.e., Web site software, customer order entry software, electronic data interchange systems, etc.) and using features these technologies offer (e.g., creating bulletin boards for collecting and imparting product info), considerable savings in customer order taking and procurement can be saved.
Partnering saves organization resources	The Internet technologies allow suppliers and even customers to perform tasks that would have taken internal resources to achieve. Allowing suppliers to do in-house warehousing or taking orders directly from customers can reduce the costs of doing business to e-commerce operations. Allows suppliers and even customers to take a more active part in product or service design by allowing timely communication between all parties. Internet technologies also permit outsourcing of parts of the e-commerce business to suppliers to be easier process.
Technology allows better managerial focus on problem solving	The use of e-commerce technologies lifts the attention from clerical-type day-to-day customer paper processing activities (e.g., invoice processing, order expediting, etc.) to focus on more critical issues in business success, such as handling order queries from customers. This refocus allowed by the clerical time savings permits departments, like purchasing, to move from a tactical problem solving group to a strategic planning group, better able to solve issues before they become a problem.
Empowerment	The e-commerce technologies permit greater access to decision-making information and encourage better training and development of personnel to handle the use of such information.

McIvor *et al.* (2000) undertook a research study that showed that e-commerce operations where uniquely positioned to successfully implement a reengineering program by the nature of change in the use of e-commerce technology throughout all businesses and their respective supply chains. Using case studies McIvor *et al.* (2000) showed that e-commerce businesses could have their supply chain operations continually benefit from reengineering programs over more traditional supply chain operations. As shown in Table 8 the benefits of reengineering an e-commerce supply chain focus on the same kind of cost reduction, waste removal, and improved productivity that have been discussed in previous chapters on JIT and lean management principles. They are suggested here, though, as applied in the implementation of a reengineering or BPR program. What can be inferred from this research is that: (1) reengineering is an ideal change strategy for e-commerce operations, (2) e-commerce operations must, more than traditional organizations, continually change to meet competitive pressures, and (3) that e-commerce operations, with their technology base, are uniquely positioned to be successful in implementing reengineering programs. In other words, an e-commerce operation has a competitive advantage in the implementation of reengineering programs over traditional brick-and-mortar operations.

Summary

This chapter begins with a description of the basic ideas and principles of reengineering and consulting management. Implementation procedures for both approaches of change were also presented. Relationships with quality and organizational change were discussed as they related to the development of e-commerce competitive advantages. A methodology used to identify when reengineering and consulting efforts should be undertaken was described along with recent e-commerce research studies that describe how these approaches can be used to change an organization for the better.

This chapter on "change" and the strategies of using reengineering and consultants fittingly concludes this book. Numerous references within this chapter tie it back to other subjects in earlier chapters. The fact is, bringing in consultants to change or reengineer an operation should not be viewed, as it usually is in a brick-and-mortar operation, as the last alternative to improving operations, but should be viewed as a first alternative. Consultants, the good ones, know when they can help a firm and can, as a result save time and effort in the process of change. In some cases, they can suggest alternatives to change that will save the disruption of what was earlier in this chapter called the "gales of creative destruction." More over, most consultants have the experience to make the process of change successful.

Many brick-and-mortar organizations have felt that their years of experience with their markets and customers have built up valuable decision-making and knowledge resources that they can extend into their e-commerce operations. The fact is, some of these resources have been ill-suited or even constraining in the changing environments found in e-commerce and have been described as the *incumbent's curse* (Chandy and Tellis 2000). What we have tried to do in this book is to take the business experiences and methodologies described in resent e-commerce research, and combine them with well-established OM business principles of change (i.e., JIT and lean management) to achieve a strategy of continuous adaptation, well suited to deal with many of the dimensions of volatility found in e-commerce operations.

◆ **Review Terms**

Benchmarking
Business process reengineering (BPR)
Change management
Continuous improvement (CI)
Consulting
Consulting management
Egalitarian culture
Gap analysis
Incumbent's curse

Information technology (IT)
Organization culture
Process flowchart
Process map
Quality management
Reengineering
Reengineering life cycle
Reengineering management
Visual management
World-wide-web (WWW)

◆ **Discussion Questions**

1. Explain how "reengineering" and "consulting" are the same
2. Explain why the discontinuous process of "reengineering" is presented with the continuous process of CI.
3. On important decisions, like a facility location, explain why an e-commerce organization might allow a consultant to make the decision rather than an internal organization executive.
4. Explain how the organizational change process in Figure 7 is like a freezing, changing, and then refreezing process.
5. Explain how reengineering and consulting can help an organization achieve a JIT or lean manufacturing type of operation.

6. Explain some of the reasons why the Internet should be used to implement BPR.

◆ Questions

1. Why is reengineering so important to e-commerce operations?
2. What are "process flowcharts" and explain how they are used in reengineering?
3. What types of activities do consultants perform for their clients?
4. Why is consulting so important to e-commerce operations?
5. What is "gap analysis" and how is it used in reengineering or consulting efforts of e-commerce operations?
6. What is an "Egalitarian organization culture" and explain how it is related to consulting?

◆ Problems

1. An e-commerce operation's executives were surveyed on how well they think they should be doing in four areas of their operations. They felt that on a 1 to 10 scale (refer to Table 4) they expect their mean performance on "quality" should be a 9, on "product service" should be an 8, on "product design" should be a 6, on "staff support" should be a 10. Below is a sample of five of their customers who rated their performance. Using the customers ratings in the table below compute the mean customer ratings and plot them along with the executive expected mean ratings in a gap analysis chart. Comment on the "gap" areas where improvement through consulting or reengineering should be directed.

CSF	Survey questions and ratings on a 1 to 10 scale for 5 customers.
Quality	How would you rate our product/service quality? Ratings: 6, 3, 10, 9, 8
Product service	How would you rate our product/service design? Ratings: 2, 4, 6, 3, 6
Product design	How would you rate our purchasing department service? Ratings: 8, 9, 8, 9, 10
Staff support	How would you rate our personnel? Ratings: 1, 5, 2, 4, 6

2. The CEO of an e-commerce operation wants to determine if she should call in consultants to fix CSFs in an organizations operation. The CEO feels that her company should score a 10 out of 10 on any operational aspect of their firm, particularly those areas that are designated CSFs. Below is a sample of ten of this organization's industrial customers who where invited to rate their performance on a set of six CSFs. Using the customers ratings in the table below compute the mean customer ratings and plot them along with the expected ratings in a gap analysis chart. Comment on the "gap" areas where improvement through consulting or reengineering should be directed to improved operations.

CSF	Survey questions and ratings on a 1 to 10 scale for 10 customers.
Quality	How would you rate our product/service quality? Ratings: 7, 3, 4, 9, 8, 8, 7, 2, 7, 8
Product/ service design	How would you rate our product/service design? Ratings: 8, 8, 9, 9, 8, 8, 9, 9, 8, 9
Purchasing	How would you rate our purchasing department service? Ratings: 1, 3, 3, 4, 2, 4, 5, 2, 3, 4
Human resources	How would you rate our personnel? Ratings: 8, 9, 7, 8, 9, 2, 8, 9, 10, 8
Supply chain	How would you rate our supply chain service? Ratings: 9, 1, 8, 2, 8, 3, 7, 5, 8, 1
Inventory	How would you rate our inventory availability? Ratings: 10, 8, 9, 8, 7, 3, 4, 8, 9, 10

References

Chandy, R. and Tellis, G., The Incumbent's Curse? Incumbency, Size and Radical Product Innovation," *Journal of Marketing*, Vol. 64, No. 3, 2000, pp. 1–17.

Chase, R. B., Aquilano, N. J. and Jacobs, F. R., *Operations Management for Competitive Advantage*. 9th ed., Boston, MA: McGraw-Hill/Irwin, 2001.

Ciampa, D., "Reengineering With Caution," *Management Review*, Vol. 82, No. 10, 1993, p. 50.

Grant, R. M., Shani, R. and Krishnan, R., "TOM's challenge to management theory and practice," *Sloan Management Review*, Winter, 1994, pp. 25–35.

Greiner, L. and Savich, R., *Consulting to Management*, New York: Prentice-Hall, 1998.

Grover, V. and Malhotra, M., "Business Process Re-engineering: A Tutorial on the Concept, Evolution, Method, Technology, and Application," *Journal of Operations Management*, Vol. 15, No. 3, 1997, pp. 193–213.

Hammer, M., *Beyond Reengineering*, New York: Harper Collins Business, 1997.

Hanna, M. and Newman, W., *Integrated Operations Management*, Upper Saddle River: NJ: Prentice-Hall, 2001.

Harrar, G., "Baldrige notwithstanding," *Forbes*, Vol. 153, February 28, 1994, pp. 44–46.

Heizer, J. and Render, B., *Operations Management*, 6th ed., Upper Saddle River, NJ: Prentice Hall, 2001.

McIvor, R., Humphreys, P. and Huang, G., "Electronic Commerce: Reengineering the Buyer-Supplier Interface," *Business Process Management Journal*, Vol. 6, No. 2, 2000, pp. 122–138

Parker, M., Strategic Transformation and Information Technology: Paradigms for Performing While Transforming, Prentice-Hall, Upper Saddle River: NJ, 1996.

Plenert, G., "Process Re-engineering: The Latest Fad Toward Failure," *APICS-The Performance Advantage*, June 1994, pp. 22–24.

Roberts, B. and Mackay, M., "IT Supporting Supplier Relationships: The Role of Electronic Commerce," *European Journal of Purchasing and Supply Management*, Vol. 4, 1998, pp. 175–184.

Schermerhorn, J. R., *Management*, 6th ed., New York: John Wiley and Sons, 2001.

Schniederjans, M. J., *Topics in Just-In-Time Management*, Needham Heights, MA: Allyn and Bacon, 1993.

Schniederjans, M. J. and Olson, J. R., *Advanced Topics in Just-In-Time Management*, Westport, CT: Quorum Books, 1999.

Subramani, M. and Walden, E., "The Impact of E-Commerce Announcements on the Market Value of Firms," *Information Systems Research*, Vol. 12, No. 2, 2001, pp. 135–154.

Wells, M. G., "Business Process Re-engineering Implementation Using Internet Technology," *Business Process Management*, Vol. 6., No. 2, 2000, pp. 164–184.

White, J., "Reengineering and Continuous Improvement," *Quality Digest*, July 1996, pp. 31–34.

Part III

Recent Trends in E-Commerce Technology

<u>Chapter 11</u> MOBILE COMMERCE

Learning Objectives

After completing this chapter, you should be able to:
      Define and describe "mobile commerce."
      Explain the history of m-commerce.
      Explain current research in m-commerce.
      Describe m-commerce infrastructure.
      Explain how banking has been impacted by m-commerce.

Overview of This Chapter

This chapter introduces and defines mobile commerce. This explains its historical origins and how it has evolved to become a critical element of e-commerce operations. A discussion of current research is presented to provide an orientation to current technology uses. The chapter also explains how the infrastructure issues related to mobile commerce.

What is M-Commerce?

Mobile commerce, referred to as m-commerce, is a quickly changing field in today's marketplace. By the time this textbook is published, some of the information in this chapter will most likely already be out of date. The mobile phone and application market is very competitive and innovation and customer's expectations have driven companies to release products at a fast pace. Companies like Apple, Nokia and Samsung are releasing new products on a yearly basis. The release of new products and technology generate the release of new applications. These applications increase the functionality and the reach of m-commerce worldwide.

This chapter discusses m-commerce from several perspectives. First, an introduction of m-commerce is discussed with figures of today's usage and statistics including a brief discussion of the difference between e-commerce and m-commerce. Next, a brief history of m-commerce is examined.   Third, the current m-commerce market is discussed. This market is examined from current research, wireless network infrastructure, and user infrastructure. Special attention is given to mobile banking and mobile payment which are two upcoming m-commerce applications.

Introduction to M-Commerce

As discussed in previous chapters, e-commerce is defined as buying and selling of products or services over electronic systems. These electronic systems include the hardware, software, and network including the internet or other computer networks. M-commerce is a subset of e-commerce and involves buying and selling of products or services using mobile applications over mobile phones (Coursaris *et al.* 2002). This definition is a little out of date since newer technologies were invented since this definition was published. This chapter takes a broader definition of m-commerce and includes buying and selling of goods and services on mobile devices anywhere and anytime. This definition does not limit m-commerce to just smart phones, but broadens the devices to tablets, laptops, and Netbooks. M-commerce has two unique qualities over other e-commerce domains: mobility and broad reach (Ngai *et al.* 2007). Mobility allows users to buy or sell goods and services virtually anywhere anytime. Broad reach means consumers can be reached at any time via their mobile devices.

The same issues of trust and security plague m-commerce as it does e-commerce. However, m-commerce is plagued with additional issues like mobile network security, network connectivity and presentation issues. Despite the additional issues for m-commerce, one of the reasons for its amazing growth and popularity is its convenience (Rao *et al.* 2003). With the proliferation of smart phones and tablets and the fact that many people carry a phone with them, consumers can purchase a wide variety of goods or service instantly. These applications can range from purchasing train tickets, sporting events, vending machines, music, videos, and books with many more possibilities in the future.

The m-commerce field is growing at a fast pace and changes constantly. Advances in wireless network technology, smart phones and tablets offer personalized services to mobile users that give pace to a rapid developing field (Tsalgatidou *et al.* 2001). Because of this growth, many companies allocate significant resources on these technologies to provide value added, interactive and location-based services such as content download, banking, and road-side assistance to customers (Lin *et al.* 2006).

Although statistics are different across studies, according to Javelin Strategy and Research (2013), 51 percent of mobile consumers own a smart phone. They estimate by 2016, almost 219 million adults in the U.S. will own a mobile device, with 72 percent of them using smart phones and 40 percent of them using a tablet (Johnson 2012). Other studies report that in 2012, the U.S. has approximately 321 million mobile subscribers (CITA 2012). The mobile market is worldwide. According to a commercial mobile website, as of 2012, China has over 1 billion mobile subscribers which gives it the largest mobile market in the world (Anonymous 2012). This towers over the U.S. market.

Some industry analyst assert the continent of Africa has the fastest growing mobile market today (Bryson 2011). They estimate over 735 million people will use their mobile phones by the end of 2012 for anything from banking to tracking animals for wildlife studies (Bryson 2011). The rural nature of the continent and the lack of proper infrastructure have led to this fast increase of mobile adoption. This mobile penetration is second only to Asia. Europe's mobile market, the birthplace of m-commerce, is currently saturated and has shown little growth over the past few years (Kuittinen 2012).

An internet technology company, comScore, compiled statistics of mobile phone usage of seven countries in 2010. The seven countries included the U.S., UK, Germany, France, Spain, Italy, and Japan. Within the mobile phone user group, 46% of Americans used internet or mobile applications compared to 41% of Europeans and 76% of Japanese (comScore 2011). Surprisingly, the same survey reported that 11% of Americans used their mobile phones to access financial services like bank accounts compared to 8% of Europeans and 7% of Japanese.

Although the statistics are slightly different depending on the study, one thing is certain: m-commerce is growing and will continue to grow. The innovation in wireless technology, smart phones, and tablets will lead to a stronger, more developed m-commerce platform for organizations.

M-Commerce History

M-commerce was first available to the public in Helsinki, Finland in 1997. Two mobile-phone enabled Coca-Cola machines were able to accept payments via short messaging service (otherwise known as SMS) text messages. Consumers were able to purchase the drink by sending a text message to the machine. The machine delivered the drink and the charge appeared on the consumer's mobile phone bill. In 1997, Merita Bank of Finland offered users mobile phone based banking. The next year Finland mobile consumers were able to download digital content to their mobile phones. This was the birth of purchasing and downloading ring tones which is still prolific today. In 1998, a Finnish mobile operator Radiolinja launched the first commercially available ring-tone service which allowed Finnish consumers to download ring tones (Halper 2004).

In 1999, two major national commercial platforms were created and deployed in the Philippines and Japan. The Philippines launch SmartMoney (http://www1.smart.com.ph/money) which is still in existence today. SmartMoney allows users to transfer money, shop online, pay bills and buy pre-paid credits for future use. NTT DoCoMo, one of Japan's largest mobile phone carriers, launched i-Mode mobile internet service. After the launch of these platforms, m-commerce took off rapidly over the next decade. In early 2000, Norway allowed users to pay for parking tickets. Japan allowed customers the ability to purchase airline tickets. Austria allowed users the ability to purchase train tickets.

In the last several years, m-commerce has grown from a simple SMS and internet approach to an application based platform. This has allowed companies to use other features of the mobile phone like the camera and mobile GPS (global positioning system) for a richer experience. For example, consumers can scan product barcodes and instantly shop for the item in nearby stores or online for a cheaper price. The mobile GPS feature allows companies to use location-based services to target and offer special marketing packages to consumers. If a customer is currently in a store shopping, the company can push coupons to the mobile user in order to keep the customer shopping. Pushing coupons to customers' mobile phones that are currently in a brick-and-mortar store is a technique used in m-commerce.

What is the Current M-Commerce Market?

Current Research

The current research in m-commerce can be divided into several subcategories. In a literature review, Ngai and Gunasekaran (2007) categorized the literature into development, behavioral issues, economics, strategy, business models, legal, ethical, context and usage. We will briefly touch on the current research in a few of these subcategories.

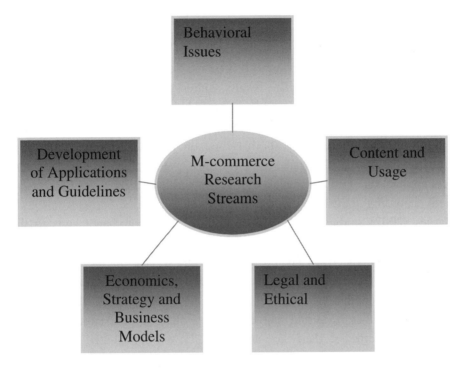

Figure 1. M-commerce research streams

Ocampo *et al.* (2003) summarizes the technologies used for the development of wireless Internet services and classifies them in terms of life cycle, engineering and managerial processes. Like other research in this area, they discuss wireless internet service characteristics that are unique to m-commerce like scalability, specific mobile services, usability on a small screen and keyboard, and device independence. The researchers highlight the fact that most businesses run their mobile sites in conjunction or on top of their existing websites. Because of this, the mobile sites need to be scalable and should be able to support mobile internet users and desktop internet users simultaneously.

Gilbert *et al.* (2003) study technology anxiety and how it correlates with gender, age and academic background and how this affects m-commerce use. For example, according to the study, females show more technophobia than males. The implication of this research suggests that wireless application developers and mobile marketers should evaluate demographics and human factors when designing and implementing wireless applications.

Magura (2003) reports on a study conducted by three researchers in China on the factors that affect the amount or likelihood of business transactions via m-commerce for Hong Kong consumers. Keep in mind that Hong Kong mobile-phone penetration rate was close to 89% in 2003 (Magura 2003). The survey examined low-involvement purchases (i.e., movie tickets) and high-involvement purchases (i.e., stock trades). The results, quite surprising, showed that low-involvement purchases require an even greater degree of convenience and security was not much of an issue for high-involvement purchases. The implication of this research suggests that companies should first understand the level of involvement in the transaction for the consumer before designing the wireless application. Different levels of involvement lend themselves to different solutions according to the Hong Kong survey.

Barnes (2002) studied how different aspects of m-commerce adds to the value chain. He examined the value chain from infrastructure and services, and from the content perspective. The infrastructure and services included examining the transport layer technology, services provided, interfaces, and applications. Content included content creation (e.g., text, audio, video, etc.), packaging (e.g., sports, news, weather, etc.) and marketing (e.g., alerts, e-mails, location based services, etc.). Barnes studied each aspect and how it contributed to the value chain.

One topic that has become well known in e-commerce and is no stranger in m-commerce is intellectual property rights. Hartung and Ramme (2000) discuss how digital rights management (DRM) systems are needed and used in m-commerce to the protect the rights of businesses. DRM systems incorporate encryption, conditional access, copy control mechanisms, and media identification and tracking mechanisms. These systems help track and improve the rights of intellectual property owners.

Nylander *et al.* (2009) conducted a survey of mobile phone users and found they were most often used in the home (31% of the time), outdoors (23%), in transit (23%), indoors (16%), or at work (8%). One interesting finding is that 50 percent of the people use their mobile phones to access the internet even though they had a computer close by.

The research above is not meant to be inclusive or exhaustive but merely a small sample of the current research in m-commerce. The breadth of m-commerce research is vast and like other technology related fields, the m-commerce field is changing rapidly. Often by the time the research is published, some of the results might already be out of date.

Wireless Network Infrastructure

In order to understand how m-commerce works, it is necessary to understand a brief history of mobile phones and the wireless mobile infrastructure. Terms like 3G and 4G are mentioned frequently and it is important to understand what these terms mean. First, let us examine a brief history of mobile phones.

Before cell phones, mobile communication was over radio telephones and citizens' band (CD) radio. This technology allowed users to communicate via radio waves in limited distances. In CB radios, users had 40 channels. This technology, though very popular among people who needed mobile communications (i.e., truck drivers), was limited by antenna size, costs, distance, bandwidth, and interference. This old technology was half-duplex, which meant that the two people communicating could not talk at the same time. One person would talk, release the button and only then could the other person talk. The cellular system solved many of these limitations by dividing areas into cells, hence the word cellular. By dividing a local area into cells, it allowed frequency reuse across a city so that millions of people could use cell phones simultaneous. In addition, cellular technology is full-duplex, which means that users can talk and listen at the same time. The first generation cell phones known as 1G were analog based and revolutionized mobile communications.

Although analog phones were a huge improvement over original radio communication, they were still limited. In analog communications, the radio wave is recorded and used in its original form. This lends itself to two issues, degradation and limited number of users. Because of these issues, analog phones did not fully use the signal between the phone and the cellular network. In addition, the analog signal could not be compressed and manipulated. Digital technology solved some of the issues of analog technology.

Digital technology samples the analog wave in given intervals and turns the wave into bits of 0's and 1's. The two big advantages of digital over analog are that it does not degrade over time and digital technology can be compressed. This compression allows between 3 and 10 digital cell-phone calls to occupy the same space as a single analog call (Brain *et al.* 2011). The digital transformation in mobile phones introduced the second generation of cellular phones commonly known as 2G.

Wireless application protocol (known as WAP) was created around the time 2G was coming out. WAP is a global standard on how wireless web should operate and has encouraged the development of wireless applications and services. WAP is still in use today with services like SMS but is fading as a technology. Although WAP is clearly not as popular as it was in the past it is still used and developed, and handsets that support only WAP are still sold (Danielyan 2003). With the proliferation of smart phones which contain fast processors and "desktop-like" capabilities, WAP is no longer needed to connect to the internet wirelessly.

The next phase of mobile technology came about when mobile broadband was introduced which is referred to 3G or third-generation cell phone technology. Mobile broadband is powered in the same way that makes mobile phones work. Instead of the digital signal containing voice data from the cell tower to the mobile phone, the digital signal carries information like e-mails, web pages, music, or video. Over the past several years, 4G (fourth generation cell phone technology) has been introduced in the market place. 4G technology allows users to connect to the internet wirelessly at very high speeds. This technology allows consumers to conduct business on mobile phones exactly how they would sitting behind their computer. Applications like Skype can work seamless on 4G technology. When this chapter was written, only a few mobile carriers had 4G networks nationwide. Other mobile carriers were only in a few test markets and were slowly expanding nationwide.

There are many different types of mobile networks. Global system for mobile (GSM) and code division multiple access (CDMA) are the two most common in the world and even in the US different carriers use different technologies. The major difference between the two technologies is how they turn voice data into radio waves and how the carrier connects to the phone. GSM is the most widely used globally. Phones that are on the GSM network use small information memory (SIM) cards that hold carrier information and the user's contacts. GSM is used in Europe and AT&T and T-Mobile in the US use the GSM network. CDMA is most commonly used in the US and in some Asian countries like China. Phones that are on the CDMA network usually do not use SIM cards. There are some phones like those developed by Research in Motion (RIM)'s Blackberry that are quad band phones that are both CDMA and GSM. In these cases, the phone works on the CDMA network but still uses a SIM card. Sprint and Verizon in the U.S. use the CDMA network. With the invention of 4G technology, two new mobile networks have surfaced. WiMax (first developed in South Korea) and long term evolution (LTE) introduced in Scandinavia that work with 4G technology and are being used in the US.

Wireless User Infrastucture

The section above discussed the wireless network infrastructure. This section discusses the user infrastructure which refers to the hardware and software the mobile customers utilize for mobile internet. The hardware refers to the device or phone the customer uses and the software refers to the applications that reside on the mobile device. The purpose of this section is not to provide the latest technology and capabilities of hardware and software since the content will already be out of date by the time the chapter is published. This section will provide key characteristics of both hardware and software and the bare minimum needed to run m-commerce.

Hardware

Hardware, in this context, refers to the mobile devices that communicate with the m-commerce applications such as smart phones and tablets. Although this chapter takes a broader definition of m-commerce to include laptops, Netbooks, tablets and smart phones, we are going to focus mainly on smart phones. Since laptops, Netbooks and tablets all use larger screens, these mobile devices can use the same presentation layer as desktop computers for displaying Web content. Smart phones on the other hand have much different presentation requirements due to the small size of the screen. For this reason, this hardware chapter will just examine the requirements and characteristics of smart phones and mobile phones.

The last decade has seen explosive growth in hardware. Following Moore's Law (1965), which states that the number of transitions on integrated circuits doubles approximately every 18 to 24 months, the size of hardware has decreased in size as the hardware capabilities have simultaneously grown. Just a few decades ago, the cutting age of m-commerce was simple text-based mobile phones and personal digital assistants (PDAs) such a Palm Pilots made by Palm which is now owned by Hewett Packard. The Palm Pilots were cutting edge as far as functionality in a small device, but were not able to connect to a mobile network. The Palm Pilots connected to a mobile phone with a cable in order to gain mobile connectivity (see Figure 2).

Figure 2. Palm Pilot connected to a mobile phone for mobile connectivity (adapted from http://www.dbyrneassociates.com/aol/cell.htm)

The birth of the smart phones soon followed. Smart phones combined the functionality of PDAs with mobile phone technology. The history of Smart phones is not well defined and several companies claim to have initiated the smart phone revolution. IBM released "Simon" in 1994 which tried to combine the functionally of email, calculator, calendar, and a clock with simple phone technology. The problem was in 1994, web browsers and fast networks were not created yet so Simon never really took off (Sager 2012). The phone was released to the public but never gained widespread notoriety. In 1996, Nokia released their 9000 Communicator in a flip-phone style that combined PDA with simple phone capabilities (Nokia 1996). Although it was similar to IBM's "Simon", the Nokia 9000 had the benefit of a more developed internet and mobile network infrastructure. In the early years of smart phones, the devices were bulky, slow and expensive. Throughout the next decade, smart phones were released that were faster, smaller, and gradually decreased in price.

Mobile devices vary in functionality, presentation, and usability. Consumers must decide what combination of features best fit their need for mobile communication. Just a decade ago, characteristics like strong voice orientation versus strong data orientation, mobility versus capability, and individual communication versus enterprise application were decisions consumers needed to make (Barnes 2003). For example, during the 2000's, RIMs Blackberry was the leading provider of enterprise mobile communications. Their enterprise activation technology allowed employees to connect to their employer's information exchange like Microsoft Exchange. Emails, calendar updates, meeting requests, notes and contacts were immediately pushed to the Blackberry device. During this timeframe, no other phone had this capability which led to RIM's big success. Other mobile devices during this time had this functionality, but other phones had to set up a "sync" schedule to connect to their employer's exchange. This made the Blackberry one the most popular devices for business employees for most of the decade. Despite the success of RIM for business employees, the Blackberry fell short of the application market for games and other software that drew in the rest of the mobile consumers. This is an example of the tradeoff consumers made between individual communication versus enterprise application and mobility versus capabilities.

Today's mobile devices combine most of the capabilities into one device. Consumers do not need to choose between mobility versus capability or between strong voice versus strong data. Devices today can support all of these capabilities which make the mobile market even more competitive. Companies like RIM who flourished in the 2000's now are struggling with the consumer market since almost all mobile devices allow consumers to connect to their employer's information exchange if the employer allows the connection.

In 2012, the major players in the mobile phone market met in Barcelona for their annual showcase in which they demo and discuss the latest trends to the market. There were five major hardware trends at the 2012 show which were quad-core processors, bigger high-def screens, mobile payments using near-field communications (NFC) and cheaper smart phones (Ricknas 2012). The first trend, quad-core processing will allow phones to have better performance on high computational tasks like full motion video games without draining the battery, which is always a problem with smart phones. In some quad processors, like the Tegra 3 made by NVIDIA, one processor is used just for simple tasks like the phone capabilities or receiving/sending emails while the other processors are used for complex tasks. This increases the battery life of the phone (Ricknas 2012).

The second hardware trend is bigger high definition screens. Smart phone screen size and resolution are an interesting trend over the past few decades. For example, the Nokia Communicator released in 1996 contained a resolution of 240 X 320 pixels. Compare that to 2012 smart phones like the Samsung Galaxy 3S which contains a resolution of 480 X 800 pixels. M-commerce applications can provide more functionally with higher screen resolution today than they could just a year ago. The wide variety in display sizes and resolution makes it difficult for M-commerce companies to develop for mobile devices. The LG Optimus 4X HD and the HTC One X released in 2012 both have a 4.7 inch screen with a resolution of 1280 X 780 pixels. A growing number of vendors are testing applications on even larger mobile phone interest to see if the market can tolerate it (Ricknas 2012).

The third trend is near field communications. NFC is a set of standards for smart phones and similar devices that allow users to touch devices and transfer data via radio waves. At the beginning of 2012, several smart phone providers had the capability of NFC like Acer, Samsung, LG, and Nokia. The problem is compatibility between the phones.   For example, users with Samsungs can transfer between one another, but Samsung cannot transfer with Acer for example. The market trend is to address this compatibility issue between phones. According to Ricknas (2012), the biggest hurdle to NFC is to change user behavior, which takes much longer than deploying the infrastructure or devices.

The fourth trend for mobile phones is growing the LTE is the standard for wireless comunication in the US market. As mentioned earlier in the chapter, LTE is a type of network for 4G communciations.   LTE has become the prominent 4G market in the US however Europe is lagging behind on LTE. The problem with LTE is that some phones are not compatible with the technology because of the processors they use. Vendors are not interested in spending the money to make their phones compatible until they are sure that the LTE market is going to be stable. This is a trend that the market will continue to watch in order to have a stable 4G infrastructure.

The final trend in the 2012 annual showcase of smart phones is producing cheaper smart phones.   Smart phones, though packed with functionality, games, applications, and capabilities, are still expensive. Vendors in the smart phone market are aware of this and they are trying to make inexpensive smart phones to hit more of the consumer market.   Although the effort is commendable, inexpensive smart phones are still in the range of $250 (USD).   Until this price comes down more, a lot of US consumers will still not be able to afford a smart phone.

Software

Historically, web and mobile phone developers created applications for a specific device, family of devices, or specific browsers. Companies would build and maintain two different websites, one for a computer browser and one for a mobile browser. For example, applications were built that were supported on IE (Internet Explorer service provider) and Google Chrome but maybe not on a mobile platform like Apple iOS. As mobile devices changed, the separate applications could not adapt fast enough. Applications that appeared normal on IE8, for example, could not even load on a Blackberry browser. This was a great concern for companies trying to stay competitive in the M-commerce market. Developers used Javascript and cascading style sheets (CSS) as tools that helped transform a page to meet the different sizes and resolutions of the different presentation layers

(Leggett 2011). However, mobile devices are not consistent in their rendering of Javascript or CSS which means the mobile applications are not consistent on the presentation.

In more recent years, an effort to standardize development on mobile applications has surfaced called the "One Web" approach. The One Web approach to web design is a broad concept that states the web should be open regardless of who you are or what device you are using. This philosophy suggests that companies should focus not on creating native applications, but instead should focus on creating experiences everyone is able to get to regardless of their device (Osmani 2011). This philosophy is fairly new and broad, so it will be an interesting trend to follow over the next several years.

Two upcoming and growing fields in m-commerce are mobile banking and mobile payments. Mobile banking is older and more established compared to mobile payment. These fields will define and shape m-commerce over the next decade. Mobile banking and mobile payment are discussed below.

What is M-Banking?

Mobile banking (m-banking) is one of the main applications of m-commerce and is growing rapidly worldwide. We define mobile banking as the bundle of capabilities a consumer can interact with his or her bank or financial institution via a mobile device. These capabilities can include checking balances, transferring funds, depositing checks via cameras, making payments to the bank, and completing credit applications. This definition is different than mobile payments in which the consumer can make payments directly to a business via a mobile payment application. We will discuss mobile payments later in the chapter.

The Yankee Group (www.yankeegroup.com), a research and advisory company, estimates that there will be 500 million m-banking users globally by 2015 (Yankee_Group 2011). Global Industry Analyst Inc., a publisher of off-the-shelf market research, estimates that the U.S., Europe and Asia-Pacific dominate the global mobile banking market (Global Industry Analysts 2010). They also state that Europe is still in the early stages of m-banking and their business model is based off of convenience and value added services rather than revenue generation like the U.S (Global Industry Analysts 2010).   Another interesting statistic is that Kenya is the world leader, as far as percent of mobile customers who use m-Banking, in mobile money services in 2012 according to Communications Commission of Kenya (2012). It is estimated that 65 percent (19 million users) are subscribed to mobile money services (Kenya 2012), compared to about 27 percent in the U.S. in 2011 (Yankee_Group 2011).

One interesting finding is the postulated reasons why Kenyans trust m-banking. Morawczynski and Miscione (2008) discovered that Kenyans do not trust banking agents with their money so interpersonal trust between the customers and the banking agents are weak. However, the institutional trust relations between the customer and Safari.com, the mobile service provider that offers m-banking, is strong. This means customers use m-banking because they believe that their money will be kept safe by the mobile service provider. Although this model is not the same in U.S., Europe or Asia-Pacific, this relationship highlights the importance in collaboration between the financial institute and mobile providers.

The main driving force behind m-banking is the financial institutions themselves. M-banking provides a mean for banks to keep their customers and to generate more payment revenue. The more convenient and the more services that are offered on m-banking, the less likely consumers are to quit using the bank. For example, several banks offer check deposits through their mobile phone. According to banks, mobile check deposits mean improved customer loyalty/retention, higher customer satisfaction, additional revenue streams (if banks charge per deposit), competitive advantages, and more importantly, lower check processing costs.

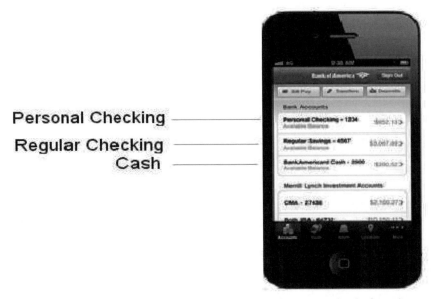

Figure 3. M-banking from Bank of America (adapted from www.bankofamerica.com)

Mobile banking has had a slow start in the industry. One of the main reasons is consumer's trust for mobile systems. Research has examined factors of why consumers are slow to use the services provided in m-banking. Luarn and Lin (2005) examined the factors determining users' acceptance of mobile banking (Davis 1985). Luarn and Lin posit that an important trust-based measurement in the context of mobile banking is needed to help explain user's reluctance. Kim *et al.* (2009) examined consumer's initial lack of trust in m-banking. They found that three variables — relative benefits, a user's propensity to trust and structural assurances — all had a significant effect on initial trust in m-banking. In this research relative benefit refers to when a new service like m-banking offers greater value to customers than existing ones like traditional brick and mortar or ATM banking.   A user's propensity to trust refers to person's disposition to rely on others in various situations. Lastly, structural assurances refer to agreements, contracts, policies, laws, etc. that are in place to assure the customer when dealing in an online environment. These three variables together affected a customer's trust in using online banking. Banks could use this information to increase the trust in their customer's to use the m-banking services. For example, by assuring the customer that policies are in place when a security breach occurs and funds are lost, the bank will guarantee funds to be returned to the account.

In addition to trust, other research has examined risk factors in adopting m-banking. Luo *et al.* (2010) examined multi-dimensional trust, performance expectancy, self-efficacy, and multi-faceted risk factors on adoption of an emerging IT system like m-banking.   They discovered that the customer's perceived performance expectation was the most significant factor in determining user adoption. This means that the user expects the system to work fast with little or no errors. In regards to the multi-faceted risk factors, they discovered that six different types of risk play a role in user adoption of m-banking. The six risk factors are financial, performance, privacy, time, psychological, and overall risks.

Lin (2011) surveyed Taiwanese m-banking users and found that perceived relative advantage, ease of use of the application, competence and integrity significantly influence attitude which in turns leads to a customer's intention to adopt the m-banking application. In addition Lin found that attitude toward m-banking applications differ between potential and repeat customers. This is an interesting find especially for banking managers where trying to attract a potential customer is different than trying to keep an existing customer.

Since the introduction of smaller tablets the line between mobile banking and internet banking is being blurred. Before tablets, mobile banking was simply internet banking on mobile devices. Since tablets combine mobility with normal internet capabilities, m-banking technically might not exist. However, Laukkanen (2007) studied the difference between internet banking and m-banking and found customers value the two differently. For example, efficiency, convenience, and safety were more important to customers on m-banking than in internet banking.

The research discussed so far mentions that trust, risk, and ease of use all play a role in increasing m-banking adoption or intention to adopt. However, how do banks increase a customer's trust in using m-banking applications? Li and Yeh (2011) suggests that design aesthetics significantly impact certain characteristics like customization, usefulness and ease of use which affect customer trust. Using previous literature in the area of design aesthetics, Li and Yeh (2011) report design aesthetics include elements of colors, shapes, language, music or animation with a proper presentation of headers, decorative font, and colorful graphical buttons. Since mobile phone screen sizes differ and are usually much smaller than computers, banks struggle to create an ideal m-banking solution. Sarker and Wells (2003) imply that physical limitations of the device to hinder trust development can be overcome by the beauty of the website aesthetics.

Other research has sought to find ways that increase trust in m-banking. For example, Belanger et al. (2002) examined privacy seals, privacy statements, third party security seals and security features on e-commerce websites. The results of their study found that customer's looked at security features more than the seals or privacy statements. Interestingly, their study also concluded that privacy and security features were of lesser importance than pleasure features like convenience, ease of use, and cosmetics. Muñoz-Leiva et al. (2010) conducted a study on m-banking customers and found that the mere presence of security and privacy seals is not in itself important in explaining trustworthiness of a website. However, they found the combination of an image denoting security arrangements together with customer testimonials is effective in increasing trustworthiness of the m-banking application. Kang et al. (2011) conducted an empirical study on banking customers and found that their trust in the offline bank (i.e., brick and mortar) transferred to the online bank. This trust reflected online trust and perceived satisfaction with m-Banking transactions.

Given the amount of capabilities offered in m-banking, the industry is rapidly growing. Research has examined the customer adoption and intention to use m-banking applications. A large number of research has examined trust and trustworthiness in m-banking. As discussed, some factors that influence trust are design aesthetics, ease of use, perceived performance expectations, and privacy features combined with customer testimonials. Banking managers need to push m-banking to their customers in order to keep existing customers and decrease internal banking costs. Trying to balance the right set of design aesthetics on the plethora of different mobile devices is difficult. Banks and other financial institutions spend a great deal of time and money on getting this correct.

What are M-Payments?

Companies realize that mobile devices are the most widely used technical device in the world, so mobile payments (m-payments) open many more channels for companies to sell their goods and services. M-payments actually started the beginning of m-commerce in Helsinki, Finland in 1997. As mentioned earlier in the chapter, customers could purchase a Coca-Cola through a vending machine and pay with their mobile phones. This launched the field of m-commerce and laid the groundwork for future innovation and services. M-payments now can be used in a variety of ways including paying for digital content (i.e., ring tones, logos, games), transportation fees (i.e., parking fees, train/airline tickets), tickets to concerts/sporting events, utilities, invoices, vending machines, and point of sale terminals (Dahlberg *et al.* 2008).

M-payments are not just the mobilization of payments. Traditional brick and mortar payments using a credit card involve a credit card swiping (CCS) device that allows the vendor to swipe the credit card. The ownership and capabilities of the device is with the seller. Even in online shopping, credit card payments are processed through software or third party vendors like PayPal. M-payments take the ownership and capabilities from the seller and moves it to the buyer, in this case his or her mobile device. M-payments can be defined as "Any payment where a mobile device is used in order to initiate, activate, and/or confirm a payment" (Karnouskos *et al.* 2004 p. 44).

Since the definition of mobile devices has been blurred over the past several years with the introduction of tablets, netbooks, e-readers, and smart phones, so has the definition of m-payments. Technically, m-payments can be made on any mobile device so tablets can be considered a mobile device in which payment can be made. However, in terms of this chapter, we will consider m-payments as only on mobile devices with mobile capabilities as opposed to just WiFi capabilities. Although the same functionality may be realized by the mobile version of the payment services as compared to the internet version, in general, designing for the mobile world is different (Karnouskos *et al.* 2004).

As previously discussed, m-payments are different from m-banking. Although banking services may allow m-payments, usually m-payments refer to services that are more general in scope, universally available, and which can be realized by other financial service providers beyond just banks (Karnouskos *et al.* 2004). These two concepts have different services and capabilities that share an intersection only with payments.

M-payments are executed with a mobile payment instrument like a mobile credit card or a mobile wallet. From a vendor's perspective, credit card swipe devices are becoming smaller and cheaper and can be attached to a mobile phone. This allows vendors to accept credit cards wherever they want to do business without being confined to a wired or wireless connection. According to MerchantExpress (www.merchantexpress.com), a credit card processing company, swiping credit cards through this terminal qualifies the vendor for lower processing fees.

Figure 4. Credit card swiper from a mobile phone (adapted from http://www.elect-mer.com/cell-phone-credit-card-swiper/)

A mobile wallet is an account that a customer sets up on their mobile device and stores his or her credit card, debit card or banking information. Customers can use their mobile phone to make payments either in person, over a mobile network or over a WiFi network (if enabled). There are several vendors who support mobile wallets including PayPal, Google, Visa, and Amazon just to name a few. Javelin Strategy and Research (2013) study rated mobile wallet services on three factors – innovation, trust and privacy. They found that Visa was consumer's number one choice for a mobile wallet followed by PayPal, Verizon and AT&T (Johnson 2012). The latest version of Google Wallet allows customers to shop mobile sites without having the customer enter in the credit/debit card information (Tode 2012).

Mobile wallets have also extended into other technologies. Mobile operator China Unicom partners with a large Chinese bank to launch mobile wallet service in Shanghai for NFC enabled phones. Participating merchants, like Starbucks, allow Shanghai customers to pay using their mobile phones by just making contact with the credit card machine (Qing 2012). Quick response codes (QR codes) are the square bar codes that contain black square dots or rectangles on a white background. QR codes can be read quickly by devices and can hold more information that standard university product codes (UPC). Customers link their credit/debit card to a mobile service and receive a unique QR code. The customers can scan their QR codes at select businesses to complete a transaction. An instant digital receipt is created on the mobile device. There are many advantages to using a mobile wallet for the customer and the vendor, however, the vendor must be able to support this technology. Until more vendors support reading mobile devices either through NFC or QR codes, mobile wallets will remain an under used service.

Figure 5. QR code sample

There are several issues with mobile payments including trust, regulatory, security, and partnerships. For example, as mobile networks expand through more partner channels, strategies to detect fraud, identify theft, and money laundering need to be identified (Merritt 2011). Mobile carries need to work with local and national authorities to identify risk factors for these type of crimes.

The more partners added to the value chain, the harder it is to detect the fraud. For example, mobile payments involve partnerships between the mobile carrier (or internet service providers (ISP) if WiFi is used), financial institutions, payment vendor (e.g., Visa) and merchant. Carriers could also need to work with banks to determine limits for daily spending. Financial institutions have established algorithms to try to detect fraud and mobile carriers can tap into this business logic themselves.

In European countries, the mobile payment value chain partners also need to worry about regulatory issues across borders. Traveling between countries is more common in Europe compared to Asia or North America, so European companies need to consider data privacy, data sharing, banking rules, law enforcement, and legal jurisdictions between countries (Merritt 2011).

The adoption of mobile payment has not been high in the U.S. compared to other areas of the world like Europe, Asia and even Africa. Crowe *et al.* (2010) examined long term and short term benefits from both the demand side and supply side to determine factors of why Americans are slow to adopt m-payments. They surmise that the in the U.S., existing payment systems work well and introducing wide-spread m-payments will lead to a low benefit-cost ratio. On the supply side Crowe *et al.* speculate low market concentration and strong competitive forces of banks and mobile carries make coordination difficult. There is also a network effect problem where consumers will not demand this service until enough merchants accept them, and merchants will not implement m-payments until enough consumers use the technology.

Kim *et al.* (2010) conducted an empirical examination of factors that influence adoption of m-payments. Using a survey of m-payment users Kim *et al.* found early adopters of m-payment value ease of use and confidently rely on their own m-payment knowledge. The study also found that late adopters of m-payment responded very positively to the usefulness of m-payment, specifically reachability and convenience of usage. This study can help merchants decide what factors are most important when trying to implement an m-payment solution. For example, it is more important for merchants to design for convenience of usage and not compatibility between devices.

In another study, Schierz *et al.* (2010) conducted a survey of German m-payment users and found different results than Kim *et al.* Schierz *et al.* found the most important factor for m-payment adoption is perceived compatibility of mobile payment services. Perceived compatibility refers to degree to which mobile payment is reconcilable with existing values, behavioral patterns, and experiences. According to Schierz *et al.*, managers of vendors wanting to implement m-payment solutions are challenged to develop and advertise mobile payment devices and solutions in a way that consumers regard them as well-suited to their individual behavioral patterns and prior experience.

Polasik *et al.* (2011) conducted a study that examined the time efficiencies of a wide variety of payment methods at a point-of-sale terminal for more than 3,700 transactions in convenience store in Poland. They examined payments using cash, credit cards with a magnetic strip, credit cards with a smart chip, contactless cards, and NFC mobile payments. They found that contactless cards without printing a receipt was the most efficient way to pay and was the first technology to beat cash as the fastest way to pay. They found that NFC mobile payments were the least efficient when making a payment. This study has not been conducted anywhere else, so the generalizibility of the results may not hold true in Western Europe, Asia or North America. However, the results are not positive for merchants or customers who want to use m-payments. If the transaction is not fast, then adoption of m-payments might not take off in the U.S.

Summary

The purpose of this chapter was to present high level ideas and trends in the market. This will allow the reader to speculate on upcoming technologies in the m-commerce space. This chapter covered the basics of m-commerce from several different angles, research and applications. An introduction of m-commerce was discussed with figures of current usage and statistics including a brief discussion of the difference between e-commerce and m-commerce. Next, a brief history of m-commerce was examined. Third, the current m-commerce market was discussed. This market was examined from current research, wireless network infrastructure, and user infrastructure. Special attention was given to mobile banking and mobile payment which are two upcoming m-commerce applications.

◆ Review Terms

Cascading style sheets (CSS)
CB (Citizens' band) radio
Code division multiple access
(CDMA)
Credit card swiping (CCS)
Digital rights management (DRM)
Global system for mobile (GSM)
Internet service providers (ISP)
Long term evolution (LTE)
M-commerce
Mobile banking (m-banking)
Mobile broadband
Mobile GPS (global positioning
system)
Mobile payments (m-payments)

Mobile wallets
Near-field communications (NFC)
Palm Pilots
Personal digital assistants (PDAs)
Quick response (QR) codes
Short messaging service (SMS)
Small information memory (SIM)
cards
SmartMoney
WiMax
Wireless application protocol
(WAP)
Wireless mobile infrastructure

◆ Discussion Questions

1. Explain how "m-commerce" is changing the business market place.
2. Explain why "mobility" is so important in today's business and consumer
   markets.
3. Explain the history of "m-commerce".
4. Explain how the research streams on "m-commerce" are developing.
5. Explain how the "wireless network infrastructure" aids the development of
   "m-commerce."
6. Explain what types of technologies can be found in a "wireless network
   infrastructure."
7. Explain what "m-banking" is used for in business.
8. Explain what "m-payments" are used for in business.

◆ Questions

1. What is the difference between "m-commerce" and e-commerce?
2. In the early development of "m-commerce" what role did SMS play?
3. How does "m-commerce" add to a firm's value chain?
4. How is a "wireless application protocol "used in "m-commerce"?

5.   What is the difference between a "global system for mobile" (GSM) and a "code division multiple access" (CDMA)?
6.   What are near-field communications (NFC) and how are they used in "m-commerce"?
7.   Why is understanding technology trends important to study in "m-commerce"?
8.   Why do you think banks are the driving force behind "m-banking"?

References

Anonymous "China passes 1 billion mobile subscribers, passes 400 Million Mobile Web Users and Overtakes US as World's Top Smartphone Market," MobiThinking, 2012.

Avgerou, C., Smith, M., and van der Besselaar, P., (eds.), *Social Dimensions of Information and Communication Technology Policy*, Springer Boston, 2008, pp. 287-298.

Barnes, S. *m-Business: The Strategic Implications of Wireless Technologies* Butterworth-Heinemann, Burlington, MA, 2003.

Barnes, S. J. "The Mobile Commerce Value Chain: Analysis and Future Developments," *International Journal of Information Management* (22:2) 2002, pp 91-108.

Belanger, F., Hiller, J.S., Smith, W.J. "Trustworthiness in Electronic Commerce: The Role of Privacy, Security, and Site Attributes," *Journal of Strategic Information Systems* (11:3-4) 2002, pp 245-270.

Brain, M., Tyson, J., and Layton, J. "How Cell Phones Work," H.S. Works, Discovery Communications, Atlanta, 2011.

Bryson, D. "Industry says Africa fastest growing mobile market," in: *Yahoo! Finance*, 2011.

CITA "U.S. Wireless Quick Facts", International Association for the Wireless Telecommunications Industry, 2012.

comScore. comScore Releases Inaugural Report, "The 2010 Mobile Year in Review"," comScore, 2011.

Coursaris, C., and Hassanein, K. "Understanding M-commerce: A Consumer-centric Model," *Quarterly Journal of Electronic Commerce* (3) 2002, pp 247-272.

Crowe, M., Rysman, M., and Stavins, J. "Mobile Payments at the Retail Point of Sale in the United States: Prospects for Adoption," *Review of Network Economics* (9:4) 2010.

Dahlberg, T., Mallat, N., Ondrus, J., and Zmijewska, A. "Past, Present and Future of Mobile Payments Research: A Literature Review," *Electronic Commerce Research and Applications* (7:2) 2008, pp 165-181.

Danielyan, E. "WAP: Broken Promises or Wrong Expectations?," in: *The Internet Protocol Journal* CISCO (ed.), 2003.

Davis, F. D. "A Technology Acceptance Model for Empirically Testing New End-user Information Systems: Theory and Results," Massachusetts Institute of Technology, Sloan School of Management, 1985.

Gilbert, D., Lee-Kelley, L., and Barton, M. "Technophobia, Gender Influences and Consumer Decision-making for Technology-related Products," *European Journal of Innovation Management* (6:4) 2003, pp 253-263.

Global Industry Analysts. "Global Mobile Banking Customer Base to Reach 1.1 Billion by 2015. ," San Jose, California

Halper, M. "The Sweet Sound of Success," in: *Time Magazine*, Time Inc., 2004.

Hartung, F., and Ramme, F. "Digital Rights Management and Watermarking of Multimedia Content for M-commerce Applications," *Communications Magazine, IEEE* (38:11) 2000, pp 78-84.

Javelin Strategy and Research. "10 Trends for Financial Services in 2013: Forging a New Frontier for Banking, Payments, Mobile and Security." https://www.javelinstrategy.com/brochure/273.

Johnson, L. "Visa is No. 1 Consumer Choice for Mobile Wallet: Study," M.C. Daily, 2012.

Kang, I., Lee, K. C., Kim, S. M., and Lee, J. "The Effect of Trust Transference in Multi-banking Channels; Offline, Online and Mobile," *International Journal of Mobile Communications* (9:2) 2011, pp 103-123.

Karnouskos, S., and Fokus, F. "Mobile Payment: A Journey Through Existing Procedures and Standardization Initiatives," *IEEE Communications Surveys & Tutorials* (6:4) 2004, pp 44-66.

Kenya Communications Commission,. "Sector Statistics Report Q4 2011/12,". Nairobi, Kenya, 2012.

Kim, C., Mirusmonov, M., and Lee, I. "An Empirical Examination of Factors Influencing the Intention to Use Mobile Payment," *Computers in Human Behavior* (26:3) 2010, pp 310-322.

Kim, G., Shin, B., and Lee, H. G. "Understanding Dynamics Between Initial Trust and Usage Intentions of Mobile Banking," *Information Systems Journal* (19:3) 2009, pp 283-311.

Kuittinen, T. "How Bad Is Europe's Mobile Tailspin?," Forbes Online, June 18, 2012.

Laukkanen, T. "Internet vs Mobile Banking: Comparing Customer Value Perceptions," *Business Process Management Journal* (13:6) 2007, pp 788-797.

Leggett, D. "Considerations for Mobile Design," U. Booth , 2011.

Lin, H.-F. "An Empirical Investigation of Mobile Banking Adoption: The Effect of Innovation Attributes and Knowledge-based Trust," *International Journal of Information Management* (31:3) 2011, pp 252-260.

Lin, H. H., and Wang, Y. S. "An Examination of the Determinants of Customer Loyalty in Mobile Commerce Contexts," *Information & Management* (43:3) 2006, pp 271-282.

Luarn, P., and Lin, H.-H. "Toward an Understanding of the Behavioral Intention to use Mobile Banking," *Computers in Human Behavior* (21:6) 2005, pp 873-891.

Luo, X., Li, H., Zhang, J., and Shim, J. P. "Examining Multi-dimensional Trust and Multi-faceted Risk in Initial Acceptance of Emerging Technologies: An Empirical Study of Mobile Banking Services," *Decision Support Systems* (49:2) 2010, pp 222-234.

Magura, B. "What Hooks M-commerce Customers?," *MIT Sloan Management Review* (44:3), Spring 2003, pp 9-9.

Merritt, C. "Mobile Money Transfer Services: The Next Phase in the Evolution of Person-to-person Payments," *Journal of Payments Strategy & Systems* (5:2) 2011, pp 143-160.

Moore, G. "Cramming More Components onto Integrated Circuits," in: *Electronics Magazine*, 1965.

Morawczynski, O., and Miscione, G. "Examining Trust in Mobile Banking Transactions: The Case of M-PESA in Kenya", *Progress in Developing Studies* (8:1), 2008, pp 13-20.

Muñoz-Leiva, F., Luque-Martínez, T., and Sánchez-Fernández, J. "How to Improve Trust Toward Electronic Banking," *Online Information Review* (34:6) 2010, pp 907-934.

Ngai, E. W. T., and Gunasekaran, A. "A Review for Mobile Commerce Research and Applications," *Decision Support Systems* (43:1) 2007, pp 3-15.

Nokia "Nokia Unveils Worlds First All-In-One Communicator For The Americas", Nokia.

Nylander, S., Lundquist, T., and Brännström, A. "At home and with Computer Access: Why and Where People Use Cell Phones to Access the Internet," Proceedings of the 27th International Conference on Human Factors in Computing Systems, ACM, 2009, pp. 1639-1642.

Ocampo, A., Boggio, D., Munch, J., and Palladino, G. "Toward a Reference Process for Developing Wireless Internet Services," *Software Engineering, IEEE Transactions on* (29:12) 2003, pp 1122-1134.

Osmani, A. "The One Web: Don't Write for Devices, Write for People," in: *Net Magazine*, England 2011.

Polasik, M., Górka, J., Wilczewski, G., Kunkowski, J., Przenajkowska, K., and Tetkowska, N. "Time Efficiency of Point-of-Sale Payment Methods: The Empirical Results for Cash, Cards and Mobile Payments," *Cards and Mobile Payments* February 17, 2011.

Qing, L. Y. "China Unicom Launches NFC-based Mobile Wallet", ZDNET, 2012.

Rao, B., and Minakakis, L. "Evolution of Mobile Location-based Services," *Communications of the ACM* (46:12) 2003, pp 61-65.

Ricknas, M. "Analysis: Five Smartphone Trends at Mobile World Congress," in: *PCWorld Australia*, 2012.

Sager, I. "Before IPhone and Android Came Simon, the First Smartphone," in: *Bloomberg Businessweek*, Bloomberg L.P., 2012.

Sarker, S., and Wells, J. "Understanding Mobile Handheld Device and Adoption," *Communications of the ACM* (46:12) 2003.

Schierz, P. G., Schilke, O., and Wirtz, B. W. "Understanding Consumer Acceptance of Mobile Payment Services: An Empirical Analysis," *Electronic Commerce Research and Applications* (9:3) 2010, pp 209-216.

Tode, C. "Google updates mobile wallet to make purchasing faster," M.C. Daily 2012.

Tsalgatidou, A., and Pitoura, E. "Business Models and Transactions in Mobile Electronic Commerce: Requirements and Properties," *Computer Networks* (37:2) 2001, pp 221-236.

Yankee Group "Yankee Group Sees Global Mobile Transactions Exceeding $1 Trillion by 2015," Boston, MA, Taken on January 17, 2013, www.yankeegroup.com.

<u>Chapter 12</u> CLOUD COMPUTING

Learning Objectives

After completing this chapter, you should be able to:
Define and describe "cloud computing."
Explain the history of cloud computing.
Explain the differences between public and private clouds.
Describe the different types of cloud computing.
Explain the relationship of cloud computing to e-commerce operations.
Describe some of the issues surrounding the use of cloud computing.

Overview of This Chapter

This chapter introduces and defines cloud computing. This chapter explains its historical origins and how it has evolved to become an important element of e-commerce operations. A discussion of current research is presented to provide an understanding of the different types of cloud computing that applied in e-commerce as well as a discussion on important issues impacting the application of cloud computing.

What is Cloud Computing?

Cloud computing is a common term in today's business and consumer market. Phrases like "to the cloud" are all too common on commercials and in boardrooms across the world. To some, the cloud just means placing data on the internet. Actually, cloud computing is much more. Cloud computing takes technology, businesses services, and applications and turns them into a self-service utility (Sosinsky 2011). In e-commerce, the cloud can revolutionize how companies can sell products or services to the world.

It is hard to ignore the growing presence of the cloud. Researchers estimate that the public cloud service market will grow about 20 percent in 2012 to over a billion dollar market worldwide (Gartner 2012) and the public cloud is just one of four different types of clouds. Cloud computing is a trend that will continue to grow, so understanding what the cloud is and how companies can use it are important.

With any new technology, there are benefits and issues. Benefits of cloud computing can include increased trust, cost savings, faster speed, greater scalability, increased security, and faster communication. Of course some of the benefits turn into issues when not handled correctly. For instance trust and security also become a bane for cloud customers and cloud service providers if not addressed properly. Other cloud problems relate to legal and regulatory issues.

This chapter will provide a high level overview of cloud computing. There are entire books dedicated to just cloud computing so condensing information into one chapter necessitates that we stay at a high level. Practical and academic research is discussed and presented throughout the chapter. First we describe what cloud computing is about. Next we briefly discuss the history of cloud computing and where the name came from. Brief statistics are offered to demonstrate the growing field of cloud computing. Next the types of cloud computing offerings are discussed followed by the different types of cloud computing. We finish the chapter discussing benefits of cloud computing to e-commerce as well as current issues related to cloud computing.

How can Cloud Computing be Defined?

The definition of cloud computing is not that straight forward. Researchers and practitioners define cloud computing differently depending on the context. We will use Weinman (2012) (who uses a mnemonic C.L.O.U.D.) to define *cloud computing* in the context of first letter of the following five characteristics: Common infrastructure, Location independence, Online accessibility, Utility pricing, and on-demand resources. Sosinsky (2011) indentifies four characteristics of cloud computing which are scalability, elasticity, low barrier to entry, and utility.

In a comprehensive definition, the National Institute of Standards and Technology (NIST), a U.S. technology agency under the U.S. Commerce department, defines cloud computing as:

> A model for enabling ubiquitous, convenient, on-demand network access to a shared pool of configurable computing resources (e.g., networks, servers, storage, applications, and services) that can be rapidly provisioned and released with minimal management effort or service provider interaction.

These definitions seem a little overwhelming and are vague on purpose. Cloud computing itself varies greatly and encompasses many different technologies and services. In the simplest definition, cloud computing allows users to access computing resources, both hardware and software, over a network.

Before unpacking the definition of cloud computing, it will be useful to understand what motivates companies to use cloud computing. Companies spend a lot of money on data centers. A data center is a facility used to house computer systems and associated components like backup generators, telecommunication networks, and storage devices. Although it depends on the size and use of the data center, it is estimated that companies spend between $10 to $25 million per year on a large data center (Hurwitz *et al.* 2009). Roughly forty-two percent of these costs are spent on hardware, software, disaster recovery, power supplies to prevent interruption, and networking costs. The other estimated fifty-eight percent is for heating, air-conditioning, property/land, and labor costs (Hurwitz *et al.* 2009).

To exacerbate the problem, many data centers are over-engineered for their particular need. Companies design data centers for maximum load although maximum load may only happen once a quarter or even once a year. Companies do this so users do not experience interruption during peak times with the fear of losing possible sales if a user cannot access the company's website. For example, online companies run their facilities at maximum capacity year round regardless of the demand resulting in wasting 90 percent or more of the electricity they pull off the grid (Glanz 2012). In addition, the consulting company McKinsey & Company found that companies were only using 6 to 12 percent of the electricity for actual computations. The rest of the electricity was wasted on keeping servers idling and ready in case of a spike in demand (Glanz 2012). To alleviate these problems, industry experts and researchers believe the answer is cloud computing. By centralizing the computing resources among large, shared data centers companies can utilize the flexible computing resources when they are needed. This will cut down on the idle computing costs that companies spend during slow demand.

Let us examine the shared characteristics of cloud computing defined by Sosinsky (2011) and Weinman (2012). One of the benefits of cloud computing is it allows companies to scale or "ramp-up" the required services when they are needed. This is referred to as scalability which is the ability of a system to handle a growing number of requests effectively. During peak sales, perhaps around the holiday season, a company can request more services from the cloud in order to accommodate the growing number of holiday shoppers. For example, in 2011, BestBuy reported a 26 percent increase in sales for the month of December on their online channel – Bestbuy.com (BestBuy 2012). In order to capture those sales, BestBuy needed to make sure their websites were able to handle the additional traffic.

Common infrastructure in the cloud allows scalability. The only way to provide on-demand resources in an economically beneficial way is through common infrastructure (Weinman 2012). Imagine two companies sharing a cloud computing service. One company sells garden and outdoor supplies and the other company sells party supplies and costumes. Obviously each company has its own peak demand in different parts of the year. The garden and outdoor supply company will probably have peak demand during the spring and early summer. The party supply and costume store will probably have peak demand starting in October and going to the end of the year. Let us also imagine that the cloud service provider will most likely place each company on the same infrastructure because this allows both companies to benefit from each others' alternating peak demand. The only way this will work is if the cloud infrastructure is on a common platform. Since the companies share the same cloud platform, the platform needs to be the same. Now picture this on a global scale. This is why common infrastructure is essential for scalability and is an important requirement for cloud computing.

Another characteristic is *location independence*. This means that an user of cloud computing services, whether it is a company or an individual, should be able to access services ubiquitously regardless of their location (Weinman 2012). Ubiquitous means something is present, appearing or can be found anywhere. The cloud user should be able to access the cloud from his or her home, work, mobile phones, etc. as long as they have network access. With the reach of the internet, this characteristic sounds a little obvious. But, imagine a cloud service provider that has one data center in the northwest U.S. but has customers spread globally.   Customers in Germany might not get the same fast service as customers in California for example.   This cloud service provider will need to create multiple virtual centers in other locations in the world to provide better services for all of its customers.

Online accessibility is another key characteristic of cloud computing. Online accessibility means there must be network access for an user to access the cloud. A network is defined as a sender sending a message to a receiver using a channel over a communications medium.   This does not mean the network is over the Internet. A company using a private cloud may use an internal, private network to communicate with its cloud service provider. Public clouds, however, use the Internet as their network. Regardless of public or private clouds, network access is crucial in cloud computing. The difference between public and private cloud will be discussed later in the chapter.

Utility pricing is another essential characteristic of cloud computing and refers to how the cloud services are priced for the user. The pricing structure for cloud computing varies greatly depending on what service is being provided. In some cases, cloud pricing is determined by usage over time. For example, how many hours is the server utilized. In other cases, cloud pricing is determined by data usage like how many megabytes are transferred over the network regardless of time. Yet another cloud pricing strategy can be based on users or licenses per time frame. For example, a company can pay for 100 licenses per month to use cloud services. Think of utility pricing as a pay-as-you-go model.

The last characteristic of cloud computing is *on-demand*. This means the cloud user can be allocated the right quantity of resources at the right time for the amount of time the user needs at anytime (Weinman 2012).   Although the definition of on-Demand is good in theory, in practice it is not clear cut. Economically, public cloud service providers are not able to provide cloud services at a very small increment of time.   For instance, most cloud service providers charge a minimum of one hour of processing time even though the user may only need two minutes. Ideally, the service provider would benefit more if larger time increments were used for pricing. Conversely, customers of cloud services would benefit more if a smaller time increment were used for pricing. Cloud service providers study the market to understand the right equilibrium of time increments to use for pricing.

Providing on-demand resources is probably the most salient feature of cloud computing. If customer demand is 100 percent predictable then cloud computing would not be needed. In this case, a company can allocate the proper hardware, software, and network access to its customers based on perfect information. However, this is never the case and customer demand can never be forecasted with 100 percent certainty. Therefore, cloud computing can help save companies money during slow customer demand by not wasting unused computing resources. Having more resources than needed can cut into margins and affect capital, profit, and/or earnings. Alternatively, cloud computing can help the company capture more sales during peak customer demand. Having too few resources can lead to slow or non-existent performance which can lead to a bad customer experience. Ultimately, bad customer experience can lead to negative word-of-mouth, loyalty and retention costs, and lost sales.

History of Cloud Computing

The term "cloud" computing most likely originated from the cloud shaped symbol used to represent the Internet in system architecture diagrams.

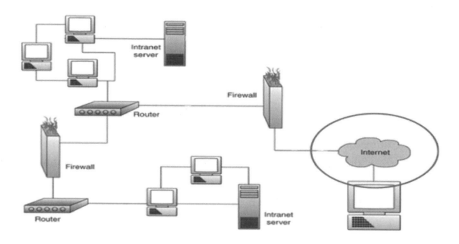

Figure 1. Sample system architecture diagram

Although the commercial use of cloud computing started in the late '90s, the concept behind cloud computing started in the 1960's (Mohamed 2009). The idea behind the "intergalactic computer network" was introduced by J.C. Licklider, one of the founders of the initial Internet known as ARPANET. John

McCarthy, a computer scientist in the 1960's, proposed the idea of computations being delivered like a public utility (Mohamed 2009). These concepts were theoretical until the commercial use of the Internet took off in the mid 1990's.

The first company to use what we now know as cloud computing was Salesforce.com in 1999. Saleforce.com offered enterprise application software via a simple website. Instead of a company purchasing large enterprise software and installing on each of the company's internal application servers, a company paid Salesforce.com to use their software on Salesforce.com servers. This reduced the expense of a company having to purchase, install and maintain commercial software in-house. The services provided by Salesforce.com started other companies to offer their software as a service over the Internet.

Amazon entered the cloud computing market in 2006 with offering *Amazon Web Services (AWS)* which offered IT infrastructure services to business (Amazon 2012). These services included storage, software, and computation services. Other well known companies like Google, Apple and DropBox started offering cloud computing services in the middle of 2000's. Companies that embraced cloud services have thrived in the past decade where their competitors have suffered. Take for example, Amazon versus Borders Books. Amazon accelerated to a market share of over $80 billion with an effective cloud strategy, where Borders Books declared bankruptcy during the same timeframe (Weinman 2012).

What is the Current Cloud Computing Usage?

Gartner Research, a large well-known research firm, estimates the public cloud services market will grow 19.6 percent in 2012 to a total of $109 billion worldwide (Gartner 2012). The research firm also estimates that North America will account for the greatest percentage of absolute growth in the cloud market. They estimate that North America accounts for 61 percent of the growth in cloud services from 2012 to 2016. Western Europe, India, China and Indonesia also expect rapid growth in cloud computing usage over the next decade.

In mid 2012 a survey, conducted by IT industry association CompTIA, of 500 IT decision-makers found that 85 percent felt positive about the benefits of cloud computing which was up from 72 percent in 2011 (Loftus 2012). The same survey showed that eight out of ten companies in the U.S. use some form of cloud technology. Respondents to the survey also indicated that they will continue to invest in cloud technology going forward. Interestingly, the move from in-house computing to cloud computing has caused a shift in the skill set needed in the IT department of companies. Instead of needing IT employees for server maintenance, cloud computing has shifted the need for IT employees to develop and cultivate more innovation (Loftus 2012).

What are the Current Cloud Computing Offerings?

Now that we have discussed the definition of cloud computing and the increasing trend for companies to use cloud computing, let us now discuss the different types of cloud computing offerings. There are many different types of cloud computing services. A company might have all the software it needs, but it does not have the proper hardware to scale efficiently. Another company might need both software and hardware. The advantage of cloud computing is that a company may purchase only the services it needs to be successful in the market. The three most recognized and universally accepted types of cloud computing services are: Infrastructure as a Service (IaaS), Platform as a Service (PaaS) and Software as a Service (SaaS). Figure 2 displays the three main cloud computing offerings and the services provided in each offering.

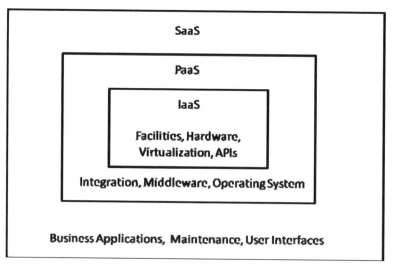

Figure 2. Main cloud computing offerings

There are more types of cloud computing services that are mentioned in the literature and mentioned by vendors supplying cloud computing services. Examples of other services include: Storage as a Service (STaaS), Compliance as a Service (CaaS), Security as a Service (SECaaS), Database as a Service (DBaaS) and Business Processes as a Service (BPaaS). This list is not exhaustive since new services or combinations of services are being introduced continuously. However, all of these services can be described by the three basic offerings: IaaS, PaaS, and SaaS.

Infrastructure as a Service

Infrastructure as a Service (IaaS) is the most basic offering and provides the smallest amount of functionality for cloud computing. In IaaS the cloud vendor provides virtual machines, virtual storage, virtual infrastructure and other hardware assets to its clients. Basically, infrastructure includes the physical facilities, hardware, abstraction, core connectivity, and APIs to connect to the infrastructure. The physical facilities include the space, cooling/heating and power supply. The hardware includes computation power and storage space. Abstraction means the vendor can create images or virtual machines out of a single piece of hardware. The advantage to abstraction is it allows each instance to share the hardware's computing resources and dramatically increase physical server hardware usage. Core connectivity provides a way, usually through an application programming interface (API), to connect users to the hosted infrastructure.

IaaS provides the basic infrastructure for customers, however, the customer is still responsible for many other items. The client or customer is responsible for everything else including providing the operating system, application software, security software, and communication to the infrastructure. Although IaaS provides the APIs to communicate with the infrastructure, the customer is responsible for developing or buying and integrating the middleware that can communicate with the APIs.

IaaS is a popular offering for cloud computing customers. According to a Gartner Research study, IaaS is the fastest growing segment of the public cloud computing services market and is expected to grow 45 percent in 2012 (Gartner 2012). IaaS offerings are ideal for companies that have custom or customized software, and well developed and experienced IT departments. Since a lot of the work falls on the IT department to build out the operating systems and middleware, IaaS can provide just the infrastructure to host all of the company's application software.

IaaS pricing greatly depends on the provider and the needs of the customer. IaaS providers usually charge IaaS services on a utility computing basis which means costs reflect the amount of resourced allocated and consumed. For example, in 2011 Amazon offered eight price bundles according to the amount of storage and memory capacity and the number of CPUs. Google on the other hand only charges for each CPU and each GB of storage and memory capacity (Kihal *et al.* 2012).

Since IaaS is a service, customers demand a guarantee that the service will be up and running when needed. The same way we demand a warranty on our car or appliance, cloud customers also demand that their cloud services will be available when they are needed. This is why cloud service providers offer Service Level Agreements (otherwise known as SLAs) to their customers. For example, the U.S. government demands their IaaS service providers offer a SLA availability of 99.5 percent. This means that the IaaS service providers must be up 99.5 percent of the time during their contract (U.S._General_Services_Administration 2012). Although SLAs are usually written into the contract between the cloud vendor and the cloud customer, sometimes SLAs may be meaningless. The IaaS SLA contracts are worded and structured in a way to make it unlikely that a customer will ever see any money back in the event of an outage that exceeds the SLA term (Leong 2012). Despite this, there can be advantages to the contractual guarantees inherent in service agreements (Weinman 2012).

Platform as a Service

Platform as a Service (PaaS) is another cloud computing offering. This offering provides the same base services as IaaS but includes integration features, middleware, and other communication services. PaaS vendors provide virtual machines, operating systems, and development frameworks. Basically PaaS is the same as IaaS except the cloud vendor provides additional services. In IaaS, the customer is responsible for installing and maintaining the operating system. In PaaS, this is provided by the cloud service provider. Development frameworks are provided to the customers so they may build their own custom software on the cloud platform. In addition, customers do not need develop or purchase separate middleware software since it is provided through the PaaS services.

According to Gartner Research, growth in PaaS is expected to continue to grow over the next several years although it is a smaller market relative to other cloud offerings. It is forecasted that PaaS will grow to a $1.2 billion global market in 2012 (Gartner 2012). PaaS is ideal for companies that have a strong core competency of application development but lack the resources or desire to maintain infrastructure and technical architecture. Companies that utilize PaaS can focus their efforts on design and development of applications without the costs and complexity of procuring and building the underlying hardware and software.

The pricing structure for PaaS varies greatly by vendors. For example, Microsoft's Windows Azure pricing is calculated based on a user's average usage during a billing cycle. Alternatively, Google's App Engine charges by incoming/outgoing bandwidth, CPU time, and/or storage. Another example is AppHarbor whose PaaS pricing is a flat rate per month based on a preset number of users in the system. Due to the large number of competitors in the PaaS vendor market, customers are wise to shop around to find the best pricing structure for their needs.

Software as a Service

Software as a service (SaaS) provides the most services for cloud customers. SaaS vendors provide all of the services as IaaS and PaaS and also include business applications, management of the applications, and user interfaces. Since SaaS provides the most services, it demands a higher price. In the SaaS offering, the cloud vendors provide the application through a thin-client interface (like a web browser). The vendors provide the entire infrastructure, operating systems, middleware, business applications and the connection to the business applications. The customers only need to provide the data needed to run the application and the rights and permissions of the user base.

An example of SaaS service is Quickbooks online. Customers using Quickbooks can log into the service from their browsers, create an account, and enter data in the system. Intuit.com, owner of Quickbooks, is responsible for performance of the hardware, software, security, maintenance, and communication from the browser to the application and back (Sosinsky 2011).

SaaS is the second largest cloud computing offering according to Gartner Research (Gartner 2012) behind what they refer to as business process as a service (BPaaS). SaaS is expected to grow to a $14.4 billion market by 2012. Although SaaS is a much larger market than IaaS, by 2016 it is estimated that IaaS will grow to almost equal the size of the SaaS market (Gartner 2012). Because of the all-in-one solution that SaaS offers, companies that use SaaS often do not have their own IT department. These companies are able to outsource the entire technology solution to a cloud vendor. This allows companies to concentrate resources on their core competencies like sales, customer service, or manufacturing.

Companies that utilize SaaS vary greatly in what services they use. For example, a small start-up company with limited cash flow many only use a few applications during their first few years like a small customer relationship management package. Alternatively large, established companies could use large ERP systems like SAP hosted with a SaaS cloud. Because of the variety of services that can be used, the pricing models for SaaS also vary greatly. Initially SaaS pricing started as a per-user/per-month sometimes with small add-on costs for extras like mobile storage (Herbert 2010). This meant that customers were sometimes being charged for services they were not using during after-hours, weekends, holidays, etc. However, the pricing structure for SaaS has evolved to more of a true usage-based model. True usage-based models mean the pricing structure closely maps to value added services and is only priced when the service is being used. This benefits the customer instead of the cloud vendor. One of the reasons this shift is occurring is because the growing number of competitors in the cloud vendor market.

Other Cloud Offerings

Although only three main cloud computing offerings were mentioned above, there are other types of cloud computing offerings. For simplicity all the other cloud computing offerings can be described as falling under the IaaS, PaaS, and SaaS umbrella. We will describe a few of the other popular cloud offerings.

Business process as a service (BPaaS) is one of the newer cloud computing offerings in the market and is becoming more popular. BPaaS is any type of horizontal or vertical business process that is delivered on top of either IaaS, PaaS, or SaaS offering (Hurwitz *et al.* 2009). Examples of business processes that can be migrated to the cloud are services like payroll, e-commerce transactions, credit checks, and printing just to name a few. For example, a smaller company may want to outsource their payroll functionality to the cloud to cut down on its human resource expenses. Prior to cloud computing that same small company would need to either build or purchase a payroll system and hire an employee to run the system. For smaller companies this is inefficient and not cost effective. Now with cloud computing that same small company can just outsource the payroll functionality to the cloud.

According to Gartner Research, BPaaS is the largest segment of cloud computing as of 2012 and is expected to grow to an $84.2 billion market. This is up from $72 billion in 2011 (Gartner 2012). This same forecast estimated that BPaaS is the largest segment of cloud computing accounting for 77 percent of the cloud market globally.

Another popular type of cloud computing offering is *Storage as a Service (STaaS)* which can fall under IaaS, PaaS, or SaaS depending on the amount of services needed. If the customer needs complete an entire end to end solution then STaaS would fall under SaaS. Conversely, if the customer can build his or her own middleware and user interface then IaaS is all that is needed. STaaS includes data backup and recovery. STaaS allows companies and individuals to store their data with a service provider on a subscription basis. Economies of scale allow the service provider to provide storage cheaper than individuals and most companies can do it themselves. One disadvantage of using STaaS is the bandwidth needed to upload and download large amounts of data to the cloud service provider. In some cases storage vendors can provide DVDs to its customers in case of major data loss in-house. Some storage providers like DropBox, iDrive, Carbonite, and MyPC Backup allow customers to access their data through the internet without having to download a client to the desktop.

Other services like database as a service (DBaaS), security as a service (SECaaS), compliance as a service (CaaS), and IT operations management (ITOM) all fall under one of the main three cloud computing offerings – IaaS, PaaS, or SaaS. Each smaller offering is just a specific type of the larger offerings. For example, DBaaS is just a specific software or service offered under SaaS.

Public, Private or Somewhere In-between?

To this point we have discussed the different offerings customers can utilize from the cloud. Now we will discuss the different types of cloud computing. There are currently four types of the cloud ranging from public, community, hybrid, and private cloud. The public cloud, as the name states, is for the public to use. Community and hybrid clouds are a cross between public and private clouds. The private cloud, as the name suggests, is for the exclusive use of a company or organization. Figure 3 displays the different types of cloud computing and where they are deployed.

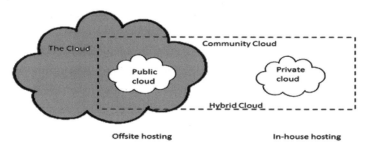

Figure 3. Offsite/in-house cloud hosting (Adapted from Mell and Grance 2011; Sosinsky 2011)

Public Cloud

The *public cloud* infrastructure is available for public use and is owned by organizations selling cloud services (aka cloud service providers) (Sosinsky 2011). This type of cloud allows the general public and companies to use service providers to gain access to services they offer. Almost always, public cloud services are provided over the internet. This means customers using the public cloud do not have a direct network connection to the service provider other than through the Internet.

The public cloud has many advantages due to the economies of scale. Multiple individuals and companies can go together to share the costs of the infrastructure, platform and software. This keeps the cost of cloud computing low and competitive. Another advantage of the public cloud is the elasticity and large scalability of the computing resources. Because so many users are utilizing the public cloud, cloud service providers can scale up or down depending on usage of individual customers. This is based on the assumption that not every user has peak usage at the same time. The disadvantage of the public cloud is the fact that it is public, and individuals and companies that use the public cloud have less visibility in the inner-workings of the service provider. Security is also a concern for public cloud users. Since data travels via the internet to the public cloud, there are inherit security risks. Also, data is stored and manipulated on servers that are not owned by the individual or company. In addition, individuals and companies using the public cloud cannot guarantee privacy in the face of legal or government action (Sosinsky 2011).

Community Cloud

A *community cloud* is where several organizations or individuals that share common concerns come together to share cloud computing resources. Common concerns can refer to the same mission, jurisdiction, security, compliance, governance, management, and/or regulations. For example, all of the departments in the State of California can share a community cloud. Community clouds are somewhere on the continuum between public clouds and private clouds depending on how big the community. The costs of community clouds are greater than public because there are fewer customers to spread the costs. For the same reason, community clouds are less expensive than private clouds (Mell and Grance 2011). The community cloud may be owned by one member of the community, shared among several members, or owned by a third party. The community cloud may be hosted locally by one of the community members or off-site by a third party.

The same advantages and disadvantages of public clouds exist in community clouds but to different degrees. As mentioned before, everything being equal, costs for community clouds are more expensive than public clouds because less users share the same expense compared to public clouds. However, security and privacy concerns are slightly eased since the members of the community have more control of the services and platform. The connection to the community cloud may be over the internet but more commonly it is through a dedicated network. Having a dedicated network can ease the privacy and security concerns because those concerns can be better controlled and monitored over a private network.

Hybrid Cloud

The next type of cloud is a *hybrid cloud*. This type of cloud combines multiple clouds (private, public, and/or community) that remain unique, but are bound together by standardized or propriety technology and are portable (Mell and Grance 2011). Basically a hybrid cloud allows companies to keep some services in-house while moving other services to the cloud. This approach combines some public and private cloud computing. For example, remote hosting of email can easily be sent to a common public cloud service where it makes more sense to keep an enterprise resource planning system (ERP) in-house in a private cloud.

An example of effectively using a hybrid cloud is how Sega used the hybrid cloud to beat the Christmas sales spike in 2012 (Venkatraman 2012). Sega produces multiple computer games and the busiest time for the company is around Christmas time. Games are built in-house and then sent to multiple teams that are in charge of finding bugs or viruses in the software. After the internal round of testing, Sega releases the games to more internal teams in addition to external testers. Sega uses external testers for variety of reasons including its limited resources during peak time and language/culture issues for an universal release. Sega turned to the hybrid cloud model to meet the demands of the holiday rush. Sega's private cloud was used to improve IT efficiency and scalability while the public cloud was used to get the games to external testers quickly (Venkatraman 2012).

Private Cloud

The last type of cloud computing is the *private cloud* which is sometimes referred to as a *corporate cloud* or an *internal cloud*. The private cloud is operated for the exclusive use of an organization. The cloud may be managed by that organization or a third party and be on-site or off-site (Mell and Grance 2011; Sosinsky 2011). The key difference between this model and other models is the private cloud is only used by one organization. Private clouds almost eradicate the security and privacy concerns of the other three cloud models since one organization and can control and manage the private cloud. However, since only one organization uses the private cloud it is by far the most expensive type of cloud model.

You may be asking yourself, why would companies move to a private cloud when they can just keep their data center in-house in the first place? The private cloud, when implemented correctly, can reduce costs, enhance service quality, and more importantly reduce the time it takes to deliver what the users need. Try not to think of a private cloud as just a data center that is managed offsite by a third party provider. The cloud offers services like scalability, virtualization, shared resources, systems management software, cluster and grid computing, and load balancing (Foley 2008). Take for example, a company with multiple departments using an enterprise-wide software program that is built in-house. Market data shows that the idle rate in computer capacity of development environments can reach 85%. Most test servers, for instance, run at less than 10% of full capacity (Santos 2012). By combining these into a private cloud and optimizing these computer resources the company can reduce the amount of hardware needed to build and test the in-house enterprise-wide software.

What Does the Cloud Bring to E-Commerce?

Cloud computing brings many benefits to e-commerce and these benefits include: trust, cost savings, speed, scalability, security and communication.

Trust is a two-edged sword when it comes to cloud computing. The negative aspects of trust on cloud computing will be discussed later in the chapter. We will now examine the positive aspects of trust. It is well established in academic literature that customers have trust issues with e-commerce websites (see Gefen 2000; Gefen and Straub 2004; McKnight et al. 2002). Industry experts and researchers have spent their careers trying to increase the customer's trust in e-commerce websites so customers will buy more goods or services online. Some ways to increase trust in e-commerce sites have included the use of third party security seals (Head and Hassanein 2002) and branding alliances with other trusted sites (Lowry et al. 2008). Companies that have not established this trust with their customers struggle with e-commerce revenue.

Companies can use cloud computing service providers for some of their e-commerce needs like payment processing or shipping. These cloud computing service providers like Google or Amazon have well established trust with customers through years of customer loyalty and brand equity. Companies using these trusted cloud service providers can benefit from their established trust with customers. For example, a lesser known company can advertise that it uses Amazon for payment processing for its online transaction thus increasing the customer's trust that the payment will be secure, trusted, and less susceptible to fraud.

A second benefit of cloud computing to e-commerce is cost savings. It is estimated that e-commerce applications in the cloud can be built, deployed and used at 20 percent of the costs of traditional in-house e-commerce systems (Loumpouridis 2009). This is due to economies of scale of using the cloud platform. These costs savings can be used to pay for other business critical needs, growth, or even passed on the customer.

Another benefit of cloud computing to e-commerce is speed. Companies utilizing the cloud can deploy an e-commerce solution to the public must faster than building it in-house. Some experts estimate deploying on the cloud is five times faster than building it in-house (Loumpouridis 2009). One reason is the hardware procurement. Most companies do not have extra hardware sitting around waiting to be used. When a company wants to deploy an e-commerce solution, then it must start with purchasing new hardware. Depending on the size, business process and departments involved, this could take months. Once hardware is established and provisioned (a fancy word for setting up the hardware), then software must either be built or purchased for the e-commerce solution. After software has been installed, other processes like user training, deployment, and business process re-engineering must take place so that the e-commerce solution runs smoothly.

Deploying the e-commerce solution to the cloud will not eliminate all of the steps, but will eliminate most of them. For example, procuring the hardware, provisioning the hardware, building/buying software, and deployment can all be eliminated. The only items left for the company are user training and business process re-engineering. These items should be left up to the company since it involves internal business processes.

Scalability is another benefit of the cloud to e-commerce. We have discussed scalability a few times in this chapter and it is one of the main benefits of using cloud computing. Scalability allows companies to ramp up the proper resources during peak demand and scale back resources during low demand. This ensures that the company does not lose sales in the case where a customer could not access the e-commerce website due to heavy user traffic. This also saves the company money by not wasting un-used computing resources during low user traffic.

Security is another benefit of cloud computing to e-commerce, but like trust it is a two-edged sword. We will discuss the negative impacts of security on cloud computing later in the chapter. Securing applications, data centers, data, hardware, and networks are a large undertaking for any company. The Ponemon

Institute, a large research firm, estimates the cost of compliance averages $3.5 million per company (Ponemon_Institute 2011). Some companies cannot afford the costs associated with securing all of the IT resources; however, it is crucial if the company wants to stay in business. Cloud computing service providers must provide these security features in order to stay in business. Companies that utilize the cloud inherit the security benefits from the cloud service providers.

The last benefit of cloud computing to e-commerce is in communications. In this context communications means between companies and/or supply chain partners. Given the explosive growth of the cloud over the past several years, more companies are moving to the cloud. This allows more effective and efficient communications between companies that are on the same cloud. Companies using a community or hybrid cloud can benefit from faster communications since they are sharing some of the same computing resources.

For example, imagine a mobile phone company (SilverCoast) that verifies a customer's credit score to determine the mobile plan options available for that customer. Since SilverCoast does not specialize in credit score checks, it outsources this functionality to a third-party vendor called CheckThisCredit. In order for SilverCoast and CheckThisCredit to communicate effectively, they must establish a network link between the two companies so that credit score checks are fast and secure. This can be done over the Internet, however, security starts to become an issue. Because of this security concerns, SilverCoast and CheckThisCredit must invest in virtual private networks, encryption software or other security measures to ensure a fast and secure transaction. Now imagine these two companies on the cloud. Now the transactions between the two companies are all on one platform without having to communicate over the Internet. This communication, or transaction, is now fast and secure and all because they are using the cloud.

What are Some of the Cloud Computing Issues?

Although cloud computing brings many benefits to companies, cloud computing has its issues. Moving to the cloud architecture is not beneficial for all companies. Organizations that have well established IT departments and existing data centers that can meet its customer's demands probably do not need to move to a cloud model. The cloud model is beneficial to those companies that do not have the IT infrastructure, resources, or existing data centers. In this section, we will discuss some issues with cloud computing. These include trust, security and legal/regulatory issues.

Trust

Trust is one of the major issues with cloud computing. Trust is a large concern in the public cloud since this model involves sharing infrastructure and/or platforms with other companies. Trust is also a concern in hybrid and community clouds since there is some sharing of infrastructure and/or platforms, but the concern is to a lesser degree. Companies using private clouds benefit from being the only company on its cloud so trust is not a major concern, unless the trust issue is between the company and the third-party private cloud provider.

We trust a system less if the system gives us insufficient information about its expertise (Khan and Malluhi 2010). Due to the lack of transparency and information asymmetry between cloud providers and customers using the cloud, trust becomes an issue. Companies sharing public cloud space cannot guarantee that its data is safe and secure since it does not have complete control of the computing resources. The lack of trust in cloud computing leads many customers and companies to avoid using cloud computing. Now the question is, how do cloud service providers increase the trust in cloud computing? Jaeger *et al.* (2008) suggests that it is imperative for cloud service providers to embrace the development of policies to ensure transparency and standards. Jaeger *et al.* go further to suggest that these policies must be addressed at the government level by either legislation that mandates greater precision in service agreements between the providers and users of cloud computing or by regulatory control from an governmental agency. They posit that whichever route is taken, it will foster user trust in cloud computing.

Cao *et al.* (2012) examined how trust affected the relationship between cloud computing and supply chain partners. Using a combination of case study and surveys they found that trust positively affected the relationship between cloud computing and supply chain partners. This means that the greater the trust between the supply chain partners, the greater the cloud computing usage between the partners. Although this type of trust occurs outside of the cloud service provider's domain, the service providers can continue to foster the trust relationship between its customers to increase cloud computing usage.

Other research is looking towards technical avenues to increase trust in cloud computing. Krautheim *et al.* (2010) introduced a new mechanisms for rooting trust in the cloud environment called the Trusted Virtual Environment Module. This tool allows cloud customers to create and run virtual environments on a platform owned by cloud service providers. This tool allows customers greater control over interfaces and security mechanisms. This greater control and transparency is likely to increase trust in cloud usage.

Security

Security is another major issue for customers using cloud computing. Security is an issue for all cloud types including private clouds since they all involve some sort of network. Security issues are broad cover storage security, data security, and network security. Subsets of these security issues can include such topics as who as access to the hardware, software, data and network, location of data, system recovery, and network attacks and intrusions. Like trust issues, security should be handled in two ways – changing business processes and providing technical solutions.

Unfortunately cloud computing technology and usage have moved in a much faster pace than local, national and global laws. Who has responsibility of security in a cloud environment? Is security 100 percent the cloud service provider's responsibility, or do customers share in some of the responsibility of security? What happens when the network between the cloud and the customer is compromised, whose responsibility is it then? These types of questions can be addressed with effective policies and governance which are still in the process of being developed (Kaufman 2009).

While the cloud computing community is waiting for laws to "catch-up" with usage, other security measures are being discussed. Wang *et al.* (2010) suggests that enabling public audits for cloud service providers is critical so that users can resort to an external audit party to check the integrity of the cloud provider when needed.

Takabi *et al.* (2010) suggests that cloud security and privacy issues can be addressed by implementing several security approaches. These approaches include authentication and identity management, access control, access policies for different domains, and a trust management framework. These approaches are both a technical solution and business process solution.

Legal/Regulatory

Legal issues arise in cloud computing because the nature of the distributed model. Legal issues like conflicting U.S. state, national and international laws, indemnification by insurance companies, data export regulations, unclear jurisdiction, and government regulations all affect cloud computing. We will discuss a few of these legal issues.

Conflicting laws across states, national and international borders poses a problem for cloud computing users and providers. An organization must know where their corporate data resides in order to make sure that the correct laws are followed. For example, European countries have stricter data privacy laws than the U.S., so companies using a cloud service provider based in Europe must follow those standards.

Indemnification (a sum of money paid in compensation for loss or injury) by insurance companies is also tricky in cloud computing (Mitchell 2012). Insurance company policies vary in coverage for losses or interruption of data caused by disasters, theft, fraud, etc. With cloud computing, the computing resources are distributed which potentially poses a problem for the insurance company and the insured.

Companies currently using cloud computing are at the risk of uncertain jurisdiction. While standards, treaties and laws are developing worldwide, there is still no simple test to determine jurisdiction for internet activities in the U.S. (Ward and Sipior 2010). Cloud computing obfuscates the problems since cloud resources may reside offsite or distributed across multiple centers. Where does the jurisdiction fall when a public cloud provider stores data in multiple places around the world for a global company?

Another issue in cloud computing is regulatory issues like financial regulations or patient privacy issues. For example, the *U.S. Health Insurance Portability and Accountability Act (HIPAA)* requires certain standards for data privacy. Another example is the Payment Card Industry Data Security Standard (PCIDSS). These regulations require cloud providers and cloud customers to work together to assure these laws are being followed. Responsibility may be blurred if multiple parties or multiple jurisdictions are involved (Mitchell 2012).

Once a problem occurs in the cloud, investigating legal issues is difficult due to multiple customers sharing a common infrastructure or platform. Multiple customers mean there are multiple computer logs and user logins which muddy the water in investigations. A cloud customer should request a contractual commitment to support specific forms of investigation from his or her cloud service provider otherwise no investigation will likely take place (Brodkin 2008).

Summary

In the chapter we discussed what is cloud computing. We then discussed the history of cloud computing and where the name came from. Brief statistics were offered to demonstrate the growing field of cloud computing. The types of cloud computing offerings were discussed followed by the different types of cloud computing. We concluded the chapter discussing benefits of cloud computing to e-commerce as well as current issues related to cloud computing.

Cloud computing is a growing field and according to industry experts it is estimated that cloud computing will continue to grow over the next several decades. The cloud is more than just placing data on the internet. Cloud computing takes technology, businesses services, and applications and turns them into a self-service utility (Sosinsky 2011). Through economies of scale, cloud service providers can host infrastructure, platforms and software cheaper than individual companies. The scalability of the cloud also provides benefits to companies during peak and off-peak demand by ensuring more revenue is captured.

◆ Review Terms

Amazon Web Services (AWS)
Business process as a service (BPaaS)
Cloud computing
Common infrastructure
Community cloud
Corporate cloud
Hybrid cloud
Infrastructure as a Service (IaaS)
Internal cloud
Location independence

On-demand
Online accessibility
Platform as a Service (PaaS)
Private cloud
Public cloud
Software as a service (SaaS)
Storage as a Service (STaaS)
U.S. Health Insurance Portability and Accountability Act (HIPAA)
Utility Pricing

◆ Discussion Questions

1. Explain why "cloud computing" is growing in usage.
2. Explain how a "common infrastructure" allows for "scalability".
3. Explain what "location independence" means.
4. Describe the history of "cloud computing".
5. Explain how "Software as a service (SaaS) is related to "cloud customers.
6. Explain what a "public cloud" is as it contrasted to a "private cloud".
7. Explain some of the benefits that a cloud can bring e-commerce.
8. Explain how trust is an important issue in clouds.

◆ Questions

1. Why is "cloud computing" important?
2. What does C.L.O.U.D. stand for?
3. What value is "utility pricing" in the field of "cloud computing"?
4. Is "cloud computing" growing or declining in use? Explain why.
5. What is the relationship of middleware and business applications in cloud computing offerings?
6. What is "Business Process as a service (BPaaS)"?
7. What is a "community cloud"?
8. What is a "hybrid cloud"?

References

Amazon. 2012. "About Aws." http://aws.amazon.com/

BestBuy. 2012. "Best Buy Reports December Revenue of $8.4 Billion," BestBuy, Minneapolis, MN.

Brodkin, J. 2008. "Gartner: Seven Cloud-Computing Security Risks," *Infoworld*, pp. 1-3.

Cao, Q., Schniederjans, D., Triche, J., and Schniederjans, M. 2012. "Business Strategy, Cloud Computing, and Supply Chain Management: A Synthesis of Resource-Based View and Social Capital Theory," in: *Decision Science Institute 43rd Annual Conference*. San Francisco, CA.

Foley, J. 2008. "Private Clouds Take Shape," in: *InformationWeek*. Online: TechTarget.

Gartner. 2012. "Gartner Says Worldwide Cloud Services Market to Surpass $109 Billion in 2012," Stamford, CT.

Gefen, D. 2000. "E-Commerce: The Role of Familiarity and Trust," *Omega* (28:6), pp. 725-737.

Gefen, D., and Straub, D.W. 2004. "Consumer Trust in B2c E-Commerce and the Importance of Social Presence: Experiments in E-Products and E-Services," *Omega* (32:6), pp. 407-424.

Glanz, J. 2012. "Power, Pollution and the Internet," in: *New York Times*. New York.

Head, M.M., and Hassanein, K. 2002. "Trust in E-Commerce: Evaluating the Impact of Third-Party Seals," *Quarterly Journal of Electronic Commerce* (3), pp. 307-326.

Herbert, L. 2010. "Saas Pricing Models in Flux " in: *Liz Herbert's Blog* F. Research.

Hurwitz, J., Bloor, R., Kaufman, M., and Halper, F. 2009. *Cloud Computing for Dummies*. John Wiley & Sons, Inc.

Jaeger, P.T., Lin, J., and Grimes, J.M. 2008. "Cloud Computing and Information Policy: Computing in a Policy Cloud?," *Journal of Information Technology & Politics* (5:3), 2008/10/27, pp. 269-283.

Kaufman, L.M. 2009. "Data Security in the World of Cloud Computing," *Security & Privacy, IEEE* (7:4), pp. 61-64.

Khan, K.M., and Malluhi, Q. 2010. "Establishing Trust in Cloud Computing," *IT Professional* (12:5), pp. 20-27.

Kihal, S.E., Schlereth, C., and Skiera, B. 2012. "Price Comparison for Infrastructure-as-a-Service." Frankfurt, Germany: Goethe University, pp. 1-12.

Krautheim, F.J., Phatak, D., and Sherman, A. 2010. "Introducing the Trusted Virtual Environment Module: A New Mechanism for Rooting Trust in Cloud Computing," in *Trust and Trustworthy Computing*, A. Acquisti, S. Smith and A.-R. Sadeghi (eds.). Springer Berlin Heidelberg, pp. 211-227.

Leong, L. 2012. "Cloud Iaas SLAs Can Be Meaningless," in: *Gartner Blog Network*, Gartner .

Loftus, T. 2012. "Survey: Rising Cloud Adoption Spurs Changes to It," in: *Wall Street Journal*.

Loumpouridis, B. 2009. "Is Your E-Commerce Operation Ready for the Cloud?" 10/19/09. Retrieved 12/19/2012, from http://www.e-commercetimes.com/story/68408.html

Lowry, P.B., Vance, A., Moody, G., Beckman, B., and Read, A. 2008. "Explaining and Predicting the Impact of Branding Alliances and Web Site Quality on Initial Consumer Trust of E-Commerce Web Sites," *Journal of Management Information Systems* (24:4), pp. 199-224.

McKnight, D.H., Choudhury, V., and Kacmar, C. 2002. "Developing and Validating Trust Measures for E-Commerce: An Integrative Typology," *Information Systems Research* (13:3), pp. 334-359.

Mell, P., and Grance, T. 2011. "The NIST Definition of Cloud Computing," U.S Department of Commerce. Washington D.C.

Mitchell, R. 2012. "Legal Issues Surrounding Cloud Computing," *Association of Business Information Systems*, New Orleans, LA, pp. 79-84.

Mohamed, A. 2009. "A History of Cloud Computing " in: *ComputerWeekly.com*. Online: TechTarget.

Ponemon Institute. 2011. "The True Cost of Compliance: Benchmark Study of Multinational Organizations," Ponemon Institute LLC, Traverse City, Michigan.

Santos, S.S. 2012. "Advantages and Options of Private Cloud Computing," IBM.

Sosinsky, B. 2011. *Cloud Computing Bible*. Indianapolis, Indiana: Wiley Publishing, Inc.

Takabi, H., Joshi, J.B.D., and Ahn, G. 2010. "Security and Privacy Challenges in Cloud Computing Environments," *Security & Privacy, IEEE* (8:6), pp. 24-31.

U.S. General Services Administration. 2012. "Infrastructure as a Service (Iaas)." from http://www.gsa.gov/portal/content/112063

Venkatraman, A. 2012. "How Sega Used Hybrid Cloud to Beat the Christmas Sales Spike," in: *ComputerWeekly.com*. Online: TechTarget.

Wang, C., Wang, Q., Ren, K., and Lou, W. 2010. "Privacy-Preserving Public Auditing for Data Storage Security in Cloud Computing," *INFOCOM, 2010 Proceedings IEEE*: IEEE, pp. 1-9.

Ward, B.T., and Sipior, J.C. 2010. "The Internet Jurisdiction Risk of Cloud Computing," *Information Systems Management* (27:4), 2010/10/15, pp. 334-339.

Weinman, J. 2012. *Cloudonomics: The Business Value of Cloud Computing*. Hoboken, NJ: John Wiley & Sons, Inc.

EPILOGUE: E-JUST-IN-TIME

Learning Objectives

After completing this chapter, you should be able to:
    Explain the differences between "just-in-time" and "e-just-in-time."
    Describe changes in marketing that have required a change in operations.
    Explain how "e-just-in-time" is an important paradigm for running e-commerce operations.

Overview of this Chapter

This chapter concludes this book and summarizes many of its suggestions for improving e-commerce operations by offering a new term to describe old principles applied in the new context of e-commerce. The new term is "e-just-in-time." Differences between the prior just-in-time (JIT) principles and e-just-in-time (e-JIT) principles are presented.

What is E-Just-In-Time?

Throughout this book we have tried to suggest a variety of approaches to improve e-commerce operations. In most of the chapters we have suggested that just-in-time (JIT) principles have a substantive and beneficial application to e-commerce operations. In this ending section we want to reinforce that connection by summarizing and proposing that traditional JIT principles can be transformed into an e-commerce related set of principles, which we will title as e-just-in-time or e-JIT.

As can be seen in Figure 1, the focus of traditional JIT principles, while advocating a focus on the customer, are chiefly applied to the operations areas in manufacturing and suppliers, while treating the retailers as a primary customer (Monden 1983; 1993; Ohno 1983; Schniederjans 1993; Schniederjans and Olson 1999; Schonberger 1983; 1988; Wantuck 1989). E-JIT on the other hand fully encompasses the final customer as a contributing part of the process of delivering a product or service. In effect, the customer is now an employee of the e-JIT

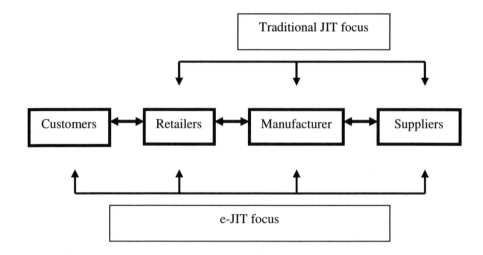

Figure 1. JIT and e-JIT compared

operation. While the tasks performed by retailers and particularly the behavior of the customer has traditionally falling into the domain of marketing, e-commerce systems are changing the marketer's role. In Figure 2, we can see that the customer and the operations manager are now performing common marketing tasks. This does not mean that marketing's role is diminished in any way. Indeed, as e-commerce is a new channel of distribution it brings with it a new level of complexity to challenge and broadening the role of marketing in all e-commerce business organizations. Since this book's is concerned with e-commerce operations management we will leave marketing to deal with its own issues and concentrate on e-JIT in e-commerce operations management.

JIT principles when applied to e-commerce operations become *e-JIT principles* by their inclusion of the final or end "customer" into a partnership with the e-commerce business organization. How does an operations manager include the final customer into a system of successful customer order completions? One might say that the only why to manage a retailers, manufacturers and supply chain partners is through the eventual inclusion of the final customer. And while traditional JIT principles (and lean manufacturing) have always suggested that the customer should be the focus of production and supply chain efforts, they never really included the final customer (they did include the retailer) as a contributing "employee." Yet, that is exactly what a customer is: a critical component in a successful customer order completion process for a product or service to its final user.

CUSTOMER: New tasks performed by customers in e-commerce	MARKETING: Traditional tasks performed by marketing personnel that are changed and redistributed in the e-commerce context	OPERATIONS MANAGEMENT (OM): New tasks performed by OM managers or operations technology in e-commerce

ORDER ENTRY: Customers place their own orders over the Web, saving the salesperson order taking time.

ORDER CHECKING: Automated order checking in Web ordering system to check inventory, prevent ordering mistakes, and confirm facility capability for shipping dates. Saves sales person's time.

ORDER TRACKING: Online movement within the production process, warehouse, or shipping area, permitting customers can tract the location of their order as it is processed. Saves sales person's time.

SHIPPMENT TRACKING: Customers gather tracking information via FedX partnerships Web technology. Web access permits customers to obtain shipping information, delivery information, and even movement through cities, saving the marketing personnel time.

PHYSICAL DISTRIBUTION PLANNING: While marketing has usually performed transportation system selection, the limited number of *WWW* transportation service providers minimizes the need for marketing planning efforts and focuses efforts of OM areas to establish least-cost partnerships with transportation firms.

OTHER TASKS: Other typical marketing tasks diminished by the new role of e-commerce include: delivery decision-making, purchase terms, order size, channel access, assortment of products, channel exclusivity, and pricing.

Figure 2. E-JIT role changes in marketing, customers, and operations management

A more obvious reason why the customer is being included in the e-commerce activities is because Internet technology has empowered customers to take a new and more active part in customer order completion activities. Clearly information technology and Web software has created a new environment that offers distinctively new markets and challenges to serve them. What better partner to have in this new market than the customers themselves. What better guidance to use in handling this partnership than the tried and eminently successful traditional JIT principles. These traditional JIT principles have been presented in prior chapters as they related to specific chapter content or related to specific critical success factors. In Table 1 we restate many of these principles and adapt them to e-commerce to include consideration of the customer. As can be seen in Table 1 the focus of e-JIT principles are considerably broader than traditional JIT principles. While e-JIT principles include all the content of the traditional JIT principles they differ from them in that they more directly including the customer in the business partnership.

Table 1. The comparison of traditional JIT principles with those of e-JIT

Traditional JIT Principle	Traditional JIT focuses on:	New e-JIT focuses on:
Seek to build-to-order	Just the manufacturer with the retailer as customer. Since retailers purchase in quantity, they usually have to maintain some inventory. For operations that operate both manufacturing and retailing, any inventory means waste.	Final or end-customer as customer. Clearly, the idea that the final customer is the desired target of production effort will more truly achieve the "pull" concept and will avoid wasteful time and money in managing inventory. This focus is more likely to achieve zero-inventory goals encouraged in traditional JIT.
Seek to eliminate waste	Chiefly the manufacturer. Eliminate wasted labor time waiting for inventory that should have been available, wasted capital in inventory that customers didn't demand, wasted motion in material handling that is unnecessary, etc.	The entire customer through supply chain. By allowing the customer to actively perform service functions (Note Figure 2) it saves time and effort while providing greater service value. The use of e-commerce technologies lifts the attention from clerical-type day-to-day customer paper processing activities for employees to focus on more critical issues in business success, such as handling order queries from customers.

Table 1. (Continued)

Traditional JIT Principle	Traditional JIT focuses on:	New e-JIT focuses on:
Seek zero finished goods inventory	Chiefly the manufacturer.	The entire customer through supply chain. Allowing suppliers to do in-house warehousing or taking orders directly from customers can reduce the costs of doing business to e-commerce operations.
Use fail-safe automated technology	Chiefly the manufacturer. Use automated technology to insure consistency in product or service quality.	The entire customer through supply chain. Use information technology that will allow greater access by customer to product and service information about their orders. Design information technology and Web site to insure quick, easy, and accurate customer ordering.
Seek long-term commitments from business partners	Chiefly the suppliers. Establish long-term relationships with members of the supply chain. A back-end approach.	The entire customer through supply chain. Establish long-term relationships with customer as a major focus. A front-end approach.
Maintain 100 percent quality inspection	Chiefly the manufacturer and suppliers.	The entire customer through supply chain. The Internet provides an easy means by which customers can not only communicate poor quality in products and service but also point out issues that can lead to further improvements in products if they are encouraged by Web site design to participate.
Maintain technology	Chiefly the manufacturer. Give all operators of technology the responsibility for maintaining and reporting on equipment performance.	The entire customer through supply chain. Customers and suppliers over the Internet can be quick to report technology failure that can inhibit them from completing their roles. Build intelligent systems to identify and correct problems automatically. Provide customers emergency software tools to permit them to correct minor problems.

(Continued)

Table 1. (Continued)

Traditional JIT Principle	Traditional JIT focuses on:	New e-JIT focuses on:
Seek to empower employees	Chiefly the manufacturer. Give personnel the responsible and authority to control production and fix quality problems that they identify.	The entire customer through supply chain. Empower everybody to identify problems and communicate them for quick resolution. The e-commerce technologies permit greater access to decision-making information and encourage better training and development of personnel to handle the use of such information.
Seek production flexibility	Chiefly the manufacturer. Seek to enhance production flexibility in employees and systems to meet with changes in demand.	The entire customer through supply chain. By working with customers and marketing, alternations in demand can be achieved through seasonal sale promotions that permit flexibility in demand, lessening the need for flexibility in production.
Seek improved quality	Chiefly the manufacturer and supplier. Where possible automate for quality consistency reasons. Also provide training and quality knowledge to employees to aid in their efforts to improve product quality.	The entire customer through supply chain. Improve information technology and Web site service to deliver service quality (i.e., reduced effort to transact an order, etc.) to the customer when using the Internet to place orders.
Seek reduced batch lot-sizes	Chiefly the manufacturer.	The entire customer through supply chain. With the focus on the individual customer orders, there is a motivation to avoid batching entirely.
Seek smaller order sizes	Chiefly the suppliers.	The entire customer through supply chain. With the focus on the individual customer orders, suppliers will have to be able to serve unitary requests in purchasing. Internet technologies also enhance outsourcing opportunities of parts of the e-commerce business to suppliers.

Table 1. (Continued)

Traditional JIT Principle	Traditional JIT focuses on:	New e-JIT focuses on:
Seek continuous improvement	Chiefly the manufacturer and supplier. Continuously find new ways to improve products, processes, people, and systems.	The entire customer through supply chain. Use Web site to include and collect customer suggestions on design and product improvements. Allow customization of Web site to permit customer-enhanced activity.
Seek to eliminate contingencies	Chiefly the manufacturer and supplier. Eliminate buffer inventory and surplus human resources to help reveal problems that might go hidden for periods of time. Identifying a problem allows it to be solved and improve operations.	The entire customer through supply chain. Encourage problem identification from the customer's perspective. Encourage and empower them to communicate problems, such as inventory stockouts and Web site failure to the appropriate department or Web master.
Improve efficiency in physical layout	Chiefly the manufacturer and supplier. Designing layouts that maximize the flow time of products from suppliers through the manufacturing operations.	The entire customer through supply chain. Emphasis here may be on improving networks (i.e., Internet, extranet, intranets, etc.) to improve all business transactions.
Respect people	Chiefly the manufacturer and retailer. Respect employees to help them to become a real partner in work effort. Respect customer's demands for products and service.	The entire customer through supply chain. Bring customer into the decision making process. Make them true partners by allowing participation in product or service design, testing, and promotion (i.e., word-of-mouth). The use of e-commerce technologies saves clerical-type day-to-day customer paper processing activities gives them the opportunity to move from a tactical problem solving group to a strategic planning group, better able to solve issues before they become a problem.

(Continued)

Table 1. (Continued)

Traditional JIT Principle	Traditional JIT focuses on:	New e-JIT focuses on:
Seek improved inventory handling	Chiefly the manufacturer. Minimize all handling of inventory movement within a production facility.	The entire customer through supply chain. Reducing the travel distance of inventory from suppliers through manufacturing to the customer. In e-commerce this may mean no retailing outlets or warehouses but direct distribution from suppliers to customers.

While the e-JIT principles proposed here are not the only important guidelines an e-commerce organization should follow, they may help to achieve a desired competitive advantage though what Schniederjans (1993) called the "productivity cycling process." The *productivity cycling process* is a means where by the elimination of production problems reduces waste and increases market share, as presented in Figure 3. The process is even more possible under e-commerce operations management since the Internet technology greatly encourages participation by all partners. Moreover, in e-JIT operations we have more partners (i.e., adding the customer) to help us find and correct problems of all kinds.

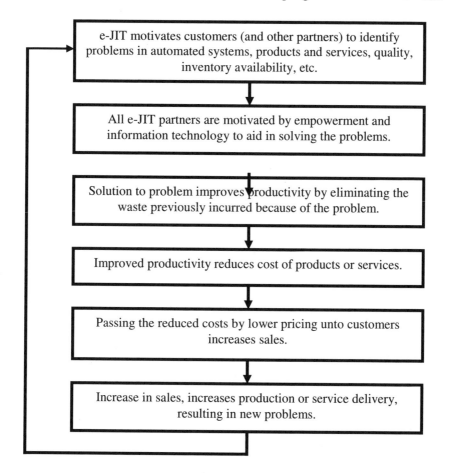

Figure 3. Productivity cycling process and e-JIT

◆ Review Terms

E-just-in-time	Operations management (OM)
E-JIT	Productivity cycling process
E-JIT principles	World Wide Web (WWW)

◆ Discussion Questions

1. Explain why are customers included in e-JIT operations.
2. Explain how the "productivity cycling process" works.

◆ Questions

1. What is the JIT "Respect people" principle difference between traditional JIT and e-JIT? Explain and give an example.
2. What is the outcome of the "productivity cycling process"? Give an example.

References

Monden, Y., The Toyota Management System: Linking the Seven Key Functional Areas, Cambridge, MA: Productivity Press, 1993.

Monden, Y., *The Toyota Production System: Practical Approach to Production Management*, Atlanta, GA: Industrial Engineering and Management Press, 1983.

Ohno, T., Toyota Production System: Beyond Large-Scale Production, Cambridge, MA: Productivity Press, 1988.

Schniederjans, M. J., *Topics in Just-In-Time Management*, Needham Heights, MA: Allyn and Bacon, 1993.

Schniederjans, M. J., and Olson, J. R., *Advanced Topics in Just-In-Time Management*, Westport, CT: Quorum Books, 1999.

Schonberger, R. J., Japanese Manufacturing Techniques: Nine Hidden Lessons in Simplicity, New York: The Free Press, 1982.

Schonberger, R. J., World Class Manufacturing: The Lessons of Simplicity Applied, New York: The Free Press, 1986.

Wantuck, J., *Just in Time for America*, Milwaukee, WI: The Forum, 1989.

INDEX